The Art of Flash® Animation: Creative Cartooning

Mark Stephen Smith

Wordware Publishing, Inc.

Library of Congress Cataloging-in-Publication Data

Smith, Mark Stephen.
    The art of flash animation : creative cartooning / by Mark Stephen Smith.
      p. cm.
    Includes index.
    ISBN-10: 1-59822-026-8 (pbk.)
    ISBN-13: 978-1-59822-026-1
    1. Computer animation. 2. Flash (Computer file). I. Title.
    TR897.7.S58 2007
    006.6'96--dc22   2006039455

Dedication

To that wonderful, beautiful reason I was looking for a job in Atlanta... my darling wife, Albalis.

(Ahem... By the way, that's how I immediately know if an unidentified caller is making a solicitation. If they can't pronounce my wife's name *properly*, it's a telephone solicitor.)

Contents

Contents

How I Met Animation

It's funny how things work out.

I never really started out wanting to be an animator, other than having a lifelong love for drawing, and now I find myself writing a "how to" book on drawing animation for Macromedia's Flash.

As far as animation, I've made no secret to my students or readers of my website (www.marktoonery.com) of how I got interested in animation.

It started out, I guess, when I was a teenager. I had written a number of short stories in the *Twilight Zone* and *Alfred Hitchcock Presents* vein, and a couple of fantasy novels that explored the premise of modernized "ringwraiths" invading a 1986 Alabama high school. Hey, I was a *student* in a 1986 Alabama high school, and writing about such things sure beat the heck out of driving back and forth repeatedly along the same stretch of road between Winn-Dixie and Dairy Queen (which seemed to be my classmates' favorite weekend pastime).

Anyway, I took some of my stories to my Methodist Sunday school teacher. What was I thinking? you may well wonder. Waving horror stories and dark, magic-wielding, wizardly epics around my Sunday morning church class? Well, our teacher was an attractive, friendly woman in her mid-20s, who raised horses on a ranch. Not your typical Southern Sunday school teacher, if there exists such a thing.

She was very supportive. After briefly reading such outlandish tales, a "typical" Sunday school teacher could have made any number of predictable, uptight replies. But not Anita. She simply suggested, "You know, your writing would be well adapted for animation. Have you ever thought about writing for animation?"

The author shares some of his early works with Anita, his favorite Sunday school teacher, ca. 1986.

"Animation?" My snobby little teenage self reacted with scarcely restrained indignance. "Animation is for children."

That was 1986.

Fast forward to two years later, when three high school friends and I decided to go on one last group outing together before our May 1988 graduation. The movie we went to see was *The Seventh Sign*. But there was a much more stunning surprise in store for the audience that far outweighed anything Demi Moore could show us.

Totally without warning, this old-fashioned cartoon music starts playing, and a baby's face, next to a white rabbit's head, zooms out of a splashy title screen reading, "Baby Herman and Roger Rabbit in a Maroon Cartoon!" It was followed by a drawing of the rabbit standing in a frying pan held by the mischievous youngster along with the words, "Somethin's Cookin'."

I had no idea who this Maroon guy was, but he had our undivided attention. That frosty teenage attitude regarding animation was already quickly melting away as the cartoon began, because my first thought was, "Y'know, this is kinda cool! I'm glad they're showing a cartoon before the main feature. Gives us a little extra for our money, with ticket prices nearly four bucks."

And then the rabbit started to *move*.

I had *never* seen animation like that. The rabbit was just standing there, counting on his fingers, but that deceptively simple animation was captivating... even downright spellbinding!

Roger (Rabbit) and me. The author experiences a career epiphany, ca. 1988.

Over the next few minutes, that poor rabbit started chasing that rotten little baby around the checkerboard kitchen floor. The camera pulled back and suddenly, there was Roger, standing in a collapsed refrigerator prop, when a live-action director stepped into the frame and started shouting at the shamed rabbit for forgetting his lines.

I don't remember the exact moment it occurred, but at some point during the cartoon I thought, "Animation! *That's* what I want to do for a living!"

We all soon realized this was a mere preview, and I knew I was going to go see that forthcoming movie when it was released the following month.

Up until that point I had wanted to be a writer, though I drew most of the illustrations for my own stories. I'd been drawing since age two — well, before two, my mother always corrects me. Having written and directed a successful high school play, *Kreechur* (about a lunatic escaping in a high school), and since I had already enrolled as a theatre major in the nearby University of Montevallo, I began my college career in drama.

Then my parents announced their move to Montgomery, a 90-minute drive south of Montevallo. I would be joining them and attending Auburn University Montgomery (where I'd already transferred my major to art) after finishing my next semester. My brother mentioned one of his coworkers (at the Montgomery movie theatre where he had just started) had a friend taking an animation class.

An animation class? Here in Alabama? How was that even *possible*?

Remember, this was near the end of 1989, before Pixar became a household name, before *Toy Story*, and about three years before *Jurassic Park* forced stop-motion animators to transfer their classic skills to the computer (or face possible career extinction). I was just about to learn, upon my enrollment, of this wonderful tool that was about to revolutionize hand-drawn animation production forever.

The computer.

Sure, I'd seen *Tron* a few years before, but that clunky video game animation (by today's standards) just never instilled in me the idea that you could use the computer to speed up, streamline, and refine the process of *hand-drawn* animation.

And that's what this book is all about.

Note

Companion files for some of the examples are available at **www.wordware.com/files/flash** and **http://www.marktoonery.com/flashbook.html**.

Acknowledgments

I'll try to keep this brief, in the interest of getting someone to actually read the names of those many individuals who were kind enough to assist me in the preparation of this book.

Thanks first of all to Wes "Kurv" Beckwith. It so happened that I was looking for a job in Atlanta, and I made an online application to a 3D studio there as a storyboard artist. Though I didn't get *that* job, they referred me to Wes (then at Wordware), who was looking for someone to write a book on Flash animation. You now hold that book in your hands. (And that, my friends, is the very nature of *networking*. Remember that when you're reading Chapter 11.)

Thanks to Beth Kohler and Tim McEvoy at Wordware for keeping me going, proofreading, and not complaining how my jobs (both freelance and full-time) delayed progress on this book.

Thanks to Kat Hagan at Westwood College (Midtown Atlanta campus, of course) for getting me involved with ASIFA-Atlanta). It's because of her I was able to meet and interview the fine folks at Turner Studios, and have a few of them to thank in turn...

Thanks to Joe Peery and Vella Torres at Turner Studios for all their work promoting ASIFA-Atlanta, and to Joe for allowing me to interview him. Our half-hour interview stretched to nearly an hour, but I was rather ashamed I had to cut it short, because although we were talking some *seriously* fun stuff about animation, my darn tape was about to run out.

Thanks to Les Harper (a Turner Studios animator) for taking time out of his busy day to show me some terrific tips in Flash; I learned more in that one hour about what a useful tool this software is than *any* written manual could ever teach me.

Thanks to Brian de Tagyos and Steve Vitale, Lead Animators at Turner Studios, for providing an informative pair of interviews during their break at an ASIFA-Atlanta figure drawing session at Westwood.

Thanks to my students James Roberge, James Bridgens, Josh Wilson, Melanie Mendoza, and Scott Pruett for allowing me to reproduce their class projects here.

And a very special thanks to the great Animation Maestro Richard Williams, animation director of *Who Framed Roger Rabbit*, for keeping the knowledge from animation's great Golden Era alive and attempting to pass it along to the next generation through his Animation MasterClass (I was there in San Francisco, '97) as well as his indispensable literary contribution to the craft, *The Animator's Survival Kit*. My greatest regret is that more of his personal work is not commercially available on DVD.

(Note to Dick: The animator from Alabama did *not* let his copy collect dust on a shelf or coffee table; it's a well-worn, floppy-paged, book-marked copy and I carry it with me to all my animation classes for easy reference and sharing.)

Section I

Girth, Thurman, and Deadbeat
© Mark S. Smith/MarkToonery.com

DRAWING AND THE ANIMATION PROCESS

Chapter 1

Introduction to *The Art of Flash Animation*

Girth, Thurman, and Deadbeat
© Mark S. Smith/MarkToonery.com

Richard Williams' Animation MasterClass

I might as well go ahead and relate this story first of all, because you'll hear the name Richard Williams peppered throughout this book. His is not exactly a household name like Walt Disney, Chuck Jones, or even the now-familiar Tex Avery, but he's won three Academy Awards, the most recent for a Special Achievement in his creation of the title character from *Who Framed Roger Rabbit*, a Disney/Amblin production on which he served as director of animation.

1997. Evidently the year I was working for KinderCare as a multi-media specialist was a busy year.

It was a matter of days after handing in my notice at American Klassic Designs, where I designed tigers ("Aubies") and elephants ("Big Als") beating each other senseless on the football field, that I was going to leave for a job at KinderCare to work on CD-ROM presentations using Macromedia Director. In fact, it may have even been the day after I'd signed my contract with KinderCare that they announced plans to move their corporate headquarters from Montgomery (my new "hometown") to Portland, Oregon, at the request of their new CEO.

A "typical" design from my T-shirt art department work (ca. mid-1990s).

To find out whether I had drawn a particular design, my friends and family knew to look for my signature, which I'd usually hide as a scrimshaw in the elephant's tusk or within the tiger's stripes. It was a habit I started when I didn't know whether they'd let me take credit for my work. Once I confessed this practice to my fellow art department workers, it became a game to find my hidden signatures.

Despite that, I stood by my notice at the former steady job, and resolutely decided to go on to KinderCare, knowing the new job was now far from permanent (it would eventually be nine months until they finally moved).

It turned out to be a good career move, because it would enable me to take an animation class from the very man who had inspired me toward an animation career, Richard Williams.

I worked in the training department and, to my delight, they would send people in our department on trips almost anywhere in the country to learn better ways to do our job! (They paid airfare, hotel accommodations, as well as your meals!) It was my first corporate experience, and I was impressed.

I was already a subscriber to *Animation Magazine*, and had noticed the ad for Richard Williams' Animation MasterClass the forthcoming June in San Francisco. I had lamented aloud to my coworkers how much I'd enjoy going to that three-day seminar, and was advised, "Go ask Bob [one of the VPs] if they'll send you on that trip. The worst he can do is say no!"

I prepared my case, memorized my notecards, and asked to see Bob. I went in, and was mentally preparing myself for rejection. "There's this Animation MasterClass from *Roger Rabbit*'s animation director. I really think if I could go to this seminar, it would really help improve the look of this CD-ROM presentation I'm working on..." I paused for a breath, expecting a speech about cutting costs and company downsizing due to the impending Portland, Oregon, move. Bob cut me off, but in a way I'd hardly anticipated.

"Oh, wow, that would be a great experience for you, wouldn't it?" he interjected with genuine enthusiasm.

"Yes... yes, it would!" I replied. I hardly remember the rest of the conversation, and was now convinced that I would be meeting Richard Williams, come June.

When the magical day finally arrived, and I stepped to the front of the theatre sidewalk, I think I was one of the first students to recognize Richard Williams when he arrived. I'd seen his 30-second appearance in the 1988 TV special *Secrets of Toontown: The Making of Who Framed Roger Rabbit,* which I still show my animation students to this day. (I'm still somewhat disappointed they didn't include that in the two-disc set release of *Roger!*)

Ironically, he was standing behind those theatre ropes when he first appeared, and a crowd that would soon top 300 animators, directors, and instructors gaped in awe. I figured he'd be standing behind ropes for the entire seminar… unapproachable, untouchable. In the animation industry, he's known as the Animation Maestro, and deservedly so. He garners somewhat the level of respect that Steven Spielberg has in the film industry.

My first view of Richard Williams in San Francisco in June 1997. Though the ropes were actually there, the pedestal has been obviously added for dramatic effect.

Moments before, we had thankfully been given name tags with our point of origin, and I saw a group of animators from Heart of Texas Productions, and figured, as I introduced myself to them, "I can let the word *y'all* slip out occasionally with you guys without getting too self-conscious."

I found out that they had done some second unit work on Bugs Bunny's *Space Jam*, and were working on another film for Warner Brothers, the soon-to-be undeservedly underappreciated *Quest for Camelot*, which I've since found in the "bargain bin" in Wal-Mart. (I bought two copies: one for myself and one to give away as a "Best Film" prize in one of my animation classes.) The Heart of Texas guys turned out to be a friendly bunch, and I greatly enjoyed sitting with them in class and hanging out with them during breaks.

At the first break, however, I noticed that Mr. Williams was gathering his notes just to the lower-left side of the stage, and that no one was yet bold enough to approach him. I shrugged briefly, and walked over to introduce myself. (This simple, seemingly bold approach would eventually reward me by extended conversations with (1) filmmaker Tim Burton on the Montgomery, Alabama, set of *Big Fish*, (2) animation director Don Bluth of *American Tail* and *Dragon's Lair* during the Atlanta Dragon-Con, and better yet, (3) my future wife, Albalis!)

Mr. Williams was very friendly, and I related the story to him of how I looked up at the screen the first time I saw *Roger Rabbit*, and exclaimed in my heart, "Animation! *That's* what I want to do for a living!"

"Oh, wow!" Mr. Williams seemed to almost blush with his reply. "Well, thank you! Thank you very much!"

I got him to autograph the cover of *Animation Magazine*, where he was depicted standing with a frame around my favorite white rabbit. His charming wife, Mo Sutton (with a *lovely* British accent), commented, "Oh, your brother took that photo of you, didn't he, Dick?"

The next three days flew by all too quickly, and I sat taking notes as quickly as possible. The problem I encountered was, while listening to those terrific anecdotes he'd tell, I'd find my mind drifting away: "Wow... I can't believe I'm actually sitting here, listening to Richard Williams, the animation director of *Roger Rabbit*, and

The Thief and The Cobbler, and my favorite Pink Panther movie titles, *Return of the Pink Panther* and *The Pink Panther Strikes Again*. This is so cool!"

The next thing I'd know, he was finished with his entertaining anecdote and had hopped back into instructional mode. I could only struggle to get caught back up. Sadly, when I got home and started looking over my notes, I discovered gaps in their sequence.

Clay Croker (the voice and animator of Zorak, the perennially evil mantis from *Space Ghost: Coast to Coast*), whom I'd met at a previous Atlanta Dragon-Con, was there at the same time. He was kind enough to share notes with me afterward, and helped fill in some gaps later over the phone, after I got back to Montgomery.

Thankfully, I found out that Mr. Williams was soon to publish his full set of notes and illustrations in the book *The Animator's Survival Kit*, which seems never to collect dust on my bookshelf.

Now that you've got an idea of who Richard Williams is, and hopefully have at least the beginning of an appreciation for his work, you'll understand why I refer to him throughout this book.

Why Animation? You May Ask

Why should we invest so much of our time and efforts in this art form we call animation? Good question, my friends. Well, here's our alternative to animation: the lowest, most base of pathetic, whimpering Hollywood executives throwing up their hands and wantonly admitting they've run out of "original" ideas, by slinging in our general direction...

the so-called "reality show."

Here's the problem I have with reality shows. When I switch on the TV, go to a movie, or even crack open a book, the *last* thing I expect — much less actually *want* — is reality. If I wanted reality, I'd switch off the TV, walk outside, and experience raw, unbridled, unedited, *truly* unscripted reality — all for the price of *free*.

I don't need an overpaid executive directly or indirectly slipping money from my pocket to fund payment on his latest convertible. Certainly not from funds garnered via reality TV.

Reality (shows) stink. Note to Hollywood: Please stop making these. It's one of the reasons I cancelled our cable.

When I allow my "suspension of disbelief" to kick in, I could care less about a group of mismatched trailer park princes and teen queens arguing about their pickup's engine problems or their nail color choices or their roommates' total lack of personal hygiene.

When I switch on the TV, go to a movie, or yes, even crack open a book, I want *fantasy*.

The same thing goes for animation. I don't care about seeing an animated series regarding a group of whiny "tweeners" (or "pre-teens," as we used to call them) hanging around their every-day neighborhood "doing nothing." I would much rather spend my escapist time in an alternate reality... in an animated wonderland, with sarcastic robots, intergalactic space cruisers, wisecracking wabbits, ill-tempered dragons, or mighty dinosaurs.

If you can achieve it in live action, why bother to animate it?
A few of my favorite things: dragons, dinosaurs, and other animated fantasies. Just for good measure, I added a few hints of reality. In addition to my self-caricature, I added my wife, my *pretty*... and our little dogs, too!

If any of those last few ideas excite you, and you feel somehow that's precisely how you'd prefer to invest your time rather than vegging out on the couch in front of someone else's bland video offering, then this book is precisely what should empower you to make that happen.

Now that we've established that animation is the doorway into that fantasy world you've always dreamed of creating, then what is the key?

Why Flash? You May Ask

Flash is a program I had heard about, but mainly in the realm of web design. And then, as time went on, I heard more and more about it. A friend at an Atlanta area animation studio had told me for years that I needed to learn Flash, but I'd been using Macromedia Director for about 15 years by that time (and it was paid for!), and I thought, "Aw, who wants to go to the trouble of learning a new animation program? Between Director painting and flipping my pages for me, and Adobe After Effects handling my compositing and camera moves, I really don't need to learn a whole new animation program."

A quick note on learning...

Frustration with new material is part of the learning process, just like stumbling and falling down is part of learning to walk before you can run. When you fall down and stub your toe, do you sit down in the mud, shaking your fist at the heavens, swearing up and down that you'll never walk again? Absolutely not! Think of all the things you'd be missing.

Although all that seems obvious, before I started to learn Flash, I used Macromedia Director, which was the first all-out "animation program" I learned to use way back in 1990, when I took my first animation class at Auburn University Montgomery. It was a great program for what I wanted to do at the time, and certainly got me to stretch my wings in the world of animation before I was capable of full flight.

But then, when I decided to move to Atlanta to join my wife (whose architectural job was by now working out), I started contacting and visiting the local animation studios. "Great work," one pair of studio executives told me. "You're easily in the top 1% of people who've ever applied here. I mean, you even wore a TIE to the interview. But we really need *Flash* animators."

After trudging wearily from studio to studio, my knuckles dry, white, and scaly from knocking on so many doors, my fingertips raw from emailing so many resumes, looking for someone who'd hire a Macromedia Director animator, it slowly began to dawn on me...

Why not just learn Flash?

Why Not Just Learn Flash?

It sounds silly now, of course, but we all have a nasty tendency to settle into our comfort zones, especially in the realm of learning, which is an ongoing process (like it or not). I taught character animation for 10 years at Auburn University Montgomery, all with Macromedia Director, but they only offered the class once a year. Now that I've learned Flash, Final Cut Pro, and other new industry standard software, I'm teaching a minimum of two classes every term at Westwood College, here in Atlanta, along with the occasional weekend workshop. Teaching, for the moment at least, is enabling me to make enough of a living part-time, while pursuing my own creative endeavors — making cartoons and movies — the rest of my waking hours, along with leisure time for my family.

My point to all this of course is simply… be prepared for the learning process.

It's essential to our survival as creative artists to learn the new software as technology continues to develop, and to make personal contacts in the animation and entertainment industry. There's not a reason in the world earning your rent money shouldn't be *fun*.

Why This Book?

In my case, when I needed to learn Flash, I bought three or four books on the subject, most of which had pretty good reviews on Amazon.com. But I ran into several problems with these other books:

- They were already out of date.
- They were written by people who either used Flash for purposes other than animated cartoons or, even if they *did* make Flash cartoons, couldn't *draw.*
- They didn't tell me what I wanted to know.

Self-portrait of the author trying to learn Flash from other books

And as I talked to some other members of ASIFA-Atlanta (the Atlanta chapter of the International Animated Film Association, from a French acronym), I discovered they too didn't care much for the other books available on Flash.

So I arrived at the only possible conclusion... I'd write the book on Flash I wish I'd had when I wanted to learn it.

My wife had a rather bemused reaction when I told her my plan to write a Flash book in this way. "You're going to write a book on a program you just learned a few months ago?"

My response was to repeat a similar scenario from (again) way back in 1990, when I'd just started taking computer graphics classes at Auburn University Montgomery. My instructor saw how enthusiastic I was about animation, and asked me if I would be interested in a position as computer graphics lab monitor. "Sure," I said with a nervous chuckle, "but is it such a good idea for me to be answering questions about computers when I'm just getting started in them?"

My instructor's response has stuck with me for years: "You'll be surprised how much you learn by helping others." And that has been *so* true. To this day, I tell my students that same story.

With that out of the way, are you ready to learn?
Here are your only two choices:

- **Yes.** Good! (Continue to Paragraph Q.)
- **No.** Too bad! (In that case, set this book down, nail yourself in a coffin, and have someone feed you through a tube slid inside a knothole. If you're not willing to learn to be fed through a tube, have them plug up the knothole.)

Paragraph Q

All right, I know it's practically impossible to learn everything you ever wanted to know about animation or Flash in one book, but I wanted to make a genuine effort to at least give you the basics within one book cover. Therefore, this book is divided into two handy sections:

- Section I — Drawing and the Animation Process
- Section II — Using Flash to Animate Your Drawings

If you know everything there is to know about hand-drawn animation (or at least more than I do, which is quite conceivably possible), you're more than welcome to skip to the second section. Really, you won't hurt my feelings… much. But there is a vague possibility there might be some useful information tucked away in the earlier pages that might make the animation process easier.

What It Is and What It Ain't…

This book is designed as a handy *beginner's* guide to start making your own cartoons, from pencil to pixel (or just plain pixel, if you so choose) with Macromedia Flash.

It's the book I wish I'd had when I started using Flash to make my own cartoons for video, web banners, or just my own personal amusement.

It guides you, step by step, from drawing storyboards, scanning them, finding voices and sound effects for your soundtrack, and creating your drawings (whether with pencils or pixels) that will move and talk… and, hopefully above all else, *act*.

I've tried to make this book an enjoyable, informative, and entertaining read by embellishing the text with original illustrations, interviews with animation professionals, and student artwork, along with a few doodles from my personal sketchbooks and yes, even restaurant menus.

As any of my students could readily tell you, I've nicknamed myself "Tangent Man," and many of the included anecdotes fall into that category. Wherever possible, such anecdotes are denoted as "Tangent Man Tales," as follows:

Tangent Man © Mark S. Smith/MarkToonery.com

Tangent Man, my not-too-terribly-secret identity, as any of my students would likely agree. He'll guide you through, or past, colorful (and optional) anecdotes that you may or may not find helpful on your journey to learning animation with Flash.

Those of you more eager to jump into Flash are perfectly welcome to leap past these sections and come back to them at such time (if any) when you're so bored you look forward to another evening of bashing your head repeatedly against the wall plaster.

This book ain't a 50-pound coffee table book subtitled "Everything You Never Wanted to Know About Flash ActionScript in 12 Oversized Volumes But Were Afraid Someone Might Tell You Anyway," and it is not intended to be the end-all, in-depth ActionScript guide.

There are plenty of other books on that very subject.

This ain't it.

Chapter 2

Learning to Draw: Tools and Tips

Girth, Thurman, and Deadbeat
© Mark S. Smith/MarkToonery.com

Which comes first? A story or your character? That's every bit as difficult to answer as "Which came first? The chicken or the egg?" (All right, the chicken, if you're a creationist, like yours truly, but that's a *whole* other book I've got to get around to writing.)

But in the realm of animation, it is tricky to say whether a character is developed by the story or vice versa. But either way you look at it, it's a pretty bleak script without characters, so let's start with character design.

Besides, if you think about it, how on earth can you start your storyboards unless you have at least a vague idea of what your characters look like?

With that said, let's move on to the fascinating world of character design, which I've tried to neatly divide into three tidy little methods.

I'd be surprised if (since you've picked up this book) you've never doodled along the edge of the page. The bored-looking "Grumbleblahs" (above, left) were done during a sales meeting. Old Man Taxbracket was probably done around tax time (go figure), and Zerg, the pointy-nosed, lizardy thing, was one of my first animation drawings done (back in about 1990) for my then all-new Amiga 2000 graphics computer! (Oh, yeah, sure... all right, go ahead and laugh!)

Three Methods of Character Design

Many people ask me… well, maybe a couple of people have asked me… okay, there was that *one* guy who asked me, "How can you possibly come up with an original design for a cartoon character?" Over the years, there have been literally hundreds of comic strips, TV shows, and animated features. Are there even any original, untapped ideas left?

Believe it or not, I genuinely believe there are. That's what excites me about the creative process. If we really put our minds to it, there is always at least one more original idea awaiting for us to discover it.

Here are three ways to find that original design for a character:

- The Frankenstein method
- The Observational method
- The Random Doodle method

The Frankenstein Method

Roger Rabbit is arguably my favorite cartoon character… along with Droopy, Daffy Duck, and Princess Elinore from Ralph Bakshi's *Wizards*. Like so many flavors of ice cream, it's just so tough to pick merely one favorite! Anyway, Roger was created with the Frankenstein method, so it's kind of hard to argue with that level of success.

When I took Richard Williams' Animation MasterClass in San Francisco (1997), he described how they came up with the design for Roger Rabbit… and better yet, *why*.

They wanted the audience to feel they'd seen him somewhere before, like he might have been an actual cartoon star whose memory had perhaps faded somehow.

So they took a Tex Avery character's cashew-shaped head with that little red cowlick of hair on top and they gave him Goofy's floppy pants, Mickey's gloves, and Porky's bow tie. He's got Brer Rabbit's feet, and they topped it all off with perhaps his only "original" feature… his ears! Roger's ears are shaped like ladles (yeah,

those flat little spoon-like thingies in the kitchen). Williams said it was really frustrating that the animators would sometimes try to draw Roger with Bugs Bunny's pointy ears. "Please, let's get the ears right! It's the only original design element he has!"

Then, to top things off, since they "wanted people to like him," they decided to make Roger the color of the American flag: red trousers, white fur, and blue eyes.

One of my own favorite characters, from a design standpoint, is A. Sezquatch, from my *Bigfoot Country* comic strip. And he, also, is the result of the Frankenstein method. Let me show you what I mean.

If you ever get a chance, try to find some of the original Popeye comic strips by his creator, E.C. Segar. I absolutely loved the Max Fleischer cartoons, don't get me wrong (before he switched over to that white sailor suit), but even the staggering animation in *Popeye the Sailor Meets Sinbad the Sailor* doesn't hold a candle to the storylines of Segar's original comic strip. Like *Lil' Abner*'s screen adaptations, they far outweighed the "assault and spinach" formula plotlines of the screen adaptations. (There are some reprints

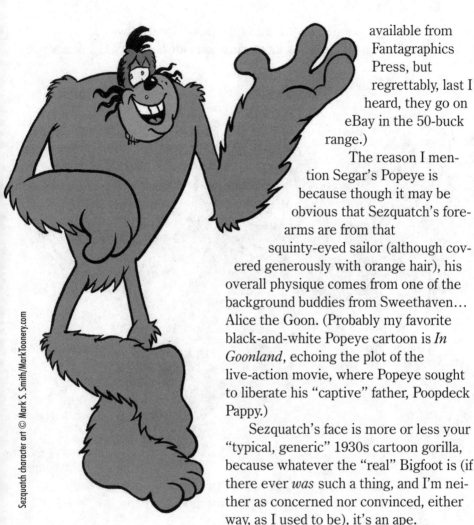

Sezquatch character art © Mark S. Smith/MarkToonery.com

available from Fantagraphics Press, but regrettably, last I heard, they go on eBay in the 50-buck range.)

The reason I mention Segar's Popeye is because though it may be obvious that Sezquatch's forearms are from that squinty-eyed sailor (although covered generously with orange hair), his overall physique comes from one of the background buddies from Sweethaven… Alice the Goon. (Probably my favorite black-and-white Popeye cartoon is *In Goonland*, echoing the plot of the live-action movie, where Popeye sought to liberate his "captive" father, Poopdeck Pappy.)

Sezquatch's face is more or less your "typical, generic" 1930s cartoon gorilla, because whatever the "real" Bigfoot is (if there ever *was* such a thing, and I'm neither as concerned nor convinced, either way, as I used to be), it's an ape.

The remaining facial feature I could suggest is perhaps that his eyebrows are heavily influenced by Wile E. Coyote's.

The only "original" element Sezquatch has is his sideburns. The first time I drew him, as a costar to BaaBraw Blacksheep in my unpublished comic book, *The Evil Plot of Dr. Ratnest*, he was missing his now-familiar sideburns. Years later, when I met my wife, she had a border collie mix named Gussi (pronounced "Goosey"), who had these adorable, wiggly little sideburns sticking out from beneath her ears.

They became Sezquatch's sideburns… and he was done. Though his building blocks originated elsewhere, my Frankenstein job worked.

"He's alive! Alive!"

While the villagers run for their pitchforks and light their torches, let's move on to the next method of creating an "original" character design.

The Observational Method

I walked out of a hospital elevator, and there he was.

A grungy ball cap barely contained a wiry nest of grizzled hair in a downward swerve past a moustache that may have once belonged to Yosemite Sam in his adolescent years. A pair of dark sunglasses covered eyes (I presume of some indescribable sort). A sweaty tank top disappeared, half-tucked, into a pair of jeans that tumbled down into messy, frayed bellbottoms just over (and this was the best part) a pair of dime-store, rubber sandals... or flops, as we refer to them in the South.

Now, remember, I caught all this in perhaps a five-second glance, at best.

If you're an artist, you've got to be prepared to not just draw fast, but to look fast, too... and take it all in.

The observational method of character design, as you've probably guessed by now, is simply observing real-life characters and putting them down on paper.

I'd just come from visiting my stepmom's sister in the hospital and, as I walked onto the ground floor from the elevator, this character was stepping into the elevator. It was hard not to stare at such an outstanding specimen of the rural Alabama experience and, as you can guess, it's wiser *not* to stare for reasons of personal safety. When observing people for drawing purposes, it's best to remain casually unobtrusive in your efforts. Try not to "draw" too much attention to yourself.

I tell my art students to never be without your trusty sketchpad, because there's no telling when you're going to run into a real-life cartoon character, who only needs a telltale outline to fully transport himself into the second dimension of Toontown.

When I am sitting at the airport, when I am waiting in a long line, or even when my wife and I eat out, I don't like to be without at least a pen so I can jot down a quick character sketch onto a paper napkin.

Recently, my wife and I went to eat at a new restaurant she'd wanted to try out. It turned out to be a "country cooking" style place (one of my favorite, with those dishes of gravy and mashed potatoes, fried green tomatoes, and the like), and an interesting character drove into the parking lot right behind us. He hopped out of his sporty little convertible and hurried past us, for he obviously had better things to do than reply to my polite "Hello."

He was in a black sports jacket, and had on an ash-colored buttonless shirt. His receding hairline rivaled my own, but his remaining snowy locks were a little more carefully cropped than my sandy brown ones. I don't know why, but immediately I knew this guy was an advertising executive. Perhaps it was the folder jutting out from his armpit, or his overwhelming, smug superiority complex. I couldn't be sure which, but very soon my suspicion was confirmed.

As you can see, Mr. Personality, on the left, was some sort of advertising agent trying to make a sale with a new restaurant owner. The two sketches on the right were done in a buffet restaurant. The top fellow was a biker in overalls. (I don't know if you can appreciate his braided ponytail.) The senior citizen below had a strangely squared, compact physique I sketched quickly as his party left the restaurant.

After my wife and I ordered and sat down to eat a late lunch, "Mr. Personality" (as I'll call him) positioned himself across the table from the owner/manager, a pleasant, polite-looking Asian-American underneath a ball cap not unlike my own.

It wasn't just the features of this ad executive that fascinated me; it was the body language that was going on between these two. Mr. Personality was leaning forward over his fancy folders of sample ads, with his fingers almost touching the opposite side of the table. Mr. Manager, on the other hand, was leaning his face in his hands. While facing the ad-man, his legs and the rest of his body were facing away from the presentation at nearly a 90-degree angle.

Perhaps you've already arrived at the same conclusion I did, even before I started eavesdropping. Mr. Manager was neither impressed nor convinced that this was the way to spend his advertising dollars.

Nevertheless, even though Mr. Personality walked out of the restaurant quietly doubting that commission he'd hoped would pay off his sporty little convertible, I walked out of the restaurant with an amusing little sketch scenario. Certainly not a finished cartoon, as you can see, but the first sketch at the top of the drawing was from my point of view, and the two sketches below were how I imagined it from Mr. Manager's perspective. All of these were drawn on a handout dinner menu.

Hopefully you can see what I'm getting at. Character ideas are all around us... at restaurants, sitting on a park bench feeding the pigeons, waiting at the bus station, or even in class.

I did some sketches while sitting in the Atlanta airport en route to my aforementioned San Francisco flight. One lady I drew, oddly enough, ended up sitting on the plane next to me. Though I can't recall whether I showed her the sketch I produced of her, I showed her the accompanying sketch of her traveling companion. She was mildly amused, at best.

And when I got to the theatre where we were all to spend the next three days enthralled at the verbal exploits and physical stage performance of Mr. Richard Williams, I found myself in a veritable amphitheater of caricatures. Cartoonists love to draw each other, for some reason, but cartoonists just love to draw... period.

Though I was pretty happy with the drawings I did of an Asian artist and Mr. Williams (who insisted that everyone call him "Dick"), I think the drawing that best exhibits the personality of the subject was this young man sitting on the front row.

Yeah, these types *always* sit on the front row. You know them.

That know-it-all in the front row

Whether you're in a college class, Sunday school, or any public forum, there's always that one know-it-all (or worse yet, more than one) who always has to pipe up.

I don't mean to sound unduly negative, but here was a room full of artists, eagerly waiting to hear the results of Mr. Williams' 30+ years of animation-experience advice, many of whom had spent their own hard-earned dollars to be there... and whatever Dick said, whatever advice the Animation Maestro himself offered us, this young man's hand would shoot up to counter-offer *his* personal approach. I wasn't the only one rolling my eyes and groaning every time young Mr. Knowitall waved his energetic palm at Dick.

There is something you may have noticed here also, from perhaps a psychological point of view, about character design. Rather than getting upset at these unpleasant types like Mr. Personality or Mr. Knowitall, rather than picking a fight or trying to win a shouting match, it's far less violent and perhaps far more constructive, and downright more personally satisfying in the end, to turn these smug individuals into cartoon characters.

In other words, instead of letting their petty annoyance factor work against your nerves, let it work *for* you and you might even surprisingly find yourself turning a profit. As a matter of fact, Mr. Grizzled Elevator Redneck (the one with the baseball cap and sunglasses, remember?) ended up in my CD-ROM presentation for KinderCare in an example on "How *not* to dress for work."

The Random Doodle Method

Okay, the first two methods we've discussed follow the general approach to drawing we've all learned instinctively, whether we realize it or not.

Drawing actually consists of two stages:

1. Seeing, and then...
2. Swirling your pencil around.

It's surprising how many of us can actually swirl our pencils around quite well, and find that our missing skill is not pencil-swirling but the *seeing* part of the process.

So if we could just swirl our pencils around without seeing, what kind of interesting results might that reward us with?

Two physical stages of drawing

Try this exercise: Get out a blank sheet of paper and a good ol'
#2 pencil. Don't worry whether it's even got an eraser or not,
because you're not allowed to use your eraser. In fact, you're absolutely *forbidden* to use your eraser in this exercise.

Sound scary? Good. Let's get started.

You're about to take your pencil in your hand (whether it's your
usual drawing hand or not doesn't really matter — you might try
this with either hand) and start randomly swirling your pencil
around in little doodles.

But here's the catch: Before you go any further, and before you
so much as set your pencil down onto the paper... whatever you
do... don't *look* at the paper!

The random doodle method

Just draw, and try not to think too much about what your hand is drawing. For the moment, you are totally unconcerned about what direction your line takes.

Put your pencil down on the paper, and start swirling it around. Do this for five or 10 seconds, alternating between slow and steady swirls and quick and erratic flicks of your pencil. Better yet, don't even let your pencil up from the paper. Just draw one continuous, flowing, wiggling, jiggling line and don't worry whether it's crossing over itself or not.

The point is to get as close to a random series of blind lines on your paper as possible.

Okay, once you're done, you can now peek at your paper.

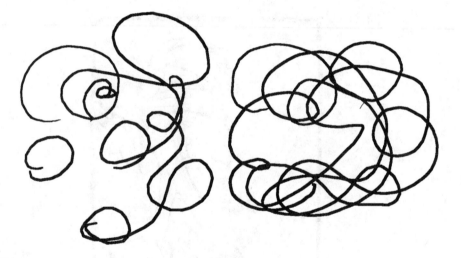

Random results of blindfold drawing

How did you do? Is it an absolute mess? That's okay; it's all part of the challenge.

Now your assignment is to start staring at that seemingly random mess and try to find some recognizable patterns. See if you see anything that resembles a face, or a body, maybe even an animal or a person.

Naturally, you might not see it at first. You may have to search through your doodles, but you'll see them eventually.

It's almost like staring at clouds in the sky. That cloud looks like a dragon, or that one looks like a sailing ship, maybe even a wolverine swallowing a badger in a duel to the death with battery-operated saxophones. (Okay, if you see that, you might actually want to seek psychiatric help; that's how I found out I was working too hard.)

Now, let's say other people were looking at this doodle, and trying to see this character that you've arrived at. They might not see it as easily as you see it; as a matter of fact, they might need some help. What sort of help would they need?

Okay, if you see an eye, maybe you could help the image by adding its counterpart eye on the other side of the face. Do you need to add eyebrows, a nose, or a mouth?

Go ahead and do that now. Your objective in this exercise obviously isn't making a finished drawing, but a beginning drawing. And sometimes those are more important than the "final."

Find the hidden critters and add lines as necessary.

Repeat this several times until you find at least one drawing you can use to begin with.

A similar approach to this is even closer to the "cloud gazing" experience. You can start out by staring at clouds and drawing what you "see," but just about any seemingly random pattern will work as well. I used to have wood paneling on my walls when I was a kid (yes, well it was the '70s), and I always remember seeing the "teddy bear" design in the wall. It wasn't a real drawing of a teddy bear, but just a wavy wood pattern that reminded me of a teddy bear.

How the ancient astronomers ever decided those constellations looked like Hercules, or any Greek heroes, monsters, or even a "big dipper" is beyond me, but it's using almost the same approach.

You may have textured plaster on your ceiling. If you don't have a textured ceiling, maybe you're sitting in a classroom or the library. If that's the case, and you look up, you may even see those little pinholes in those ceiling panels. Are there any interesting characters residing there, just waiting for you to stare at them long enough for them to begin to stare back?

Do you have carpet on your floor? Has it been disturbed by someone's footprints recently in a pattern that reminds you of a towering ogre's profile? How about a rock formation in a city park or zoo? There was a tiny, almost imperceptible tear on the wallpaper of the bathroom in our last apartment that few would have noticed, but right next to that tiny tear was a slightly discolored blob that made me think of a prehistoric monster, with horns like a musk ox and tusks like a wild boar on steroids.

By this time, you may find yourself getting some ideas. Y'know, you'd better jot those ideas down before you forget them.

You *might* be able to use one of them.

Mutant wild musk ox/boar on steroids

My Drawing Process and Tools

There's one thing I have to say up front. I learned one of the greatest secrets to making your drawings better from that Richard Williams fellow you hear me going on about. He calls it "Lesson #1," and I will recommend you read his book by either picking it up on Amazon.com or checking to see if your local library has it.

Anyway, he can explain how this lesson was forever ingrained in him by master animator Milt Kahl (who animated perhaps my favorite Disney villainess, Madame Medusa from *The Rescuers*, and the most impressive realistic tiger animation on Shere Khan — without a reference model), and his drawings tell it better than I can, but I'll let you in on the secret without further ado...

Ado!

(Okay, sorry, I had to get in just one last further *ado*. I just couldn't help myself!)

Lesson #1: Unplug. Turn off that TV, unplug that stereo, and take those earphones off.

Set them aside. Leave them there.

I have to work in silence. Ever since I took the Animation MasterClass from Richard Williams, I've had to work in silence. In his book *The Animator's Survival Kit*, Richard's got a terrific caricature of the incident between himself and Disney's Milt Kahl, explaining — at the top of his lungs — the importance of working in silence. The members of his class get a hysterical performance of Mr. Williams himself recreating the "incident."

In summary, a photo of himself after the "incident" shows Mr. Williams wearing a shirt reading (on the back, to discourage interruptions), "Animation is concentration."

Up until the time I took the class, I liked working with instrumental music (usually movie scores or classical) playing. But after receiving this groundbreaking revelation, I noticed that I worked better in silence. I could focus, and do better and more productive work, in a shorter amount of time.

Concentration requires quiet
even if quiet itself requires a creative approach.

Oddly enough, when I got back to my job after attending that class, I found even the most casual conversations between my coworkers were highly distracting. I solved the problem with a pair of ear protectors I had bought for working with noisy power tools. (Sorry, folks, but it's true. I hope my former coworkers don't read this.)

Okay, now that you know the condition under which you're supposed to work — silence — we can go on to the tools you'll need to get started.

Here are the three basics I think you need to draw animation:

Mandatory Animation Supplies

■ Light blue (*not* "non-repro blue") Col-Erase pencils

■ Acme-punched animation paper (one ream of student bond is fine for starters)

■ Acme plastic peg bar (you can tape it to a drawing surface to keep it steady)

And here are some more possibilities, depending on your personal approach and preference:

Optional Animation Supplies

■ Pilot Precise V7 Rolling Ball ink pen (black)

■ #4 or #5 brush for inking (probably the smaller you can stand, the better)

■ Small jar for water to rinse brush

■ Waterproof black ink

■ Tiny jar or lid for an inkwell

■ 100% cotton cloth for drying brush

■ A light table

Yeah, that light table — easily the most expensive item on the list, but you can buy a small light table for about $30 at most craft stores like Hobby Lobby or Michael's. Then you can attach a $6, plastic animation peg bar with household glue or even tape it along the bottom (or top edge; your choice) of the light table. You might even consider using drafting tape to attach the peg bar, and then you could remove it whenever needed. Or you can go ahead, splurge, and buy a small light table with the peg bar already attached in the $70 range.

Animation Pencils

The secret of my drawing method (which is hardly what I'd call a secret) is a small, obscure, friendly-looking utensil called the Col-Erase light blue pencil. (Available from www.cartooncolour.com at $8 per dozen, at the time of this writing.)

OH, DO YOU MEAN...

NON-PHOTO

NOPE → BLUE?

Oh! THEN YOU MUST MEAN THE

LIGHT BLUE

Col-Erase Pencil

YES

Thurman and Deadbeat © Mark S. Smith/MarkToonery.com

Almost immediately, people leap to the conclusion that I mean "non-repro blue pencil." Absolutely not. Although it has the same effect, it's a bit of nitpickery, but essential nitpickery. Though the light blue doesn't reproduce either, it's slightly darker (than non-repro blue), but just enough so that you can see through your blank sheet of animation paper to your previous drawing.

And the reason I insist on Col-Erase is essential. Something about that almost magical little eraser keeps it from tearing up your paper, even after multiple erasings. Better yet, you can ink right on top of the Col-Erase pencil. With many other kinds of pencils (especially the *vile* non-photo blue), if you try to ink directly on top of them, their consistency is chalky and it lightens up your ink too much so that when you scan, you'll waste *way* too much time cleaning up the mess.

However, if you're fortunate enough to have a light table, you can pretty much see through as many sheets at a time as you like, which would make this argument pointless.

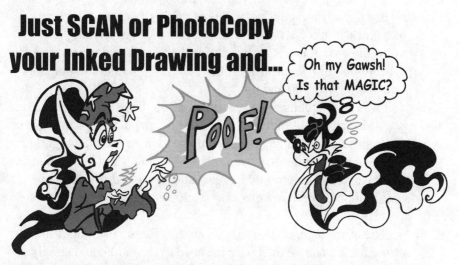

When you draw in light blue (or non-repro blue, for that matter), and then try to either photocopy or scan that drawing in black-and-white line art mode, what's going to happen? Exactly! The blue lines are going to disappear.

So this is what I do: I do my animation drawings with a light blue pencil so that I can ink directly on top of the original sheet of paper. Even though the delightful eraser (its namesake) allows you to erase to your heart's content without shredding your paper.

Animation Paper and the Acme Peg Bar

For years I resisted using professional animation paper. You can probably guess the reason if you've already looked it up on even a great place like www.cartoonsupplies.com — the cost.

One of the first things I saw when exploring the possibility of doing animation for fun and/or profit was how animators used something in drawing (especially on those interviews or Disney specials on drawing animation) called an *animation disc*.

It's a large, unwieldy metal disc that is attached to your desk and has the advantage of rotating to enable the ease of drawing characters at different angles. But of course, like anything that makes life easier, it has a price. And when I was looking in the back of *Animation Magazine* at the time, that price was in the neighborhood of $300 to $500 and up.

I was a struggling college student at the time, so I quickly came up with an alternate method that both held my drawings in registration (more or less), and gave me a place to keep them all together at once: a three-ring binder notebook. As a matter of fact, it became a personal challenge to find larger and larger notebooks as time went by, just to keep my growing stacks of animation sequences organized.

The advantage, of course, was cost. A three-ring binder might set me back a couple of dollars in those days, and I could simply use a standard three-hole punch (a one-time fee of about $15 or so) on a pack of typing paper, which was thin enough so that I could see through two or three drawings at a time without a light table.

The disadvantage, naturally, was keeping the drawings in registration with each other. The holes created by the paper punch were considerably larger than the wire rings, and the drawings have a tendency to slide around a bit as you draw.

As you start to draw animation, one of the things you'll quickly appreciate is how important it is that the drawings stay in registration with one another. If the drawings do slide around, a character that's supposed to be standing perfectly still might slowly begin to drift left or right. An amusing error perhaps, but unintentionally so.

Fortunately, an inexpensive solution awaited me after taking the Animation MasterClass. I found out that manufacturers produce a plastic peg bar that went for about $3 apiece back then. (They're about $3.50 to $6 now, depending on your supplier.) With this knowledge in hand, I eagerly made the purchase of a plastic peg bar.

The Acme peg bar and its accompanying paper consists of one peg in the center, and two rectangles on either side. The reason for this, of course, is to keep the animation drawings firmly rooted in place as you draw, rearrange, and flip your drawings to test the motion of the character.

Now that I had an animation peg bar in my possession, I knew it was time to buy some official animation paper. The first place I discovered was www.cartooncolour.com, thanks to their ad in the back of *Animation Magazine*. I found their 12-field animation paper, at 10½" x 12½", would suit my purposes. It was about $26 a ream, and I soon found out there was a problem.

Like most desktop animators, I scanned my animation drawings into the computer even then. But my scan bed was the usual, just-barely-over 8½" x 11" size. Often, my animation drawings were too big for the scanner, which made me have to scan a drawing twice because part of an arm or a leg was just hanging off the edge of the scan area. When that happened, after scanning in the offending character art twice, I then had to copy and paste the pieces back together. And as many animation drawings as you'll soon find are necessary for a scene, that is an unnecessary bit of time-consuming work!

Fortunately, I discovered the other website you've already heard me mention, www.cartoonsupplies.com, which offered student animation bond paper conveniently sized just for a desktop scanner. Better yet, at a mere $8.95 a ream!

You can guess where I've been buying my animation paper since.

I'll mention one last thing about animation paper before we get started actually drawing. There's been a big controversy over the years whether you're a "top-peg" animator or a "bottom-pegger." All this means is that some people prefer to draw with the pegs at the bottom of the page, and others with the pegs at the top of the page.

The advantage of being a top-pegger is that you can flip the drawings as you test the action to watch it progress.

Personally, I'm a bottom-pegger, because I prefer to simply "roll" the drawings back and forth by placing my left fingers between five or six pages at a time.

Whichever you choose, especially if you're working with a friend, fellow student, or assistant, choose one and stick with it throughout an entire scene. When I was subbing for an animation class last term, I was simultaneously amused and horrified (a disturbing and confusing feeling) when I saw that during a class exercise, two students were sharing the tasks of animating and inbetweening the same scene. The cause of my conflicting emotions was that while the student acting as the animator (doing the key drawings of the scene) was using the pegs at the top of the page, his assistant (or in this case, "inbetweener") was using the pegs at the bottom of the page. I'm sure they would have figured out the error if I'd let them be, but I much preferred to go ahead and save them some grief by pointing out the problem before it went any further.

I've even had some students want to draw with the pegs on the side. Forget that right away. Whether you're drawing animation for the Internet or for video, or even film, remember the orientation of the viewing screen or monitor. It's in landscape mode, or sideways. If you try drawing your character in an opposite orientation to the destination of your animation output, you may end up inadvertently cutting off your character's head or feet.

Learning to Draw

You probably have some basic experience drawing, as do most of us who are interested in animation or cartooning, so regardless of your level of expertise, let's just go over some simple, basic tips that will hopefully help you refine your technique.

START OUT
DRAWING LIGHT!

DON'T START
OUT TOO DARK!
THIS WOULD
TAKE **FOREVER**
TO ERASE THESE
GUIDELINES!

When you draw, whether it's with a good old #2 for rough sketches or with a light blue Col-Erase for finished animation draw-ings, always start out light. That way, when you make mistakes, and let's face it, you will, they will be easier to erase if the pencil marks are lightly shaded at the beginning. Otherwise, if you're bearing down on your pencil, grinding into the paper like you're giving it a tattoo, it's naturally going to be more difficult to erase.

Three Methods of Character Construction

These are not to be confused with the three methods of character design, which we've already covered. However you've arrived at the design for your character, now it's time to draw that character, over and over and over again, while still remaining consistent in the overall look, using one of the following methods:

- The Grid method
- The Gingerbread method
- The Geometric construction method

The Grid Method

First off, if you've got a book that tells you how to draw characters using a grid, do you and me both a favor, and either chunk it in the garbage or donate it to the library for some other hapless, misfortunate soul to discover the wrong approach to constructing a character.

Grids are fine if you're six years old, and have no real desire to draw that character in any other way than the way you see it already drawn.

Mark and Jayle © Mark S. Smith/MarkToonery.com

Grids are fine if you've got a finished drawing you're trying to reproduce at a different size, but animation producers aren't hiring animators who can only draw that perfect drawing of a character in that one given pose that's already been done. You need to be able to draw a character in a myriad of poses and with different facial expressions, with different physical, emotional attitudes.

A grid won't help you there.

The Gingerbread Method

When I was young, this is basically how I drew. I would start with the outlines of the character, like a gingerbread man, and then I'd fill in the features as I went along, like putting frosting features on my flat little character.

And right away, that's the problem you'll encounter with the gingerbread method. A flat, two-dimensional character, which looks just like that... a flat, two-dimensional character.

Yeah, yeah, I know... this is hand-drawn animation. I know it really *is* only two-dimensional characters that we're dealing with. We only have that x-axis (width) and y-axis (height) at our disposal. But we're trying to give characters that *illusion* of the third dimension, that illusion of the z-axis... that illusion of depth.

So how do we do that?

I'm so glad you asked. Fortunately, we have one last method of character construction.

The Geometric Construction Method

I know the title sounds a little fancy, but basically it just means that you construct your character out of basic geometric shapes, like circles, ovals, cylinders, and occasionally rectangles (use these sparingly). You're even allowed to use fruit and other yummy shapes like oranges, pears, cashews, and cucumbers.

Again, we come back to the reason why we use these geometric shapes.

First of all, they're easy to animate. Remember, you're going to be doing a lot of drawings on these characters… and I do mean a *lot*. So right away, you'd better decide to make your character relatively easy to draw by constructing it out of shapes that are easy to draw *repeatedly*.

You also have to be able to turn these characters in space, and a character that's built out of a series of circles and maybe a pear is going to be much more easily drawn from different angles. Also don't forget that (depending on the style in which you're working)

this character is going to be pushed and pulled around by outside forces, and squashed and stretched by gravity. Once again, far easier to accomplish with basic geometric shapes.

A final reason for basing your character construction on geometric shapes is visual appeal.

It has been noted that the appeal of Disney's most famous mouse is that he's built out of circles. A circle has been called the most geometrically perfect shape, and perhaps that is why Mickey has been such a success with generation after generation of fans.

Now that you've hopefully settled on the third (and I truly consider it the *only* viable) method, let's start with the most obvious feature of a character: the head.

I like to draw a character in what's called the 3/4 view. Obviously drawing a character in profile is not something you want to do in every single shot. Drawing directly in a frontal view is better than profile, but if you turn the character roughly halfway between a profile and frontal view, you've got the 3/4 view.

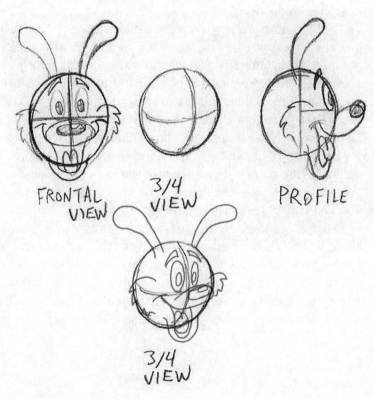

FRONTAL VIEW   3/4 VIEW   PROFILE

3/4 VIEW

As I mentioned earlier, we know very well that we're drawing two-dimensional characters, but we're always trying to give that illusion of the third dimension.

Drawing your character in the 3/4 view is probably the most important step in achieving that illusion.

Start out with a circle. To ensure that I'm drawing the character in that 3/4 view, I like to place these little perspective "guidelines" on the face. One that goes directly down the center of the face, between the eyes, and all the way around the back of the head back to where we started. The other guide will run perpendicular to the first line you drew, crossing the former right around the nose and at the very back of the head.

If you're working with a #2 pencil, you can erase these guides later. If you're working with the light blue Col-Erase pencil as I suggested, you don't even have to worry about erasing. Should the character turn out well enough so that you wish to ink him, and either scan or photocopy later, the blue lines will naturally disappear in reproduction.

You'll probably want to place the eyes sitting on that second guideline we created. Since we're drawing in 3/4 view, notice that perspective dictates that we need to make the character's eye, the one farther away from us, slightly smaller than the eye closer to us.

If you don't believe me, try drawing them the same size. Suddenly the eye farther away looks bigger than the one that is close (see the figure at the upper left on the following page), even though we know we've drawn them the same size. I have to "cheat" a bit and make the far eye smaller to give the eyes the illusion of being "the same size" (see the figure at the upper right).

The laws of perspective sure are weird, huh?

Okay, depending on the particular features of your character, go ahead and fill those in either according to the example on the following page, or use details of your own choosing. Here, we're using a sort of traditional 1940s animated character, but of course, style will vary according to your personal taste. You've got to start somewhere, and this is as good a style to start with as any.

As you start to flesh out the rest of your character, you're going to start to ask yourself questions: What kind of character is this? Tall, short, skinny, fat, or muscular? How old is he or she? Is the character generally a happy individual, or angry, maybe even sullen? What time frame is this character from? Is this a well-to-do, zoot-suited party player from the 1940s, or is he a peasant from the Dark Ages? Obviously, costume is going to play a role here as well in determining your character, so these are all questions you'd better be prepared to answer.

When I was drawing characters back in high school, I found myself making up stories about them that practically wrote themselves.

The Gargoyle and Cathy © Mark S. Smith/MarkToonery.com

For instance, that's the Gargoyle. If you just look at him once, he looks like something that hopped off a ledge from the Notre Dame cathedral. But at second glance, he's actually a party animal... he's got a weakness for being a ladies' man (or a ladies'... well, *whatever*) and making wisecracks at inappropriate times. He's a practical joker, and if his "boss," The Dark, were to tell it, the somber overlord would describe the Gargoyle as something between a flying bodyguard, tomcat, and court jester all rolled into one.

Did I mention his tail has poisonous spikes?

Do the same thing for your character. Give him a back story. How did this guy become the Gargoyle, for instance? He used to be a typical teenager named Marty at an Alabama high school back in 1986. Then his best friend Mark Johnson found a magical amulet (a sinister talisman from a forgotten North American civilization), a fearsome metallic basilisk with ruby eyes, coiled into the shape of an ampersand (the "&" symbol) turned on its side. Marty wished he could be a shapeshifter, and now the gray-green gargoyle is his favorite form of choice.

Easy, huh?

Now back to our little generic 1940s character. We'll give him those thin arms common to the era, as well as those little white gloves. Why do they all wear little white gloves? Good question. I always figured it was to help conceal the fact that they only had a thumb and three fingers, as opposed to our four fingers and a thumb. The reason this is done (most likely) is to reduce the work for the animators. If you think about it, since there are 24 frames per second for film, and 30 frames per second for video, and you've got to do a drawing for each one of those frames (as long as the character isn't standing perfectly still), you start to see why very early in the animation industry, people began to look for shortcuts to speed up their work process.

If you figure drawing one less finger on one hand would be 24 less fingers you'd have to draw per second of film, then double that for the other hand, that's 48 less fingers you have to draw... again, per second! (Multiply that out across 60 seconds per minute in a six-minute cartoon, or even a 75-minute animated feature!)

Right away, I hope this helps you appreciate one of the most important aspects of character design... simplicity!

When I was at the Animation MasterClass, Dick was taking questions, and I was still fairly new to animation (only seven years to his thirty-plus), so I thought, "How can I come up with a good, sensible question? Well, I got my degree in graphic design, so I suppose I'll ask him a design question."

"Dick," I asked, after he pointed to my raised hand. "What's your favorite character you've worked on from a design standpoint?"

"I'd have to say the Thief, from *The Thief and The Cobbler,* just because he has such a simple design." Since that comes from a bona-fide animation genius, I'd say that was a pretty darn good answer.

I'd have to say as a comparison, about the same time *Batman the Animated Series* came out, a new *X-Men* cartoon came out. With Batman, they came up with a terrific "look" that had the characters simplified to a level of streamlined simplicity so the artists could focus less on "drawing all those little detail lines" you see in the comic book, and could channel their creative energies onto giving the characters a better performance in fluid motion.

On the *X-Men,* they tried to go with the look of "drawing all those little detail lines" and attempting to get the characters as close to their original comic book designs as possible. While doing so, they had to focus on "all those little detail lines" rather than the fluid performance of the character, and they ended up being stiff-limbed and kinda clunky-moving.

I really need to mention this here as we approach drawing your first model sheet, because this book's goal, as you recall, is to teach you to import your drawings into Flash. Not only will a simple character be easier to animate with fewer lines, but it will honestly download faster and move faster with fewer lines.

So please do keep that in mind as you're designing your character.

Legs on our typical 1940s character aren't too different from his arms, relatively thin, but perhaps just a bit longer than the arms. Feet are kept simple, like the rest of the character, and we'll leave him barefooted for no particular reason. Notice we can get away with giving him even fewer toes than he has fingers. If you don't believe me, count how many toes Fred Flintstone has. Three! You think I'm kidding? Count them and see.

With our first character drawing done, now we need to take this a little bit further and do at least two more drawings from the basic angles: 3/4 view (which you hopefully just completed), profile, and back view. You may want to do a full frontal view, just to even things out.

When drawing a model sheet, it's best to draw all your views of the character at the same size, and standing on the same horizontal line. Many studios even place what I call a "head ruler" across the sheet, just to show how many "heads high" a character is. That's a further precaution that helps you keep the proportions consistent on the character, regardless of whether you're a one-man independent animation crew, or have a staff of hundreds that will all be drawing the same character. (Naturally, you'll soon discover how many assistants you have depends on how many zeros are in your animation production budget.)

You may wish to add to your model sheet, depending on the size of your sheet of paper, the character in various moods, attitudes, and positions. Facial expressions are handy to include.

What you'll also quickly realize is that it's unlikely you'll get any of these drawings right the first time; that's perfectly all right. For now, you're in an exploratory process to develop a character that, if properly drawn, can enthrall hundreds, thousands, or perhaps even millions of happy viewers.

An early Jayle Bat model sheet. Note the "head ruler" behind Jayle, which indicates she's roughly 4½ heads tall. A model sheet should include a turnaround, preferably with front, back, and side views of the character. It should also show the character in various attitudes of happy, frightened, bored, angry, and any other emotions she's likely to run through during your cartoon.

It's kind of interesting to see how Jayle has developed over the past 10 years. Oddly enough, the "frightened" image still looks most like how I currently envision the character.

A.

B.

(A) If you have two characters, it may be best to use contrast to your advantage. Even though Laurel and Hardy dressed almost identically, the contrast between thick and thin made them visually amusing to look at.

(B) Variations. When developing a character, don't be too quick to choose your first drawing. Experiment with those anatomical proportions! See how many variations you can get, starting with the same shapes (circles) and the same ingredients (1930s bulb-nose, gloves, hair).

(C) See what I would've been stuck with if I'd stopped at any of my first three drawings of Jayle?

C.

Jayle studies © Mark S. Smith/MarkToonery.com

Basic Character Types

Naturally, as I've stated before, I don't expect to be able to tell you every possible character type and body description (in a book of this scope), but I would like to discuss a few basic characters to get you started: the hero, the heroine, the wacky sidekick animals, and the villain/monsters. I'm sure we could name plenty of others, but as I can see you chomping at the bit to leap into Flash, we'll stay simple with these four.

Basic Hero Construction

The hero is a guy who may have an everyday build, more on the slender side (like the caricature of yours truly), or any variation of these, but generally, in the category of the animated film, we're talking about the Charles Atlas/knight in shining armor type.

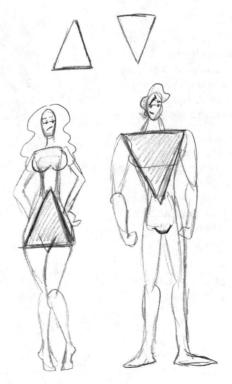

Basic gender geometry

One of the most basic differences between males and females is what I call the "appeal of the inverted triangle." (*Ahem!* Now, be nice!) With the male, and even more so in the hero, you'll want to have a triangle pointing downward. The broad shoulders taper down to a narrow waist.

In the female, there is a significant difference. And to quote Pepé Le Pew on that very subject, *"Vive le difference!"*

The female's basic overall form starts from a flat-bottomed triangle, or a standard pyramid, pointing upward. Her narrow shoulders and waist widen out to the hips, which are the widest part of the body. But more on that later.

As for the hero, you'll probably want to keep him at least reasonably muscle-bound, or at least enough so that he's prepared for the challenges he'll face in the adventures you're about to lead him through in your cartoon.

SLIGHTLY PIGEON-TOED (INWARD)

IN SOME CASES

Basic hero and heroine

A good rule of thumb I've read about drawing muscular characters is to try to keep most of your muscles on one side of the arm
or leg... and that's the side with a bulge on it, or at least something
of a curve. The other part, closer to the bone, will have a tendency
to be more straight.

Again, depending on the physical tone of your hero, he may
have a thick neck, a lantern jaw, and the traditional six-pack just
below his rib cage.

Additionally, you'll note that one difference between the more
realistic characters and the more cartoony characters is the number
of heads tall. We have a tendency to think of the head taking up
more space on the body than it actually does, but that's mostly psychological. Since we focus generally on the face (during a
discussion with someone), we think it's larger in proportion to the
body than it really is.

On adult males, we're generally about six to seven heads tall,
and not too far from that on women. Naturally, we're all different,
and that's what makes us interesting as real-life individuals or cartoon caricatures. These are obviously just general rules of thumb.
And remember, it's best to learn the rules of anatomy first... and
then break them only as necessary.

For more detail on drawing heroes, I'd check out a great book
by Ben Caldwell called *Action! Cartooning*, and its companion book,
Fantasy! Cartooning. They're great reference, whether you're
drawing heroes, heroines, villains, or fantasy creatures.

Basic Heroine Construction

Once upon a time, my brother (who is also an artist) was looking through my sketchbook. He was enjoying my pictures of monsters and silly cartoon characters, but he had to stop and slightly mask a grimace. "I hate to say this, Mark, and no offense, but... you really need to work on your women. They're really not... well, all that *attractive*."

I'm one of the few artists who will allow you to see some of my earlier lousy drawings, but here you go. I think he was probably talking about a drawing not unlike these:

Not my best female drawings, from an early sketchbook.

At this point, I had two choices: I could (A) get angry and/or indignant, throw myself into a serious tantrum, and never ask his opinion again. Or I could (B) grow as an artist, by weighing the opinion he had offered as diplomatically as he was then able, and taking a careful, scrutinizing look at my work.

I went with choice B, and looked carefully at my *attempt* at an attractive woman.

Hmm… (Sigh.)

As much as I hated to admit he was right, well… he *was* right. My women needed some serious work.

So, I practiced. I looked at photos, and tried to figure out and analyze what unique, individual features made each woman attractive. I tried to inject that into my designs. Here are some of the observations I collected from my own opinions regarding feminine physical charm, and from other artists over the years.

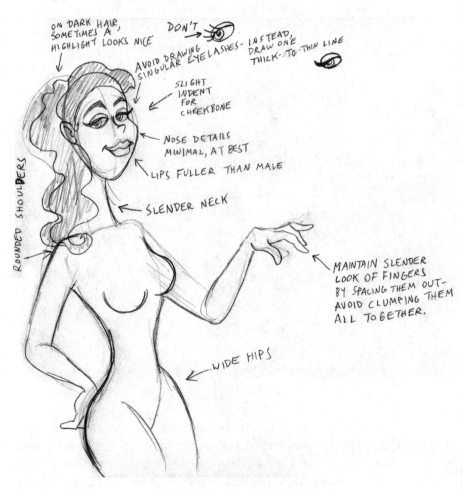

Helpful tips in drawing females

Overall, when drawing women, again make sure the hips are wider than the shoulders, which are generally more soft and rounded than her masculine counterpart's. The neck also has a tendency to be more slender, and the hands are longer and more graceful.

One of the foremost features to be considered is the face. And since the eyes are, as they say, the "windows to the soul," that might be as good a place as any to start. I have a tendency to draw the eyes on women larger than I do on men. When possible, I like to draw the iris as a separate shape from the pupil. Normally the iris, or colored part of the eye, is the first thing to be lost during the simplification process of caricature. Otherwise, the larger the pupil, the more alert (and sometimes even the *younger*) the character.

Keep the eyelashes as a single, thick and thin line. Think how mascara thickens the eyelashes and tends to clump them together. Ask yourself, how often can you count individual eyelashes when standing three feet away from someone? Avoid drawing the little cartoon eyelashes whenever possible, except perhaps for a moment of comic effect.

For a more attractive woman, also put as little detail in drawing their noses as possible. As weird as it sounds, look at those fashion commercials, when they flood a model's face with light, or when they're interviewing an aging model/actress. They'll either overlight or soften and even blur the picture so those wrinkles and detail lines disappear. One of the first things to go is the nose. Don't believe me? Look at those two foundations of feminine teen beauty (well, in the cartoon kingdom, anyway), Betty and Veronica. Find a picture of either one and look at their noses. Not only are they missing the bridges to their noses, they don't even have nostrils. They just have a little right triangle, a triangle set on its side. In other words, less is more!

The same basic rule for drawing eyelashes applies similarly to drawing hair. As one of my first drawing instructors told me, avoid drawing the individual hairs, and instead approach hair as a mass. Because even though it is composed of those tiny fine lines, gravity (and air, especially wind) tends to treat hair more as a mass, so we as artists should do the same.

For my first art show, the 1988 Atlanta Fantasy Fair, I had done a number of drawings, mostly in pencil (not the best recommendation for an art show, especially as light as some of them were). One in particular I recall was a mermaid, or rather a variation I called a Mermayden. Instead of her body tapering to a single fish tail, she had two legs (and knees) like most human females, but instead of feet she had fins, beginning pretty much at her calves.

In any case, another artist was kind enough to offer me a few words of advice on drawing female hands. Besides keeping the fingers relatively long and slender, it's best to avoid drawing all the fingers clumped together (a fist would be the obvious, inescapable exception); otherwise the hand is in danger of looking too massive. Instead, cluster them together in groups of two or three.

Legs are widest at the thighs, tapering down to the knees, flaring out again slightly at the calves, and then down again to the ankles.

Naturally, all these general guidelines for drawing men and women are just that… general guidelines.

As I've grown older, I've also found that the general appearance of women I find attractive has changed as well. When I was a teenager, I was attracted to the "Morticia Addams" types. Of course I've always been attracted to brunettes, but when I was younger, they were taller and more slender. Phoebe Cates and Jennifer Connelly were (and still are, at the time of this writing) probably the best live-action examples.

I've noticed in the past 10 years or so, however, that I like women who are described as a little "curvier." Look at the Frank Frazetta women from the 1970s, on the covers of *Vampirella* and those old *Conan the Barbarian* novel covers.

Some people may get "wowed" by Jessica Rabbit, but I think if we ground the female character with just a *bit* more realism, we're likely to be a bit more successful. My favorite female cartoon lead in the past few years was (from the vastly underrated *Road to El Dorado*), the native girl Chel. Likewise, look at Princess Elinore in Ralph Bakshi's *Wizards* for another example of an attractive female with some curves.

A woman doesn't have to be a total walking stick figure to turn heads, folks!

I'm probably one of the few people involved in the media who will tell you this: Just because idealized men and women are portrayed physically a certain way in popular entertainment doesn't mean that's the way we're *supposed* to look. Remember, animation is largely a *fantasy* world.

If the famed Barbie doll were a real woman, and walking down the street, she would get more than a few casual glances. Because if a human female were actually as tall proportionately as that popular toy, which is regrettably given to little girls around the world at an impressionable age, she would be seven feet tall.

Wacky Sidekicks

The wacky sidekick characters, much like the 1940s character explored earlier, have a tendency to be shorter and fewer heads tall. Your wacky sidekick could be any number of silly forest or barnyard animals walking upright or down on all fours, goblins, insects, or even humans.

If you can stick a pair of eyes and a mouth on it, you can make it into an animated character. As a matter of fact, if you take into account characters like *The Addams Family*'s Cousin Itt, and perhaps better yet, the Flying Carpet from Disney's *Aladdin*, even those details may not be needed for a particularly talented cartoonist. You can get a surprising range of expression with a minimum of details. And that's something else I like about animation.

Of all of the expressive art forms, I think animation has the greatest storytelling potential. With animation you can give anything a range of emotions, whether it's an anthropomorphic bat-girl, a pompous teapot conducting a symphony with a spoon, or even an animated flour sack, hopping and scrambling across the room to get away from a rampaging eggbeater.

As I often tell my students, if you can do this scene in live-action, why bother to animate it? You're going to a lot of trouble, so make sure your trouble is worthwhile.

Such is the case of the wacky sidekick.

Wacky sidekick sketchbook sampler

Even though your main characters may be more realistic, like Fred and Daphne, you may very well find the wacky sidekick can provide a helpful role in an otherwise serious drama... and contribute more than their potential marketing future. (Yeah, we all know the wacky sidekick will have *great* merchandising sales potential as a Beanie Buddy!)

Seriously though, even Shakespeare knew the benefit of having an amusing character in an otherwise deep drama. Think about the

Fool (or Jester) from *King Lear*, or the Nurse in *Romeo and Juliet*. Especially after moments of heavy tragedy in a play, a wacky sidekick can relieve the tension.

Generally, the proportions of the wacky sidekick are an oversized head (but try not to overdo it, or the character will end up looking like a frightening Mardi Gras escapee), hands, and feet. (Think about how puppies look, with oversized paws that they later grow into.)

Just be careful, though, because if you overdo it with the wacky sidekick, you'll end up with an annoying, or worse yet, a downright obnoxious sidekick... like Jar Jar Binks from *The Phantom Menace*, Orko from *He-Man*, or the most despicable, the most contemptuous, the absolute worst of them all... *yecch!* Yes, I mean, of course... Scrappy Doo.

The Villain

One of the first things Disney Studios realized in dramatized animation was that often your hero is only as strong as your villain.

A villain, like any other cartoon character, can be human, animal, cyborg, or any other conceivable being capable of rational, or for that matter irrational, thought.

While your hero and heroine (and even supporting characters) have more everyday proportions, your villain is often a character with which you can have a little more leeway.

They can be thinner, with drawn features and bags under their eyes, suggesting they've lost sleep pondering tomorrow's big plans of subjugating the masses to their cruel authority. The hands can be skeletal, pointy, as if to indicate the similarity between their fingers and the talons of a bird of prey.

Just as easily, you can go in the opposite direction, like Jabba the Hutt. They've gorged themselves on the finer things in life, and are now bloated sacks of fat. Maybe they're so oversized, just like the giant aforementioned space-slug himself, they often send underlings to carry out their nefarious missions of destruction.

Although certainly a true villain may not be apparent from the outset of the story (just as in real life), things that they say or do, or even from our artistic viewpoint certain design cues, may act as hints that these are less than trustworthy individuals.

Color cues go as far back as the heyday of the Hollywood Western, where the hero wore a white hat and the villain wore a black hat. We can even look at more subtle clues: Perhaps there may be a certain off-color hue to their skin, like the pale green of Snidely Whiplash or the Wicked Witch. Maybe though they're not dressed in black, instead wearing colors or trimmings like dark purples (they imagine themselves royalty) or reds (the color of blood).

All character art © Mark S. Smith/MarkToonery.com

A sampler of villains and villainous types and beasts
that carry out their evil bidding.

Even the lines of their design could be more harsh, angular...
something that suggests the cruel point of a dagger.

Don't underestimate the value of a worthy villain. A weak villain makes things too easy for the hero. And what makes a strong
story is a believable conflict... it's what keeps us interested.

I learned from watching cliff-hanger shows like *Dark Shadows*,
and even back when I was reading *Spiderman* comics, that if any of
the characters ever got their problems permanently solved I'd lose
interest and stop watching.

Avoid *established* stereotypes altogether; instead, *build* on these
existing stereotypes by modifying them, or try creating a *new* stereotype altogether. Be a trendsetter. But make your characters
interesting to watch, and maybe even suggest a moment of sympathy to the audience by showing why they went wrong.

One villain that stands out in my mind is Hades in Disney's
Hercules. The villains in their most previous films (Scar from
Lion King, Jafar from *Aladdin,* and that forgettable guy from
Pocahontas... what was his name again?) had been snobby, stuffy,
upperclass British types. While a few of the early character studies
of Hades looked in danger of taking this beaten path yet again,
someone made the suggestion to go 180 degrees away, in the opposite direction of a scheming villain... they made him a New York
business executive.

I'd never seen that done before and I think it worked particularly well. But I'll repeat what I said at the beginning of this section:
Your hero is only as strong as your villain. So make 'em strong.

Whatever character types you've come up with — heroes, heroines, wacky sidekicks, and/or villains — make a model sheet.
Whether you're working by yourself or with a small studio, you
need to keep all these drawings consistent, regardless of whether
we've got one, several, or dozens of artists working on them.

So now, from your various drawings on various sheets of paper,
photocopy and cut and paste or scan and assemble your final model
sheet in your graphics program of choice, like Photoshop.

When you've got a model sheet of your character, or better yet,
several original characters that look like no one else's, you may
want to seriously consider registering them with the U.S. Copyright Office.

Copyright Registration: Protecting Your Creation

When I went to a portfolio show at Westwood recently, I met a young artist whose comic book pages were proudly displayed and meticulously detailed in full color. She had fairies, lovely girls, and handsome young men in stories not unlike those old 1950s romance comics (except they had fairy wings) that were quite well drawn.

"Have you ever submitted your work to get published?" I asked nonchalantly.

"Oh, no," she replied. "I'm afraid someone would steal my work and walk off with my characters!" She shook her head somberly, a worried look clouding her face.

"Well, why don't you just register them with the copyright office, so nobody can steal them, and *then* submit your work to get published?"

The cloud disappeared immediately. "You can do that?"

"You can do that," I assured her. "Just go to www.copyright.gov and look for the Visual Arts Form VA, which allows you to register any collected work or characters with the copyright office. It's a one-page form, and simple to fill out. All you have to do is print out that form, make a photocopy of your work, and mail it all to the address they have there with a check for $30, and they'll send you a receipt in a couple of months or so." Melanie was writing down the website as fast as her fingers would allow as I spoke. "That way, in the unlikely case someone does try to steal your original characters, you can sue them... and win."

Thus ends my free commercial for the U.S. Copyright Office.

Now that you've got a character registered and ready to work with, and while you're waiting for your receipt from the copyright office, let's do the next logical step: place that character in an actual story.

Thorn © Melanie Mendoza

Melanie, a student from my character design and 2D animation classes at Westwood College, has an interesting style. It kind of reminds me of a cross between those old romance comics of the 1950s and the more modern anime/manga-inspired fantasy stories.

Chapter 3

Thumbnails, Storyboards, and Layout

Girth, Thurman, and Deadbeat
© Mark S. Smith/MarkToonery.com

As a matter of fact, I stress to my students the importance of storyboarding… even in live action. If you think about it, it's kinda weird that most live-action movies (at least the ones worth watching) start out in storyboard format.

My problem with people jumping onto the computer and wanting to get started typing right away is this: I truly believe, on some subconscious level, they believe the computer is going to somehow do the thinking for them.

It's not. They need to rely on that computer that is far more impressive (in most cases, anyway) sitting between their ears.

Here's a quick counter-example case study. Sometimes I need to learn to follow my own advice.

I was working on my latest public service announcement (hereafter abbreviated as PSA, the TV industry official acronym) for the Georgia Public Library, and had been given a rather lengthy three-page, fully typed manuscript that I had to somehow shave down into both 30-second and 60-second versions for television.

I had already taken care of the first part of the problem while standing in line for my driver's license (never go on Saturday,

folks). I always carry my sketchbook and a modicum of drawing supplies with me whenever I know I'm going to be standing in line or in a waiting room. (As one of my cousins said, a bored Smith is a dangerous thing, and he's right!) In this case, while shuffling forward at a frozen snail's pace, I was crossing out line after line, until I could read the whole storyline in 60 seconds or less.

Your friend in any waiting room is your sketchpad.
Don't leave home without it!

My next task was to put the storyline into visual form, because first and foremost, television is a visual medium... and animation is no exception. So I tried doing the storyboards full-size. After 45 minutes I managed to have four fully un-colored panels penciled. And they weren't terribly exciting.

Thankfully, my intellectual lightning struck, illuminated my brain, and reminded me to take my own advice: Start out *small*... with thumbnail sketches.

Thumbnails

The advantage to working in thumbnail format is that you take yourself out of "prettyboy artist" mode and force yourself to think in "gritty layout artist" mode. In other words, instead of concerning yourself with making a pretty, finished drawing, you're instead forcing yourself to think in terms of layout. Can you tell what the character is doing on a series of drawings two inches wide and an inch-and-a-half tall? If so, I'd say you've got yourself a rather successful storyboard.

Getting back to my example with the storyboards for the library project, once I made up my mind to start out in thumbnails, I was done in roughly half an hour with about 27 tiny storyboard panels. They may not have been pretty, but they helped me decide that I only needed about three pages of character drawings that I could switch out arms and legs on to make my 60-second commercial.

That brings me to one of the finer features of Flash. Armed with my 27 thumbnails, I was able to take my scanned drawings and prepare my storyboards directly inside Flash.

I can't stress enough the importance of starting your work out small.

As artists, we have a natural tendency to try to make a pretty, finished drawing (well, some of us, at any rate). What I mean by that, though, is we want to spend too much time in fine artist mode, and not enough time in graphic designer mode.

For instance, when you start out drawing small, you're forcing yourself to leave out details. Most artists want to dwell too much on details at this stage, which can cause problems when you're attempting to create a visually dynamic screen layout. A dynamic screen layout that showcases your action should be your focus at this stage; you can have fun with the details later.

I like to use the word *dynamic* in connection with whatever I'm working on. It means packed with energy, and that's exactly the same kind of drawings we need to produce, particularly in comics and animation.

All character art © Mark S. Smith/MarkToonery.

> HEY, SEZQUATCH! DO YOU BELIEVE IN BOOGLEYMEN?
>
> ZZT...
>
> DEADBEAT! YOU COME UP TO MY CAVE AT 3AM AND WAKE ME UP TO ASK ABOUT BOOGYMEN?
>
> DO YOU HAVE ANY IDEA WHAT I'LL DO IF YOU *EVER* WAKE ME UP AGAIN?
>
> BEAT IT, BUDDY! ...I JUST SAW SOMETHING *WAYYY* SCARIER...

The original *Bigfoot Country* comic strip I decided to develop into a Flash cartoon, *Midnight Sneak*.

Let's take as an example my thumbnails for the *Bigfoot Country* short *Midnight Sneak*. Just to keep things nice and tidy, I've also included the original comic strip that inspired the short cartoon, a four-panel comic strip that chronicles Deadbeat's encounter with a boogeyman, and his semi-successful visit with Sezquatch for help. Although I liked this comic strip (at least enough to turn it into a short cartoon, anyway), I found the four-panel setup and "payoff" didn't really work as well as I would have liked. I really wanted to slow down the pacing at the beginning, but keep the punchy ending fairly close to the inspirational strip.

Animation just seemed like a natural subject on which to experiment with my newfound toy, Flash.

All character art © Mark S. Smith/MarkToonery.com

Thumbnails. It's best to start out small before doing full-blown storyboards.

As you can see, I could have easily spent some serious time drawing meticulously detailed layout drawings, nice and pretty, as fully rendered storyboards. But I decided against that for several reasons:

- Time (It's seldom on your side, especially in any kind of video production.)

- Simplicity (I'm not showing these storyboards to any clients; that's really the only reason for doing full-color, full-size storyboards, for client approval. Since I'm doing this as a cartoon "just for myself," I'm not even going to do full storyboards. I just need the thumbnails for a planning tool.)

Since I was only doing this "for myself," I did about four rows of blue lines on my paper, trying to stay close to the aspect ratio of the final output video, at a roughly 3:4 size. (That means if my video screen is three inches tall, it's about four inches wide.)

Back in the old days, when I got started in video production/animation, you only really needed to know one size for a computer/video screen: 640 x 480. Simply put, that's a video screen 640 pixels wide by 480 pixels tall. But lo and behold, digital video had to come along and complicate matters. Now I tend to make my movies 720 x 486 (for DVD), although there are numerous aspect ratios you could choose.

The four original storyboards clearly overgrew their four panels, which is one of the reasons I didn't really pursue doing *Bigfoot Country* as a newspaper strip. And sadly, the newspaper comic strip, perhaps the most unique contribution to the newspaper (and ironically the one section almost everyone, regardless of age, makes a point to read), is becoming a victim to its parent newspaper. Like a boa constrictor, the other sections of the newspaper are trying to force the comics smaller and smaller, less and less legible, restricting the creativity and storytelling space of its artists. True, a newspaper strip does have the potential to pay more in the long run — a successful newspaper cartoonist feasibly can become a millionaire overnight, but as Eddie Cantor once said, "It takes twenty years to become an overnight success!"

Anyway, the kinds and scopes of stories I wanted to tell with the characters didn't really fit within the four-panel constraints.

Zombie Skunk Ghouls Halloween Special Preview sample page

When my brother offered me a chance to contribute half of a comic book, I jumped at the chance to tell longer stories with these *Bigfoot Country* characters that I'd come up with. And now I'm having a lot more fun animating them… in full color, with Flash.

As for the thumbnails under discussion, I added the opening shot of Deadbeat approaching Sezquatch's cave, which wasn't in the rather limited strip of origin. It turned out to be a good place to add some opening credits. It also seemed to be a good place to let the "spooky/silly" music set up the mood for the cartoon, and was a fun spot to add in a sneaky tiptoe walk cycle.

Having Deadbeat zip into the mailbox for a hiding place served two purposes:

■ Forcing the body into an impossibly small-sized container (not to mention popping one's head out again) is usually good for a laugh.

■ Showing Sezquatch's name on the mailbox lets you know where Deadbeat is going; even if you're not familiar with the characters, you can even get the idea that Sezquatch (a purposeful misspelling of Sasquatch) is most likely a talking Bigfoot… that gets mail somehow. (Despite the fact that few really believe in him!)

At some point, it hit me that it might be funny for Deadbeat to still be cautiously tiptoeing (for paranoid reasons that soon become obvious) even after he got inside the relative safety of Sezquatch's cave. And better yet, he could still be zipping from hiding place to hiding place.

Again, one of the great things about animation is that you can make the impossible seem perfectly plausible. I decided to have Deadbeat zip into Sezquatch's bookshelf (another chance to make some inside jokes about the possible titles that would be on hand), and then peek out from the shadows between two of the books. Besides being another quick gag (and hopeful laugh), making a character's eyes blink is, as you can probably guess, one of the easier things to animate.

Originally, I had Deadbeat reach his finger out, almost in slow motion, and tap Sezquatch on the shoulder to awake him. One of the things to remember about animation is that the faster something moves, the fewer drawings you need. The slower something moves, the more drawings you need.

Here's the example I often give in class: When most Wile E. Coyote cartoons have the characters freeze into place, the fake Latin name (like *Carnivorous Vulgaris* or *Speedipus Rex*) appears below each character. Usually, they'll pop back into full speed immediately. On my favorite Coyote cartoon, however, they ever so slowly went into slow motion, and then, moment by moment, the action returned to its maddening pace. Although I didn't understand at the time (watching as a child back in the mid-'70s), the reason Chuck Jones didn't do this in more cartoons is that having the characters move convincingly in slow motion requires a whole bunch of drawings... even more so than the usual 24 frames per second (that's for film, and 30 fps for video)!

Apart from the economical reason of drawing Deadbeat's hand reaching in slow motion (you'll see ways around even this later when we discuss tweening), I was trying to keep this cartoon down to about a minute. A minute seems to provide the pacing that I'm comfortable with for my *Bigfoot Country* cartoons; and from experience with the previous shorts I've done with the characters, I know it takes me roughly a couple of months to complete 60 seconds of animation.

I later cut this, mainly so I'd have time to replace it with the "bookshelf peekaboo" shot later. I really liked that drawing, and wanted to see it animated.

Speaking of eyes popping open, I liked the eye-dea (whoops!) or the idea, rather, of a close-up of Sezquatch's eye popping open. Pretty much this whole cartoon is about what an unpleasant person the otherwise nicest individual can be when disturbed from their "beauty sleep." And believe me, some of us (yours truly in particular) need it more than others.

Sezquatch's eye pops open in the original thumbnail storyboard (left), and then in the finished symbol (right) traced, cleaned up, and colored over the same drawing.

It was probably about here that I think I started realizing at least one of the reasons this cartoon appealed to me was personal experience. My wife and I bought a sheltie (a Shetland sheepdog, which looks like Lassie but is about one-third the size) about three years ago. This dog and I are on very good terms; she's been the first inside dog I've raised from a pup, and during normal waking hours we're the best of friends. But for some reason, she goes through spells when she wakes me up at three or four in the morning. (Starting to sound familiar?)

Though I don't react as harshly as Sezquatch does here, being roused from much-needed slumber makes me every bit as cheerful. (I think this is why I like this cartoon so much.)

Deadbeat very sheepishly asks his big buddy, "Hey Sezquatch, d'you believe in Boogleymen?"

His friend solemnly replies, "You come up to my cave and wake me up at 3 AM... to ask me about the Boogeymen?"

By now, Deadbeat is starting to suspect disturbing his otherwise best pal during the middle of the night may not have been the wisest solution to his imminent dilemma. His nervous nod was originally going to be a rattling cowbell sound effect, but all I could find was the "squeaky plate rub" sound effect from my Hanna-Barbera CD library. I ended up liking that better, because it sounded more wimpy... almost more like an apologetic nod.

Here I decided to cut to a close-up of Sezquatch's face and his clenching fists to fully display the rising anger about to be unleashed. "Do you have *any* idea what I'll do to you..." (Here I added a ratchet-like sound effect of his cracking knuckles.) "...if you *ever* wake me up AGAIN?!" I added an echo to emphasize Sezquatch's displeasure.

Here was where I really wanted to milk this shot (linger) of Deadbeat's nervous reaction; this wasn't quite the answer he was hoping for. He's obviously placed himself in an awkward situation that he doesn't know how to extract himself from.

Sezquatch © Mark S. Smith/MarkToonery.com

A peek at things to come... My original thumbnail storyboard sketch (left), and the image I traced directly from the drawing (right), via my 9x12 Wacom digitizing tablet in Flash. If you don't have one, *get* one. *Heck*, get a smaller one if you have to! If you're a student (or an instructor), you can get a great deal from a website like AcademicSuperstore.com.

My familiarity with classical music (at least in the realm of Saturday morning cartoons) came in handy here. I wanted to have some sort of underscore that helped to draw out Deadbeat's indecision of what to say next. It just so happened that I had bought a music library CD (Mix IV) from Sound-Ideas.com on their monthly "blue plate special" (which varies, naturally) that had one of my favorite classical pieces, a short selection from Strauss' *Tales from the Vienna Woods*... an almost wimpy little string whine (you can tell I'm not musically inclined by my terminology) that went perfectly with the nervous expression on Deadbeat's face.

How do you get yourself out of an awkward moment like that? I've experienced dozens (if not hundreds) of such moments personally, and oddly enough, I can't remember how I got out of a single one of them. It just made sense then, dramatically, to cut directly to the next shot...

A surprised-looking Boogeyman. Of course the full gag comes out here. Believe it or not, Deadbeat really did see an actual Boogeyman... he wasn't just imagining things... and now Mr. Boogeyman seems every bit as surprised and awkward as Deadbeat did seconds ago during Sezquatch's unexpected response.

As far as the design for the Boogeyman, he is naturally some sort of a ghostly apparition. My favorite cartoon ghost as a kid was from *Casper the Friendly Ghost*'s publisher, Harvey Comics. No, not Casper himself, but his mischievous pal, Spooky the Tough Little Ghost, was always my favorite Harvey star. Of course, back then I knew Spooky from the comic books, and didn't realize his voice was sort of a tough kid, since he spoke out of the side of his mouth... sort of like a slightly less nasal version of the so-called "Boss Weasel" from *Roger Rabbit*.

Deadbeat's voice is sort of what I always thought Spooky would sound like... a tough, wisecracking kid who somehow ended up with the larynx of a much older man. All his harsh "Boo!" sound effects have worn on him, giving him a somewhat gravelly voice.

My other Spooky influence here on the Boogeyman's look (hearkening back to my Frankenstein approach to character design) is his derby (which is my favorite piece of cartoon wardrobe to draw), and perhaps the less obvious freckles... maybe even the "1930s cartoon ape nose." As for the rest of the body, I have a vague recollection as a kid of the first comic book I remember owning... an issue of the Flintstones (which had Fred using something like the teeth of a live Stegosaurus for a pencil sharpener on the cover). It had a non-Flintstones-related, one-page cartoon in the back. A pair of kids were staring into a dark room, and one kid warned the other not to go in: "There's a Boogeyman in there." In the next-to-the-last panel, the Boogeyman made his appearance, with a ghostly "Hi" word balloon. If I were to see it again, I'm sure these two (mine and theirs) would look little if even remotely alike, but the general description sort of stuck with me over the years because it was the only Boogeyman I'd ever seen convincingly depicted.

Don't forget... for special moments in your cartoon, or even for backgrounds, you can import images you've either drawn by hand (like this example, which was done with Prismacolor art markers and colored pencil) or created in Photoshop. For cartoons that might be posted on my website, I make sure to "Save for Web" in Photoshop, with a moderate compression of quality (to assure faster download time) and import into Flash as a JPG. For instance, at 30% Quality, it would reduce this 1.58 MB image way down to 79K (that translates to a much, much faster download!)

The reason for this particular Boogeyman's astonishment is that his intended fright victim is now heaving a succession of suitcases toward him (the literal cartoon translation of "sending someone packing") and ushering him hastily offscreen. However scary Mr. Boogeyman thought he was, the sight of Sezquatch's disturbed rest is something "wayyy scarier."

And I thought I'd end, inspired by the *Ren and Stimpy* show, with a somewhat detailed illustration of the character, as opposed to a flat-colored animation drawing. He's been stuck on the side of the road, his thumb out in classic hitchhiker position, with the words "The End" floating above.

I had already planned for a sticker to be placed on his suitcase, which I naturally assumed would be too small to read in its final position onscreen. It reads, "Boogeyland or Bust!" It didn't really bother me if it couldn't be fully read by the first-time viewer, because I've got plenty of hidden gags in my cartoons that few but myself would appreciate. But then I showed the first pose test (which we'll discuss shortly) to my character design and development class.

One of my students said, "Well, couldn't you just start in really close on the suitcase sticker, and then pull back to the wide shot of the ghost sitting by the roadside?" Thank you, Paul. Great idea.

See why it helps to get a second opinion sometimes? And still being at the planning stage, it's easily added. I would have only been able to slap my forehead in disgust if someone had suggested it after the cartoon was otherwise complete. Once someone makes a helpful recommendation, it just seems so obvious! Why didn't I think of that?

All right. Now the thumbnails are complete, and we've got a pretty good idea why it's important to start out small. The smaller the picture, the easier it is to tell what's going on and make changes. That leads us to the next portion of our discussion.

Storyboards

When you're coming up with a screen layout, the composition of the frame is every bit as important as the animation itself that will take place within it. In some cases, the layout is perhaps even more important. If you've got the greatest animation in the world and some foreground object in the layout is obscuring that terrific animation, or if something you overlooked is causing the audience to look anywhere except at that great animation, especially in a quick shot, it's wasted effort. And as much effort as animation takes, we want it to be appreciated.

While we're on the subject, let me mention an ongoing argument I had while still at the T-shirt shop. (Isn't it amazing how many "Don't-let-this-happen-to-you" anecdotes I always seem to have on hand?)

There was this salesperson named, for our purposes here, MaryAnn. MaryAnn was a former soccer coach and had a classic aggressive personality. How she got into selling T-shirts is anyone's guess, but our ongoing argument was this:

I'd set up a design — very seldom would it be what I later considered a spectacular design. That was pretty much dictated by the short turnaround time in which customers would want their T-shirts; a common inside joke we had at the time was, "Would you like fries with your T-shirt order?"

MaryAnn would come into the art department, lean over me at the computer screen, and say, "It looks great, but center that text."

Disgusted yet again, I'd say, "Okay, how many times have we had this discussion? It's not about whether or not the design is centered... it's all about *balance*."

Many times I fought the inclination to blast her with the following sarcastic reply. "You know what? You got me. You got me, and you got every single individual who ever graduated with any kind of art degree. We thought we could scam the rest of the world, but MaryAnn, you're just too smart for us. Okay, we'll admit it... you caught us. You're absolutely right. Every class I ever took in two-dimensional graphic design, electronic layout, and advertising art class... we'd show up every day, semester after semester, quarter after quarter, and each instructor would repeat, for two hours solid, 'Whatever you do, center *EVERYTHING*!'"

Although I never shared this cynical blast with MaryAnn, my students and other artists (for some reason) find this scenario as amusing as I do. Go figure.

Here's something I learned at the University of Montevallo. While I was there, still in my fine arts degree mode, I took a class called Integrated Arts. We spent about two weeks in each area of the fine arts: visual arts, theatre, music, and film. I appreciated the visual arts and theatre sections well enough (I was already steeped in information about both), but the two areas I hadn't much experience with at that point (in formal education) grabbed my interest far more than I expected.

The music section gave me an appreciation for classical music. It's difficult to ignore the contribution of classical music to animation. So many of us have become familiar with musical works (if not the titles and composers) like Wagner's *Ride of the Valkyries* (*What's Opera, Doc?*), Rossini's *Barber of Seville* (*Rabbit of Seville*), and perhaps most of all, Franz Liszt's *Hungarian Rhapsody Number Two* (*Rhapsody Rabbit*). Thus began a lifelong appreciation for classical music, and not just the pieces that happen to underscore cartoons.

The film appreciation section of the class brought me a respect for film composition that I would otherwise never have enjoyed (even in the British film class I later took at Auburn University Montgomery, they didn't discuss the topic of the next section).

The Rule of Thirds

All righty, now take that computer screen, TV screen, or film screen, and divide it into three sections horizontally by drawing two lines across at even intervals. Now divide it further by drawing two more lines vertically down across the first set of lines. You should have something that looks roughly like a tic-tac-toe grid, or maybe even a Rubik's Cube. You've got nine squares in front of you.

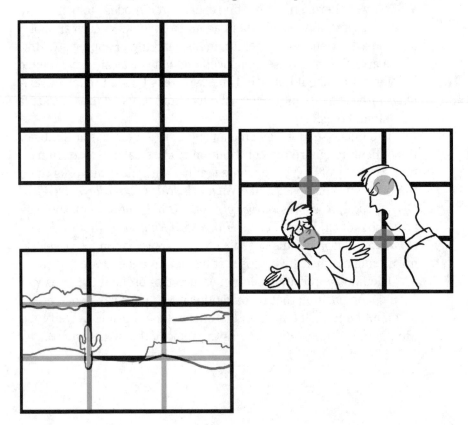

Rule of Thirds: By dividing the screen both horizontally and vertically into thirds, the linear intersections provide key focal points to place items or characters.

Note how the upper-right intersection is the most authoritative focal point, and the lower left is the least. The father is evidently saying, "So you deny that you ate all the jam *and* that you gave me this lousy haircut during my nap!?"

Also note how you can use it as a guide when setting up shots with landscapes, creating a more open, and perhaps in this case, bleak and empty feeling.

Okay, do you see where those lines intersect at those four points? Those intersections are the best place to put items of interest when you're composing your camera shots.

I've heard it said that it's useful to place your character's eyes along that top line for the best framing reference.

In my film appreciation class, the instructor also pointed out how to place characters who are talking to each other, or even in an argument. The most authoritative intersection to place a person's head is in the upper right. In that same shot, if someone is losing the argument, place their face in the lower-left intersection. But you couldn't set up every single shot in the scene like that, naturally.

Make It Painfully Obvious

Some of my favorite layout drawings come from the background layout genius Maurice Noble. How one man can manage to come up with so many variations, from cartoon to cartoon, of the Coyote's painted desert escapes me altogether, but he managed to do it time after time.

One shot that you always manage to see in every Coyote cartoon is the inevitable shot of the accident-prone protagonist falling off a cliff. Then you'd see Maurice Noble's background of the edge of the cliff, and the Coyote plummeting downward, following the perspective lines perfectly.

Did you ever notice how those lines pointed precisely to wherever the Coyote was falling? You probably didn't, but those not-altogether-subtle lines were pointing downward, exactly the direction the Coyote was falling, and exactly where we needed to be looking in the shot.

In one particularly clever shot from my film appreciation class, there was a little boy playing in a vacant lot, most likely where a motel had been torn down. There was a rusty sign that had probably once been lit up with "Vacancy," but all that remained was a giant arrow pointing downward to the entrance of the long-gone structure.

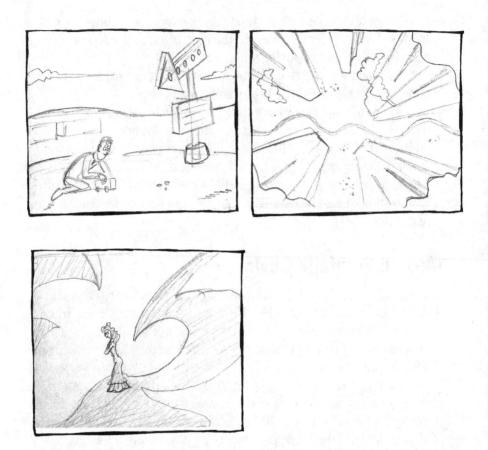

Painfully obvious layout shots. Use setups like this on key moments to draw a viewer's attention to the right spot onscreen. Is there any doubt to the direction a coyote would fall in the shot on the upper right?

However, the director of photography had been clever enough to place the little boy on that exact spot to which the arrow pointed. He had guided our eyes carefully and precisely to where he wanted us to look. Of course, this would be downright exhausting were we to do this with every single shot, but at those key dramatic moments during a scene or a character's introduction, the occasionally "painfully obvious" layout doesn't hurt.

Basic Camera Shots

The basic camera shots include the wide shot, full shot, medium shot, close-up, and extreme close-up.

Although it may strike the reader as odd, the primary reason I talk about thumbnails before discussing camera shots should be obvious. As I already said, it's best for your camera shots if you do your thumbnails first. Then do your storyboards full-size and (if you're going to show them to a client) in color.

Chances are your clients may not be able to fully visualize the final result — otherwise they'd probably do the storyboards themselves — so it's best to help them get a better idea of what the final product will look like by showing them in full color. According to Richard Williams, showing the client pre-production art and revisions only slows down the production process. The fewer revisions from the client, the faster you can finish the project!

With that out of the way, now we can break down each camera shot in depth.

Here's the illustration I generally give in my classes when discussing film, animation, or any dramatized screen entertainment for that matter:

Let's say we have a character (who once again looks suspiciously like a self-caricature of yours truly), and he's going to show his portfolio to an animation studio.

How do we start out this film?

It's best that we establish the location of where this film takes place, and the most common sort of establishing shot is a good place to begin.

The five basic camera shots

The Wide Shot

The character is a barely perceptible speck in the foreground of this image, because the main "character" in this wide shot is actually the castle, we could say. Yes, out in the gloomy foothills of Rumania's most famous land territory (commonly referred to as Transylvania), the clouds are gathering around the spires of a castle as our hero approaches the drawbridge.

As with most scene setups, your camera shot is going to be determined by the action going on within it. In this case, since we're establishing the locale of the story, it's best to begin with this wide shot of the castle.

An establishing shot can tell your audience within a second or two where your story is taking place, like with a national landmark. Let's say that we begin with a shot of the Eiffel Tower. Where is the next scene taking place? France. We start with a shot of the Roman Coliseum? Italy. The Statue of Liberty? New York. Mt. Rushmore? Gotcha! (Well, some of you anyway. That's in South Dakota, in case you didn't know.)

An establishing shot can also be used to set the mood for a scene. For example, in the movie *Irish Jam*, they added a clever little touch every time they showed the manor home of the nasty land baron who was trying to snatch everyone's property out from under them. Whenever they cut to his house, they chose a shot behind a gnarled, crooked branch. And there was always this raven sitting there, ominously watching. I thought it was a nice mood-setter.

The Full Shot

Well, we know *where* our character is, now let's take a better look at *who* our character is.

For this, we'll cut to a *full shot*. A full shot is pretty much what it sounds like: We get a good view of the full body from head to toe. We can see that our character is almost all the way to the drawbridge by now, and that he's a dapper young chap in his um… (ahem!) early 30s, with a good head of hair, and he's proudly marching up to the old castle with his portfolio in hand.

A full shot may very well have more than one character in it, and like the other shots to come, variations abound; but we're just getting started, so bear with me.

The Medium Shot

The character comes to a door with a gargoyle-faced door knocker and he knocks on the door. Since he's come to a stop now, we don't really need to see his feet standing perfectly still in this particular shot, called the *medium shot.*

All the action going on here is from the waist up, so that's pretty much how the medium shot is set. Also notice, much like the comic strip, we're perfectly able to use sound effects "visually" (for lack of a better term) with the "knock-knock."

The Close-Up

In the *close-up*, we focus primarily on the character's face. It may show as much as a bit of the shoulders, but our central concentration is the face, or sometimes more specifically, a particular facial expression, like a reaction to an event or situation. In this case, the character is waiting for the door to be answered.

I even go a little bit further with visual notations by sticking a single musical note coming forth from our hero's pursed lips to show that he's whistling while he waits.

Again, I added another sound effect at the bottom of the screen: "Creeak!"

I usually ask my students during this example, "What's happening here?"

"The door's opening," they'll reply.

"How do you figure that?" I'll ask.

"Because of the sound effects of the hinges."

"What hinges?" I'll say. "How do you know there are hinges? I didn't even draw any hinges on the door in that shot." And as a matter of fact, you don't even *see* the door at all in that shot. I've already established there's a door when he knocked on it in the previous medium shot.

Naturally, my point is that you don't have to draw every single action, nor every single detail. Setting up the scene in this way serves two purposes:

■ It's simpler to use a sound effect that gets the point across without having to draw a door opening outward, which requires some 3D drawing skills. And it therefore saves time by simply using the sound effect to suggest the door is opening.

■ In cases like this, it's more dramatic to suggest what's about to happen rather than show it. Especially when our next shot is...

The Extreme Close-Up

Yes, quite possibly the most overused shot in all of horror film-dom has got to be the *extreme close-up.*

The primary difference between the extreme close-up and the plain old close-up is that while a close-up shows the character's *face*, the extreme close-up usually focuses in on a particular *feature*, in this case the eyes.

In this example, judging by the character's reaction, which we see in his eyes, we're pretty sure that whoever answered the door... well, let's just say it ain't exactly Alice the Housekeeper from the *Brady Bunch*.

Are we always going to see these five basic camera shots in this particular order? Absolutely not. That would get exhausting, if not downright monotonous. Just like picking out which shot is appropriate for which action, the order of the shots serves the dramatic needs of the individual scene.

Let's look at another use of the extreme close-up, and how it's appropriate within a given scene. An extreme close-up is not necessarily a shot of a facial feature. It could be a shot of a character's toe that's just been stuck with a tack, or the tag number of a car's license plate; just about anything to which the director needs to draw particular attention.

1. (MED SHOT)
   JANET SITTING AT BAR,
   LARRY IS HITTING ON HER

2. (CLOSE-UP ON LARRY)
   MOTIONS BACK TO "HIS PLACE"

3. (CLOSE-UP ON JANET)
   SHE GLANCES DOWN TO HIS HAND...

4. (EXTREME CU OF WEDDING RING)
   RING DOES EXAGGERATED "GLEAM"

5. (CLOSE-UP ON JANET)
   SHE ROLLS HER EYES.

Artwork © Mark S. Smith/MarkToonery.com

Other use of the extreme close-up (or XCU)

Let's say a girl is considering the motives of a particularly per-sistent admirer while she's sitting at a bar. He's got a smooth smile and a confidently raised eyebrow, but she glances down at his finger.

And we see in an extreme close-up... Uh-oh! He's wearing a wedding ring. We can even add a little special effect of a gleam on the ring as it catches the light.

We cut back to the girl's expression. She realizes she'd best move on and await a more sincere and, well... more suitable suitor.

Other Useful Camera Shots

Though some of these shots are primarily used in live action, they can also come in handy in animation. I forget which film it was, but I was watching some anime, and the main character was going on and on about all the horrible things that had happened in the last mutant robot war and how for centuries the people had suffered under the hands of the cruel, overbearing warlord, and while this character was going on and on and on, I suddenly noticed the cam-era had cut back to a wide shot of the landscape, and all you could see were the characters as tiny little dots moving along the landscape.

Could you see their lips moving?

Of course not! You could barely see their *legs* moving! But it suddenly occurred to me that they had very cleverly concealed the fact that not a whole lot of animation was going on (if any at all), while they needed to cover this major piece of plot exposition.

It is common in anime to have very few mouth positions... sometimes quite literally only two (open and closed)!

Cutaway Shot

A *cutaway* is a shot that shows something... anything else... other than the main action. A character could begin a long speech and, to dodge the arduous task of animating all that dialogue (like perhaps a two- or three-minute soliloquy), you could cut to a shot of the landscape or perhaps a shot of an abandoned car, while the characters discuss the horrors of the last civil war, which left the once-lush countryside a bleak, barren desert.

Cut-in Shot

A *cut-in* is extremely similar to the cutaway shot. However, one of the primary differences is that usually the cut-in shows something that is more directly related to the main characters talking... perhaps even the very persons involved in the conversation. For instance, let's say you have two characters discussing a troublesome teenager, like a mother and the boy's school principal. The principal could be saying he's warned her son about missing classes, that he's keeping bad company, and so on. Even though the scene starts out with the principal's face showing he's talking to the mother, we then cut to a shot of the mother's hands, wringing worriedly and twisting at a handkerchief as the principal describes her son's latest run-in with his math teacher.

Over-the-Shoulder Shot

An *over-the-shoulder* shot (OSS) is seen exactly as its name implies. The camera is positioned as though someone is standing behind one of two participants in a conversation.

① (WE COULD START WITH THIS SHOT)

PRINCIPAL: PLEASE UNDERSTAND,
MRS. WILSON...

② (THEN CUT TO THIS REACTION SHOT)

PRINCIPAL (O.S.): THIS ISN'T THE FIRST
TROUBLE WE'VE HAD--

③ (THEN CUT TO THIS "CUT-IN" OF HER HANDS)

PRINCIPAL (CONTD.): --WITH YOUR
SON, LAWRENCE...

④ (THEN CUT TO A "CUTAWAY" OF THE DESK)

PRINCIPAL (O.S.): I LIKE TO THINK OF MY-
SELF AS A FAIR MAN...

Cut-ins and cutaways. If you look at (3), you'll see an example of a cut-in. It "cuts in" to the main action, in this case, a nervous mother's hands fumbling with a handkerchief as the principal tells of her son's latest troublesome exploits.

In (4) we cut "away" from the main action (the two characters) to an item that may be either symbolic (in this case, the "scales of justice") or indirectly related to the main action.

1. POV- A "POINT OF VIEW" SHOT THAT SHOWS SOMETHING FROM THE CHARACTER'S POINT OF VIEW.

2. OSS, OR AN OVER-SHOULDER SHOT, GIVES US A VIEW OF HOW A CHARACTER LOOKS FROM BEHIND ANOTHER CHARACTER.

3. A "NODDY" SHOT OF A CHARACTER NOT SAYING ANYTHING, BUT JUST NODDING HIS HEAD IN REACTION TO DIALOGUE.

More camera set-ups that can assist greatly either in animation or live-action scenes: the POV (point-of-view), the OSS (over-the-shoulder), and the "noddy" shot, which shows a character nodding understandingly to an OS (or off-screen) character's dialogue.

Point-of-View Shot

A *point-of-view* (POV) shot has the camera positioned as though it's the main character, and allows you to see something as though you're looking with the character's eyes. If the character is typing at a computer screen and pauses typing briefly to look down at a spot of jelly someone dripped on the keyboard, you'd likely see it from the typist's point of view.

Noddy Shot

A variation on a cut-in, a *noddy* is a particularly popular shot with news crew photographers. Again, if you're dealing with a long-winded bit of dialogue, it helps to break up an otherwise extended single shot of the speaker. This is simply a shot of the interviewer (or listener, in a dramatic conversation) nodding or reacting to what the speaker is saying. In live action, it comes in quite handy when you need to edit a three-minute response (to a single question) down to about 15 seconds.

Camera Pitfalls to Avoid

Jump-cut

Though it's more likely to happen in live action than animation, I have seen it happen. Let's say you have Mr. Long-winded Response again, but we only have footage of him talking and nothing else in the room... no cutaways, no cut-ins of his hands, no sweat dripping down his brow in an extreme close-up, nothing. Went on for four solid minutes and we need to edit this down into a six-second sound bite. Even if he were sitting perfectly still (which people seldom do) and talking, and we had to cut his conversation in mid-sentence and then resume with his ending, there would be a jarring, visual jump. His mouth would be in a greatly different position where we cut out those few words, and perhaps we'd catch him in mid-blink. Even if there was no discernible change in the dialogue, most likely some drastic change in the image would give away the fact we'd done an edit.

Believe it or not, that can happen in animation just as easily. Especially if we've got more than one animator working on the same scene.

If we cut from the wider shot of the cat with his hand up at the left to a close-up with his hand at half-mast, there will be a noticeable discrepancy called a *jump-cut*.

If the animation has already been completed for both shots, we may have to ask the assistance of the editor (or ourselves, if we're a one-man show) to insert a *cutaway*, like the shot of the moving taxi at the left, between the two mis-matched shots.

Let's say we have this cat standing with his hand out, hailing a taxi in a full shot. We then cut immediately to a medium shot, and his hand is now suddenly down by his side. That's a *jump-cut*.

In animation, one of the easiest things in the world should be to hook up one shot to the next. It is important to pay careful attention to your storyboards, and if you are working with others, always make sure you know each character's position, on every first and last drawing of the scene.

A fixer-upper might be a cutaway, perhaps to the cab, and then back to the cat in a different pose, but it's best to avoid this in the planning stage. Doing so creates extra work for the editor, who has to fix someone else's mistake. If it just so happens that you're the editor, don't make your job more difficult than necessary.

(Redwood tree)

(Woodpecker)

Basic Camera Moves

Tilt up or tilt down means to move the camera in a vertical direction, as the cat looks up the tree to see the bird (upper left).

Zoom in and Zoom out

Truck in and *Truck out* can be a little trickier to explain, especially in animation. Think of the "zoom," which is an effect that happens by adjusting the lens of the camera. Truck in or out means you physically push or pull the camera backward or forward in relationship to the subject, as though the camera were on a track.

(Taxi)

Try to avoid having cars moving at an angle, like this car's 3/4 move (left). In that case, items in the background may move in perspective, which presents a drawing (and therefore time-consuming) problem. Instead (when budget is an issue), consider showing the car in perfect profile (right), which is much easier (and quicker) to use with a panning background. A *pan shot* moves in a perfectly horizontal, left to right or right to left direction.

Also note how repeating items like the trees could be easily duplicated in Flash. Remember how Scoob and Shag always ran past the same painting (several times) when running down a long hallway? Well, now you know why!

Camera Moves

Zoom In/Zoom Out

The most widely overused terminology in the industry, and quite often misused, is zoom in and zoom out. If you zoom in on a picture, it's not a physical move of the camera so much as an adjustment of the camera lens that focuses in on a particular object. When you zoom out, it gives the impression of backing away from the subject.

Truck In/Truck Out

Also referred to as pushing in and pulling back, because here you physically are either pushing the camera in closer on the subject, or pulling it back, farther away from the subject.

Tilt Up/Tilt Down

You tilt the camera up to get a better look at something "over your head." Let's say that crazy tomcat just lost track of the woodpecker he was chasing for his lunch. He turns around, and notices it's flown to the top of that great redwood tree. As his eyes trace a pathway up the great trunk of the tree to the topmost branch where the bird is sitting, the camera tilts up to the woodpecker's resting place. Naturally, a tilt down is in the opposite direction.

Pan Left/Pan Right

You swivel the camera left or right. You might pan with a character that is walking past the camera, or you might actually follow the character during a walk cycle, when the character essentially "walks in place" (which is easier to animate) while the background pans behind the character.

Camera Transitions

The Cut

Up until now, we've pretty much *cut* from one scene to the next. A cut is basically taken from the old days of film terminology. When the film editor came to the last frame in a scene, he would literally cut the film with a pair of scissors at that last frame, and then attach the next frame to it with film paste.

A cut is generally used between every shot within a scene. It implies that there's no passage of time between one shot and the next. It can, however, be used for dramatic impact between two scenes.

A *fade-in* to a scene has the effect of light filling the picture (sunrise).

A *fade-out* has the effect of light leaving the picture (sunset).

A *dissolve* is yet another useful way to imply the passage of time, where one image becomes transparent and blends into another.

Fade-In/Fade-Out

A *fade-in* is what happens when you fade in from black at the beginning of a scene. In traditional film or video, you're opening the aperture on the lens and allowing light to begin feeding into the camera. It has the same effect as the sun coming over the horizon and filling the landscape with light.

A *fade-out*, as you've probably guessed, is the exact opposite. It comes at the end of the scene, and looks as though the sun is disappearing over the horizon and the landscape (or room, or scene) and filling the screen with black.

Dissolve

A *dissolve* is what happens when one shot becomes transparent and begins to reveal the next shot beneath it, so to speak. It usually implies a passage of time, or could even be added to a special wavy effect, as though a character is dreaming or recalling past events, and often is accompanied by a phrase like, "I remember it as though it was only yesterday..."

Blur Pan or Zip Pan

Another nice way to imply a passage of time is with a *blur pan* or *zip pan*. Another director I had the privilege of working with, whom I'll call Frank (since that was his name), said that whenever he would send one of his cameramen out on assignment, he'd tell him to make sure to lock down the camera on its tripod, start recording, and give the camera a quick little spin (making sure it doesn't fall over, of course). The reason he did this was to create a blur pan.

If you'd like to see a quick example of this in professional productions, look no further than good ol' *Green Acres*.

1) WE CAN CUT IMMEDIATELY FROM THIS MEDIUM SHOT TO...

2) THIS "ZIP PAN" OR "BLUR PAN", WHICH WILL IMMEDIATELY CUT TO...

3) ANOTHER SHOT OF THE CHARACTER IN A DRASTICALLY DIFFERENT SETTING

A *blur pan* or *zip pan*, whether in live action or animation, offers a quick (and cheap) transition between two drastically different scenes or settings. You can achieve it by a few frames of spinning a live-action camera, hand-drawing a bunch of marker lines on white paper, or even using the "Filter... Blur...Motion Blur" filter in Photoshop on just about any photograph.

Mr. Douglas is talking to his wife, who tells him that Mr. Kimball just lost his job. "Mr. Kimball lost his job?"

We could show Mr. Douglas storming out the door, getting into his car, driving down to the County Agricultural Office, marching up the steps, talking to the secretary, and sitting in the waiting room reading a magazine. Or, we could simply cut to a blur pan, and then cut immediately to Mr. Douglas with his finger waving in front of

Mr. Kimball's former supervisor, exclaiming, "I demand that you give Mr. Kimball back his job!"

Since we are dealing with a half-hour sitcom, and all those traveling and waiting shots aren't terrifically entertaining, I'd suggest we stick with the blur pan transition. Even more so in animation, when you would be required to meticulously animate every one of those thrilling travel details.

Layout and Backgrounds

There are three words of advice I've heard repeated by expert after expert who has been kind enough to take the time to talk to a pesky little animator in his (ahem!) early 30s: "Keep it simple."

It's no different when it comes to planning your backgrounds.

Some great advice came from a guy named Rob at a Montgomery advertising agency. Though he could never seem to find anyone willing to pay what animation was worth (one of the reasons I eventually left Montgomery), he always enjoyed looking at my work, and asked me to bring him anything new I had to show him.

Before I got my scanner, I had my old Amiga 2000 computer (once upon a time produced by Commodore), and had something called a *genlock*. Before we had the technology to burn our cartoons and movies directly to DVD in a computer, if you wanted to transfer your computer signals over to video signals (even for something as simple as dubbing your computer cartoons to VHS), you had to have a genlock to translate the signals. That's what it did.

Since I didn't have a scanner, I would videotape my backgrounds with my camcorder, and overlay my animated Amiga character graphics onto those hand-drawn backgrounds with the genlock.

What I was showing Rob was a dragon that was basically flying in place. I made it appear as though he was moving by moving the background (essentially what we still often do in animation) behind him. This made it look as though he were flying over the animated forest meadow.

Rob was watching this, smiling, and he said, "I hate to tell you this, but as much as I like that background, which is really well-drawn, your character's just getting lost in there!"

He was right. Even if I had a cool character, he was getting lost in the cool background.

In order to fix this, know where your action is taking place in a given scene. Leave space for your characters to move around in there. Don't get too detailed with your background if it's going to interfere with your character.

Here's how I like to create my cartoon backgrounds:

Backgrounds: Sezquatch's cave

This background was created with a combination of markers and colored pencils, the latter of which really helps achieve the gritty look of bare stone that you might imagine to be in a cave.

I also like to leave plenty of "space" for the characters to move. Although you can hardly appreciate it here, the caption on the photo of the Loch Ness monster in the background reads, "Sorry, not my best photo! (Haha!) Love Nessie."

Art Marker Backgrounds

For backgrounds I'll color with art markers, I start with my patented technique of beginning with the light blue pencil. (Okay, it's not really patented, so you're welcome to use this approach for free.) I'll make a layout drawing with that pencil, working from my thumbnails and/or storyboards. If it looks as though it's going to work, I'll ink it with my trusty ink pen and make a photocopy of my inked layout drawing.

I photocopy it at this point for three reasons:

- Just like scanning a blue pencil and black ink animation drawing, it makes the light blue line disappear.

- I'm paranoid. Since I'm about to hand-color this background drawing, I like to have a backup in case I mess up.

- I'm going to be doing part of my background drawing with color art markers. If I tried to put those markers directly on the original inked drawing, it would bleed into the black ink. For some delightful reason, it doesn't do the same thing on a photocopy. You can color all you want over the black photocopied areas, and it doesn't bleed.

All right, now that I've made a photocopy (or two) of my cleaned-up line drawing, I can start to color while hopefully enjoying myself, and not worrying too much about messing up the black-and-white copy.

The color art markers I prefer are Berol Prismacolor markers. Let's face it, the color markers you buy in the toy store or craft department of the local discount store are harsh, fluorescent, and/or aren't even close to the colors you want in your background, at least not if you want your character to be seen in front of it.

Go to an art supply store to get these markers. Though you might get a couple of dark colors like ultramarine for a deep midnight sky or Nile green for a mucky river, I'd stick with the mid-range colors and pastels... colors that will help your character stand out. I'd get a couple of browns and tans for tree bark, at least three or four greens for grass and shrubbery, and some various reds and oranges. Though I'd get maybe a yellow and blue for the heck of it, one color you shouldn't expect to find anywhere is a sky blue. Oh, the marker label may very well claim to be sky blue, but to this day, I haven't found one that can both cheerfully and truthfully live up to those expectations. When it comes to the sky, I'll generally just leave the area blank, and later, after scanning the rest of the image, come up with a more believable sky blue in Photoshop.

Yeah, now's the fun part. Just like the good old kindergarten days of yore, go through and color just as you like.

But you're not quite done, no matter how well you stay inside the lines. Because once you've done a thorough job of coloring those outlined areas, and covering up the worst of those blank white spaces, you're going to go back to add shadows and highlights… with colored pencils!

Why all this trouble to use real-world objects to color our backgrounds when we've got all these digital coloring toys at our disposal? The answer is simple, really. Once again, we want our characters to stand out from the background. And since we'll be filling our characters with mostly flat colors and the occasional gradient once we get into Flash, these real-world, imperfect colors will make the digitally colored characters "pop out" from them. You can scan your background in Photoshop (at 72 dpi for screen purposes), and resize it or even compress it as a JPG if you're making a cartoon for the web, which will take up less memory.

Once done making any necessary Photoshop touch-ups, go to Save for Web… and then find a compression that's small enough while still preserving the look of your background without getting too many of those chunky compression pixels in there. Click the Four-up tab in the upper left-hand corner of your screen, which will allow you to view four different compression option previews at once.

Naturally, this is just one approach to making your backgrounds. You're perfectly welcome to apply whatever technique you like to colorize your backgrounds.

You may even find another technique that works for you, such as scanning black-and-white line art, filling the black lines with a blue-gray color in Photoshop, and then beginning to add your fill colors. Maybe painting your backgrounds with acrylic colors gets the best results! Sometimes I'll find one brand or another of acrylic craft paints are on sale for 25 cents a bottle, and that's hard to beat!

Of course, you're just as certainly welcome to make your backgrounds in Flash! All the techniques we'll soon be discussing for adding colors to characters can just as easily be applied to background objects like trees, skies, and cityscapes.

Chapter 4

Soundtracks and... What's an Animatic?

Girth, Thurman, and Deadbeat
© Mark S. Smith/MarkToonery.com

Once we've got our thumbnails done (mainly for our own planning purposes), and our storyboards completed, colored, and pretty (mainly for the benefit of our clients and/or coworkers — if any), and the layouts/backgrounds done (or sketches handed over to our background designers), we're ready to move on to the fun part.

Okay, you got me, what about animation isn't the fun part? (Boy, you are new to this cartooning thing, aren't you? Oh, wait a minute... that's why we're all here. The learning thing... Right!)

When I introduce the act of making a soundtrack and the subsequent pose test (aka the *animatic*) to my students, that's when they really seem to have fun.

Now that you pretty much know the storyline of your cartoon, you should have a pretty good idea about the dialogue, sound effects, and music needed.

Now where do you get these?

BaaBraw & Morris Rabies, Detective © Mark S. Smith/MarkToonery.com

The Dialogue Track

I usually like to start with the dialogue recording. Before the built-in microphones on computers came along (like the one on my iMac) and got to the stage where they're actually decent and of near air-worthy quality, I used to go to a sound recording facility to record my audio.

Yeah, that's kind of expensive for the amateur or the student animator. Believe me, I know and understand completely. But if you're a professional, or can afford the rates they charge (which vary from city to city and studio to studio), and/or you've got a client that's particularly picky (and believe it or not, people who are spending money on your services can be), it might not be a bad idea to invest that small portion of your profit margin into a recording studio session. They'll even likely burn your session to CD as part of the service.

My very first job was in radio, so attention to digital audio quality is something I try to be aware of.

As a matter of fact, I'd written a high school play titled *Kreechur*, about a cannibalistic lunatic getting loose in a high school. (I look back at my life and honestly can't believe some of the stuff people not only let me get away with, but actually *encouraged* me to do, bless them!) I made myself an audio cassette with a handheld, old-fashioned 1970s recorder, which my friends and I used to make "radio plays" (such as recreations of *Inspector Gadget*, Jonathan Winters' Little Boy character, and *Skeeterman*, an original creation). I used the deepest, darkest, scariest voice I could muster, which I now refer to as my "lousy Christopher Lee impression." I spoke into the built-in microphone and described the creepy happenings at my fictional Parkerson High School while suitably spooky music played through the speakers of my LP stereo. All this I somehow

Kreechur © Mark S. Smith/MarkToonery.com

Portrait of the lunatic that escaped in Parkerson High School, based on a play I wrote and starred in as the title character, *Kreechur* (1987).

managed to fit into 30 seconds, which is the perfect length for a public service announcement. That's what encouraged people to go see this play I'd written. Since it qualified as a PSA (promoting a school event), the radio station, WEZZ-FM, was able to justify playing this ad for free.

I had to admit that I didn't really listen to WEZZ-FM, the Clanton station, regularly as a teen. When I wasn't listening to horror movie soundtracks on old-fashioned vinyl LPs (CDs didn't become popular until after my senior year in high school), I was more of a Casey Kasem's Top 40 kinda guy. The reason I mention that, is on those rare occasions I did listen, just to hear my commercial… uh, ahem… PSA being played, well, I didn't hear it. So I dropped by the radio station (which happened to be five minutes down the road from me) to see why they hadn't played it.

Rob, the programming manager, informed me that they actually had played it several times, but I had probably just missed it. In fact, he told me if I'd keep my radio tuned to the station on the way home, he'd play it before I got to my driveway. Before he made good on his promise (which he did, incidentally), he asked me, "By the way, who did that voice on your spot?"

"Oh, that was me," I said. "Just sitting by my stereo, and a creepy movie soundtrack LP in the background."

"Not bad," he said. "If you're interested in a job, me and my buddy are looking for someone to work nights and weekends for us, just so we can have some time off occasionally."

"You mean work as a DJ?" I asked.

Again, I've been richly blessed throughout my career. And that was my first weekly paycheck. It gave me some more experience doing voices (I'd done puppet shows at church since age 10, and I was 17 at this time), it gave me my first experience writing for broadcast (believe me, squeezing information with even minimal entertainment value into 30 seconds is a challenge), and it gave me my first experience with sound effects… which we'll discuss shortly.

Tangent Man © Mark S. Smith/MarkToonery.com

Before my evil alter ego, Tangent Man, takes us any further away from the subject of cartoon voices, let's steer sharply back onto that road.

If you happen to have a range of character vocalizations, even one or two, it's probably best to do your own voices. Working in radio and puppetry gave me a good start and range of characters. As a matter of fact, radio, puppetry, and animation have one thing in common: One person can assume literally dozens of roles within a single production, depending on their imagination, vocal versatility, and editing ability.

There are plenty of animators who do their own voices. Walt Disney was Mickey's first voice artist. The story goes that he kept trying to demonstrate to voice actors reading for the part what he wanted, until someone finally suggested, "Well, gosh, Walt, why don't you just do it yourself?" And that's exactly what he did until the late 1940s.

John Kricfalusi, the creator of the controversial *Ren and Stimpy* show, performs the voice of Ren Hoek, the irascible asthmatic Chihuahua. And that voice is simply his interpretation of character actor Peter Lorre (whom I best remember for his role of the unwilling and somewhat evil doctor from *Arsenic and Old Lace*). Again, nobody could give John K. the performance of Ren with the intensity he wanted, so he simply decided to do it himself.

Tony Anselmo, another Disney animator, took over the voice of Donald Duck after the original voice actor, Clarence Nash, died.

Like character designs, there should be inspiration abounding all around you for character voices. One of my classmates (who was a costar in our high school's aforementioned 1987 production of *Kreechur*) did a hilarious interpretation of our vice principal, who was the self-appointed hall monitor. Imagine Fozzie Bear speaking after taking a deep breath from a helium balloon... and then being possessed by the evil spirit of Jerry Lewis' Nutty Professor. Now imagine that character saying, "Get back to class, you lousy little..." Through a staggering coincidence, I just discovered that very classmate is a weatherman for CNN here in Atlanta.

My point here is that doing imitations of someone you know is a great starting place for an original character voice. My brother heard Mark Hamill (whom we all know and love as Luke Skywalker, and now is perhaps best known as the Joker's voice on *Batman: The Animated Series*) speaking on the subject of voice acting. He said, "Never forget that a bad vocal impression... is an original character voice all its own."

Normally, I'll do all my male character voices myself for a couple of reasons:

■   Like John K., few people can give me the intensity of the character voices I'm looking for. And nobody else understands the character better than its creator.

■   I'm a cheapskate. I'll admit it. I don't have to shell out another chunk of my already-marginal profit margin to somebody else if it's something I can do myself.

Occasionally, I will get someone else to do a male voice for me. I was pretty happy with my Deadbeat Skunk voice for the two reasons I just mentioned. However, on my first *Bigfoot Country* cartoon with a voice track (the *Zombie Skunk Ghouls Halloween Special Preview*), I was never terribly satisfied with my Sezquatch voice. It was just my deepest possible voice, and even my wife said that it sounded too deep... it sounded forced, like I was trying too hard. It sounded like a kid trying to impersonate his father on the phone. I even slowed down the pitch a bit (using an old version of SoundEdit 16), but it still sounded fake. I just had to get somebody else to do Sezquatch's voice for *Midnight Sneak*.

I enlisted the help of my friend Tony Beckham, cofounder of the Montgomery improvisational comedy troupe Brain Freeze. He had acting and writing skills, and he had timing, delivery, and personality that came shining through whether on stage, on camera, or just through his voice. It was perfect.

I knew the guy was talented. I was working the camera when we auditioned him and the rest of the applicants for our ABC-32 Spot Team (our local screen personalities, since the news department had been closed down). We recorded 87 interviews, narrowed those down to about a couple dozen, and then down to maybe half a dozen, and finally the three we were looking for. Tony was one of the three, and later became the semi-official "Spot Team Captain."

When I let my students watch the first pose test for *Midnight Sneak*, they even said, "I almost thought you *somehow* got John Goodman to read that part!"

When it comes to female voices, unless I want a silly, bimbo-type voice for comedic effect (which I can sorta do... well, kinda), I'll enlist the services of my sister-in-law, Melinda Smith. Melinda has a beautiful voice and has done some professional backup singing. My wife even says that all my female characters have a tendency to look like Melinda. If it is, I promise it's unintentional. Melinda's own voice is pretty darn close to Jayle Bat, the semi-official mascot for MarkToonery.com.

My favorite story about Melinda was when she was doing the aforementioned *Zombie Skunk Ghouls Halloween Special Preview* reading for me. For some reason, I suppose because I wanted the reading fresh, I hadn't shown her the script until we started recording. (Jackie Gleason had a similar preference; he preferred not to do rehearsals for *The Honeymooners*, it's been said.) For the first time ever, Melinda read the line, "I dunno, girls, a rural skunk graveyard is no place for our annual sorority pajama party." Immediately after reading that line, she burst into laughter at the ridiculous implications. It let me know that the laugh I was working for had paid off. Naturally, in the editing stage, I cut off her uncontrolled laughter, and I had to make the cut quick. But it was worth it!

One of my favorite recording sessions from Jayle's voice actress Melinda, and the best compliment she ever gave me.
Before: "I dunno, girls, a rural skunk graveyard is no place for our annual sorority pajama party..."
After: Melinda's completely unrehearsed reaction to the first time ever reading the script for *Zombie Skunk Ghouls Halloween Special Preview.*

Recording Dialogue at a Professional Studio

If you don't know where to begin looking for a recording studio, apart from the obvious Internet search, you might want to thumb through your local yellow pages. I'd recommend trying audio production, video production services, and maybe even call your local TV or radio station for help. Be sure to tell them that you're recording voices for a cartoon, and even *more* so if it's really a student project... they may even cut you a deal on their regular rates.

Besides that, you never know when someone is looking for animation services, or voiceovers, for that matter. Make sure if you do use a TV station or video production facility, you offer them a copy of the cartoon once you get finished. You just might find yourself making some useful contacts... maybe even your first animation services sale!

If the stations don't provide the services themselves, they may be able to recommend someone who can.

It's tempting to let family and friends do your cartoon voices for you; hey, they might even be pretty good!

But just remember that stage fright doesn't just happen when someone's on stage, or even on camera, for that matter. There is such a thing as mike fright. Someone who is perfectly at ease speaking or even performing for friends can just as easily be intimidated by that little microphone or that little red recording light.

Such fear can actually be audible during a recording session. One of the most difficult things in the world is reading lines and making them sound like they're *not* being read. Naturalism is one of the hardest things to fake convincingly... at least if it doesn't come, well... (ahem) naturally. Despite that, make sure your actors have a chance to rehearse before the clock starts ticking (and those hourly rates start adding up) once you start the actual recording session.

Usually I try to get at least three takes for each line, preferably accenting a key word somewhat differently... maybe even accenting a different key word each time. As long as the budget allows, I'd also recommend listening to the burned CD *before* allowing the actors to leave the studio. It's cheaper, and less aggravating for everyone's collective schedules, to retake a few lines while everything is still set up. For instance, you might not have realized it during the otherwise best take of a particular line that your lead actress was rustling the pages of her script or her jingling earrings were picked up on the microphone. (Seriously; it happened to Cyndi Lauper during the recording session of *We Are the World*!)

Especially double-check the CD if you've talked a friend or family member into doing your voices for free. (When your voice actors aren't getting paid, you'll find their schedule is slightly less flexible. Go figure!)

If you have decided to do most or all of the voices yourself, and you can actually pull it off, let me add a suggestion from Mel Blanc's technique. As most cartoon fans know, Mel Blanc justifiably earned the nickname the "Man of a Thousand Voices" by providing vocal characterizations for well over 90% of all the *Looney Tunes* characters... Bugs Bunny, Daffy Duck, Foghorn Leghorn, Pepé Le Pew, and Taz, to name just a few of my personal favorites. (About the only exceptions were Elmer Fudd, performed by Arthur Q. Bryant, Witch Hazel by June Foray, Granny and Mama Bear by Bea Benaderet, with additional characters such as Junior Bear by Stan Freberg.)

At first, the producers had Mel record all the character voices in sequence. For instance, he'd read a line for Porky, then a line for Daffy, then a line for Porky, then Daffy, and so on.

It took about a day and a half to get through a recording session for a six-minute cartoon in that way. Mel actually made the suggestion himself to record one character voice at a time. Record all of Porky's lines, then go back and record all of Daffy's lines. Even in those days, before digital editing, all you really needed was a sharp knife blade and a piece of tape to perform an imperceptible edit. (That was something audio editing had in common with film editing, even then.) Using Mel's technique, they were able to shave down their recording session time from a day and a half to an hour and a half.

And if you're paying a recording studio by the hour, well... that can have a rather significant impact on your production budget.

Recording Dialogue at Home

When I first got started mixing my own sound effects, I bought a $30 microphone from Radio Shack and a mixing board for about $75 or so (if memory serves me accurately). I tried not to get the cheapest mike I could find. (You get what you pay for... or worse yet, you'll get what you *don't* pay for.) The same goes for the mixing board. I naturally couldn't afford the most expensive, so I got something in between. I figured each would last me a reasonable amount of time, and I didn't get rid of them until well after I had my digital recording system in place.

Once I was able to record my audio on my home computer with a built-in microphone, I used a program called SoundEdit, which was originally packaged with Macromedia Director. Nowadays, the program of choice seems to be Audition, and since that's also an Adobe program (like Flash itself), you may wish to consider it.

There are any number of programs you may decide to go with, and in a book whose focus is drawing animation in Flash, we couldn't possibly explore *every* software possibility, so I'll recommend Final Cut Express. Though primarily a digital editing program, its audio capabilities are well worth the price I paid for it, used, on Amazon.com (I think in the $50 neighborhood for a "used" copy). iMovie, which ships with any Mac that has a DVD burner, might also suit your purposes. Both are capable of recording, editing, and mixing broadcast-quality audio.

Don't worry, all you PC folks out there; I know I have a tendency to be "Mac-centric," but you shouldn't be troubled by this. Most PCs come with their own home video editing capabilities (they were bound to catch up with Macs someday... heh-heh)! My wife has a PC... that's why I jokingly tell people I'm in a mixed marriage. I'm a dedicated Mac user and she's PC. Her HP Pavilion included a program that's supposed to be the PC equivalent of the aforementioned Mac programs, MovieMaker, which can import a wide variety of video, image, and audio formats.

Naturally, there are many programs you could use to record and edit your audio, and I recommend reading the instruction manual that came with your audio editing utility of choice.

I will part, however, on this subject of home sound recording, with a few helpful tips:

1. If you have a noisy or even barely audible heater/AC, make sure you turn it off for the duration of your recording session. But if it's low enough, and not *too* noticeable, your music track might actually drown it out (if added later).

2. The same goes for a ticking clock near your computer, or a potentially noisy furry friend that may have to go into the next room — as long as that doesn't send her into a barking frenzy (in my case). Remove any possible sources of unwanted background noise, and don't rustle the pages of the script while you're reading. Place a stiff cardboard backing behind your paper if necessary.

3. Also, sad to say, some computer disk drives (like internal CD players) have a nasty tendency to start whirring when a disc is inserted. If this is the case with your computer, take it out.

The Music Track

I'll admit it, when I worked at the Clanton radio station, I was just in a whole world of audio ecstasy. When I started working there, I naively told them that I had a few LPs of sound effects they were welcome to use (in those days, along the lines of Halloween sound effects). Well, first of all, they already had their own sound effects library... and music library. Second of all, I found out you can get in some serious trouble if you use music or sound effects intended for home use in a for-profit production like a TV commercial. And if you pay special attention to the copyright notices on DVDs nowadays, you'll notice it contains a message warning that "unauthorized duplication or presentation, even without monetary gain" is punishable by law. That means even if you don't *intend* to make a few bucks, even if you're just making an unauthorized copy for your own personal use, you can still get fined in the neighborhood of $250,000... and/or get put in jail.

Myself, I like my freedom and what few bucks I do have, so I try to keep my sound effects and my software clean. I'm against software, video, and sound piracy, because:

■ I earned the money to pay for my software, video, and sound effects library, and I don't see why anyone else should go to less effort than I did to get theirs.

■ As a creative artist who depends on royalties for my income (this book, my children's book, *The Lost World Adventures*, my cartoons being downloaded via mobile phone devices, etc.), the thought of myself or any other deserving artist being deprived of rent or grocery money makes me sick... and that's putting it lightly.

In any case, later at the radio station, I discovered my first music library on CD. It was a library called Canary that consisted of about 15 CDs. It had a wide variety of music styles, from contemporary to jazz, with a few scary and silly music tracks as well. There was even a disc full of digital sound effects! (My personal favorite at the time was a cut on CD number nine, called "Poltergeist." It was the sound effect that convinced me to purchase the whole library.)

When I called the publisher to get a price quote on that CD, they told me I could either pay $50, and get that one CD, or I could pay $200, and get all 15 CDs in the set. I was a college student by that time, and most "off the shelf" CDs you could buy in a record store were in the $20 range. However, having worked at the radio station, I knew there was a difference between CDs intended for home use and those that are intended for broadcast purposes. I bit the financial bullet and (since my parents were paying my rent at that time) shelled out a weekly paycheck or two for that whole library. Looking back, I don't regret it. Especially if you consider what other college students spent their money on: sports cars for showing off to people who don't really care about them, stereo equipment to impress friends at expensive parties, and vacations that send them on a downward spiral into credit card debt. At least with my initial CD library investment (start simple and straightforward; don't go overboard!), there was a reasonable chance of a return.

Broadcast music, incidentally, falls into one of two categories: needle-drop fees and royalty free. If you have a choice, take royalty free. Here's why:

The term needle-drop fees obviously comes from the days of the LP record albums, when a diamond-tipped "needle" dropped onto the record, and the little wobbly knobs encoded within the grooves of the album sent the sound waves up the needle, through the stereo arm, and out the speakers. A needle-drop fee means that every time you use the sound effect or recording, you are obligated to report each use to the publisher, and they charge you a fee. That's a bit of a time-consuming hassle, and can be costly. That's obviously why, if given the choice, royalty-free music and sound effects are preferable.

Royalty free means that once you pay a given price for a CD, usually $70 to $150 for those that are really worth using (I'm sure you can find some cheaper that might feasibly work), you're done paying for it.

Do be sure to read your licensing agreement. Though you're done paying for it, you may still be requested to report certain broadcast or duplication uses. In these cases, it's usually just for the purpose of making sure that the composer (or sound effects studio) gets the royalties they deserve for their hard work.

My personal favorites and recommendations:

If I had to do it all over again, I'd probably start with these two simple, basic CDs from Sound-Ideas.com: *Captain Audio* and *Mzzz Music*.

Both go for $29 each (at the time of this writing), and have the distinct advantage of being CD-ROMs vs. audio CDs. Besides the obvious price tag advantage (they're cheaper than Sound-Ideas' own best discs and even beat most of them by at least $100), they're already in WAV format. That's a sound format that seems to work equally well with either Mac or PC audio platforms. That also means you can directly import them into Flash without having to go through a secondary program like iMovie or Final Cut, and then export them as AIFF files (another common audio format).

Anytime you can save yourself an extra step is usually a good thing.

Now if I had a few more bucks burning a hole in my pocket (which is seldom a disadvantage I suffer), I would perhaps take steps forward by getting a slightly larger music library with slightly longer cuts. Most of *Mzzz Music*'s cuts don't last longer than 30 seconds, and for the beginning animator, that should be a perfect starting place. However, if you want to get longer clips, you might want to get one of their mix libraries. The one I have is *Mix IV*, which has 10 CDs that range from pure everyday household sound effects to jungle, nature, and even a few cartoony sound effects. The music CD in particular that got me was their Comedy and Children disc (Mix #31), which was precisely what I needed. It's great for animation. Also, they have a few dramatic, sports, historical, and dance CDs, each with a variation of cut lengths from 30 seconds to 60 seconds, and sometimes even 10- or 15-second cuts. Ten seconds is the standard length for a TV or radio station ID.

When I re-edited our live-action horror-comedy, *Late MidAfternoon of the Living Undead Insurance Salesmen, Politicians, and Telephone Solicitors*, I bought another pair of Sound-Ideas CDs that came in quite handy. Their *Classic Drama Music*, a two-CD set, had scores from the era of the movie we were obviously parodying, the *Night of the Living…* oh, something-or-others. Anyway, that set has music tracks of the silent movie era, 1950s and 1960s television styles, and even some 1920s jazzy music that I used to redub my cartoon *Cooksey the Cannibal and the Boiglah.*

I also like Music Bakery, and you can find them at MusicBakery.com. At the time of this writing, their standard mix CDs go for about $70 each (they seem to have an ongoing sale, which certainly doesn't bother me). There's usually about three or four terrific cuts at best on these so-called variety/legacy CDs (as I believe they call them), but then there are about as many cuts of varying length that just don't do anything for me, usually along the lines of "easy listening," which I very seldom use.

But that's not necessarily a problem at Music Bakery. (Before I risk sounding negative toward these guys; I'm actually quite fond of a number of their CDs.) They also give you the option of buying CDs by category (drama, orchestral, international, etc.), so you don't end up with a lot of those "unused" music tracks.

The advantage of putting your soundtrack together digitally is that, if you can't afford a composer (or can't find a musician friend to write a score for your cartoon), it's relatively easy to cut the music to your needs. You can cut the music at an appropriate music sting or naturally occurring pause, or even fade it up and/or down into your next sequence.

When I put together my soundtrack for *Midnight Sneak*, I used four different music pieces. It opens with Shadow Tag (track 77) from Sound-Ideas Mix IV CD #31, and then when Sezquatch gets angry, it changes to some rather intense, dilemma-type notes from another track on that same CD. When Deadbeat reaches that moment of an awkward pause, I use those few whiny strings from *Tales from the Vienna Woods* (CD #34 , track 23, also from Mix IV), and then whirl right into track 84 from the Holiday selections on that same disc, as Mr. Boogeyman is sent on his rather abrupt exit.

I edit music before adding my sound effects (which come last), because, in those otherwise awkward pauses, music can sustain or shift a mood as necessary.

Legend has it that Alfred Hitchcock, one of the twentieth century's greatest film directors, doubted the success of the now-acclaimed shower scene from *Psycho*... at least until they added composer Bernard Hermann's signature slicing violin strings.

And the rest, as they often say, is history.

Editing Sound Effects

The last thing I'll do for my soundtrack is add sound effects.

With the pacing provided by the dialogue track and the music track, we've got a pretty good idea about the flow of the cartoon. We can also start to sense where to place the sound effects.

As I discussed during the music section, a couple of basic sound effects CDs will help you get started. If you're really into sound effects, I'll add another few CDs to your wish list, from our good friends at Sound-Ideas:

- *The Hanna-Barbera Lost Treasures*
- *Jurassic Dinosaurs*

The first CD is absolutely delightful. You'll have to listen to it once just for fun, because you'll remember the animated scenes that once accompanied these now-classic sound effects. Then listen to it again, and wonder to yourself, "How in the blazes did these

Two of my favorite sound effects categories rolled into one: dinosaurs and wacky Saturday morning cartoon sounds.

people *make* those weird sounds?" Now listen to it one more time, and plan how you can use those sound effects to your own production's advantage.

You're perfectly welcome to purchase the four-disc set of the otherwise complete *Hanna-Barbera SoundFX Library* (for $495, at the time of this writing), budget permitting, naturally... or you can get the single *Hanna-Barbera Lost Treasures* CD for $129.

As a matter of fact, I got my *Hanna-Barbera Lost Treasures* CD for less than that because (as I may have already mentioned) one of the truly appealing reasons to visit Sound-Ideas.com every 30 days is that they have a blue plate special that changes monthly. I could be wrong, but I think I got the *Lost Treasures* CD on sale for somewhere between $70 and $95. And if even that wasn't enough for you, if you lose your chance the first time around to get a previous month's blue plate special at that special price, at the end of the year (sometimes December or January), you can most likely catch it at that price again during their "All You Can Eat Special," when the previous year's titles go on sale at one time.

What I particularly like about that *Lost Treasures* disc is that it has a nice *variety* of useful sound effects. Obviously most of the sound effects are cartoony in some sense, along the lines of Yogi and Scooby style, classic Saturday morning cartoons... boings, splats, falling down stairs, and exaggerated diving board plunges into a pool. But they've also got some rather nice science fiction sound effects, like the types you'd hear in *Space Ghost* and *Jonny Quest* adventures... laser blasts, transporters, spaceships, and so on. They've also got a variety of animal sound effects that can double as monster effects... elephant roars, camel grunts, and gator hisses.

The second disc I mentioned was, of course, *Jurassic Dinosaurs*. Speaking as a verifiable dinosaur nut, it's pretty obvious why anyone would want to invest in some prehistoric-sounding Rex roars, Apatosaurus grunts, raptor hisses, and eerie jungle bird ambience sounds. I kid you not... they even have a fire-breathing dragon sound effect sequence. Not only do they provide you with the mixed elements, but they also give you the individual tracks that make up the sequence as well.

All that would have been enough, but they've also got a few science fiction sounds thrown in on that same CD. A werewolf transformation, a robot, and fairy wings in flight. They don't actually fit in with the Jurassic Dinosaur category, but who am I to complain?

From whatever source you choose, you can place your sound effects in your Timeline by importing them (if they're already in WAV or AIFF format), or you can simply drag them over from your sound effects/music CD onto your hard drive. They should then copy over as AIFF files, which you should be able to import in a program like Final Cut Express or Final Cut Pro. (Again, because there are so many different sound editing programs out there, it's best to check your user's manual for actual details.)

A program like Final Cut will allow you to pick out the sound effect you need, even if it's embedded within a sequence of other sounds. For instance, let's say that I've found a cut on one of the CDs with a slide-whistle sound effect, like an object falling down to the ground, and it's followed by an earth-shattering crash of metal and glass. For whatever reason I don't necessarily want the sound of that silly slide-whistle. I'm making an adventure cartoon and don't want silly... in this case, I want melodramatic. But I do need that metal and glass crash.

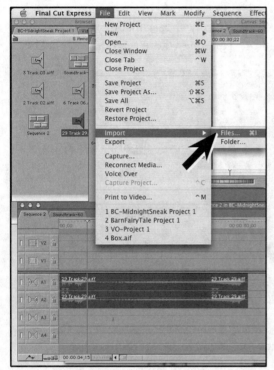

Final Cut Express (not to mention its fully loaded counterpart, Final Cut Pro) is just one of many audio and/or video editing programs you can use to mix and edit sound effects for your cartoon's soundtrack.

Here, I'm about to import a sound effect.

In the case of Final Cut Express, after going to **File | Import**, I'll place the sound effect in my Timeline by dragging it down into the first two audio channels. (Video channels are listed as V1, V2, etc., and audio channels are listed below as A1, A2, etc. Most audio channels you'll find work in pairs for stereo.) I'll select my Razorblade tool, and place the playback head (a line common in most audio and video programs, that displays your current position in the Timeline) along the point where the slide-whistle ends and the crash begins.

I'll click there, then select (with the Arrow tool) and delete the first part of the sound effect, the silly slide-whistle. Now I can move the effect to that point in the Timeline where the crash is needed.

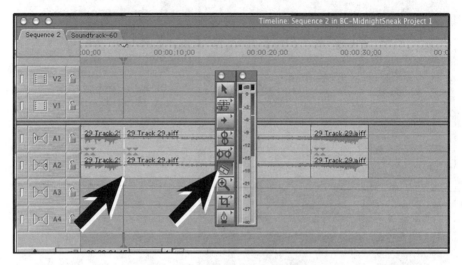

In Final Cut, you can clip off parts of the sound effect or music track that you don't need by using the Razorblade tool (right) to slice sections of the soundtrack (left).

If the two effects are too close together, perhaps with the whistle continuing into the crash, or some other such audio calamity, there is most likely another tool at your disposal. In the case of Final Cut or iMovie, you can simply fade your audio in or out, to the point of subtlety that most viewers won't notice a problem.

The editing process really amazes me, whether it's audio or video. You can hand the exact same raw footage of cover shots, dialogue, and even sound effects and music to two different editors, and two weeks later, each of them can hand you back two entirely different films.

One of the most basic things I'll say about soundtrack editing is hopefully the most important: "Keep it simple!"

The main thing is... is the main thing you're trying to say in each scene getting across to the audience? In other words, one of the things I would grade my character animation students' final project on was this question: Can a first-time viewer tell what's going on in this film?

You're not going to have the luxury of sitting behind every first-time viewer when they see your film to explain to them what's happening. One of the basics of comedy is that if you have to *explain* a joke, it's probably not that funny to begin with.

On the subject of soundtracks, I'll usually try to let someone else listen to it before I consider it done... and don't explain ahead of time what they're about to see. One of my own common self-criticisms is that I have a tendency to let the music get just barely too loud where you have to strain to hear what the character is saying.

And no matter how cool the music track is, no matter how amusing I personally find that particular sound effect, if I can't hear the character's dialogue, I'm obviously missing the mark.

Again, keep it simple. In animation, like all good comedy, or even good drama, for that matter... only *one thing* happens at a time. That's all the audience can take in, anyway... and they are paying the ticket price, or buying the product your commercial is selling, or purchasing your DVD feature... so just give them one thing at a time to focus on. And if something crazy has happened, don't be afraid to give the audience a moment to catch up, to chuckle for a second or so, before going on to the next gag. That's the basis of those pauses from really talented classic comedians like Groucho Marx, George Burns, and Jack Benny. They knew just when to give that questioning glance to the camera or audience, as if to say, "I can't believe I'm seeing this, can you?"

Timing is one of those things you're working on at this stage, and that can make or break any film, animated or live action. Some people say you're either born with it or you're not. I don't necessarily agree. Like drawing skills or math, you learn it or you don't... but perhaps some are more eagerly inclined to learn certain skills than others.

If you keep these things in mind when you put together your soundtrack, chances are your completed film will be that much easier to follow and enjoy.

Importing Soundtracks in Flash (Formats)

Once you're happy with the pacing in your cartoon, you've let a couple of friends listen to it, and you've carefully weighed in your mind which of their suggestions are helpful and useful (and which should be politely or diplomatically disregarded), you can export your soundtrack as a sound file, either in AIFF or WAV format.

When your soundtrack is at this point, legible, entertaining, and in a file format that you can actually use in that magical program we've been hinting toward all along... then... yes, *then* you're ready to go into Flash!

Animatic, or "Pose Test," Defined

Now hopefully you're ready to assemble your animatic.

Ah, but what is an animatic, you might well ask? Well, since you asked... an animatic (or "pose test") is perhaps best described as an onscreen comic book with a soundtrack.

Bigfoot Country art © Mark S. Smith/MarkToonery.com

The animatic or "pose test." Imagine watching a comic book on video, reading one panel at a time. With every line of dialogue, the panel changes to the next picture.

The level of detail an animatic has depends largely on budget and client preference. I'll usually just scan in my colored storyboards (generally colored with colored pencils and the occasional art marker set), import them directly into either Flash or Final Cut, and start pasting them onto the soundtrack. In that way, I can make adjustments so that with every new line or phrase of dialogue, or every new action or its accompanying sound effect (however often needed)... every time one of these dramatic changes take place, we're looking at a new picture onscreen.

Other good places to change a scene are on a music sting or accent, a cutaway to a character rolling her eyes at another character's line, or even a lingering pause on someone not quite certain what to say (like Deadbeat in the *Midnight Sneak* example after Sezquatch yells at him).

For that particularly picky client, or even perhaps for your own inner perfectionist's benefit, you may decide to get a little more detailed with your animatic, and start doing some additional key animation drawings for your testing purposes.

As a matter of fact, the best thing to do at this point may be to look at an example.

I scanned in my thumbnails (which you can do just as readily with your slightly prettier storyboards) at 300 dpi (that's dots per inch), which in this case comes in handy two ways. First of all, it enables me to print them out original size at print-quality resolution, if necessary. That's helpful if I decide to color them for some reason and print them out. Secondly, since these tiny little storyboards are scanned at 300 dpi, that means if I take them into a web- or video-ready program like Flash (which is set at 72 dpi), my formerly tiny 300 dpi storyboard will now almost fill the 72 dpi screen.

If you care to try this for yourself, you'll soon discover that a two-inch thumbnail scanned at 300 dpi will almost fill your screen when brought into Flash. This two-inch thumbnail gives me a good start for my animatic, and will later serve another purpose, as you'll see, when I get ready to animate (should I choose the so-called "paperless animation" approach to drawing 2D cartoons).

Hopefully you've scanned your storyboards and saved them all into a single folder. Once you've done this, you're finally ready to dive into Flash. But first let's discuss acting theory. If you just can't wait, jump over to Chapter 6.

Chapter 5

An Actor with a Pencil... Um, Pixel

Girth, Thurman, and Deadbeat
© Mark S. Smith/MarkToonery.com

A Few Words on Acting

The late, great Chuck Jones is the cartoon director best known for his definition of an animator: an actor with a pencil.

And that's very true.

Every shape we draw, every muscle we bulge, every flip of the hair or curl of an index finger, every subtle squish of flesh or rubber ball that contacts a hard, flat surface... all that is channeled from our brain, down our arm, into the tip of our pencil or digitizing stylus, and translates into acting.

Does that sound intimidating? Good. Let's get started with a couple of theories on acting and drama before that intimidating factor sinks in.

Deadbeat and Mark © MarkToonery.com/Mark S. Smith

Comedy vs. Tragedy: The Power of Sympathy

Think about that classic symbol of drama: those two masks that you often see sculpted in bas-relief over many a classical theatre proscenium arch... the two masks of Comedy and Tragedy.

You'd think that's one of those things that's painfully obvious, but let's consider one silly little fact: Tragedy and comedy have a lot more in common than you think. As a matter of fact, anything you watch, whether it's a cartoon, a play, or television sitcom or soap opera, falls into one or the other of those categories of drama: tragedy or comedy.

And what makes it worse, or ironic, or something like that is a famous quote (which I've heard attributed to both Mel Brooks and W.C. Fields, but both were brilliant comedians) that goes something like this: "Tragedy is when I cut my finger. Comedy is when you walk into an open sewer and die."

Yikes! Sounds cruel, doesn't it? And to a staggering degree, it really is.

But think about it like this: A little boy who is dressed in dirty, ragged clothes is rubbing his belly, obviously from hunger. He looks over and sees a cart of apples sitting out in front of the grocery store, with a sign that reads, "Apples 4/$1." The little boy licks his lips, and reaches into his pockets and turns them out. They're empty. But he looks down just 10 feet ahead of him and sees a crumpled dollar bill on the pavement. He rushes to pick it up and smiles, licking his lips as he looks over again at the sign, and starts toward the grocery store. Then as he heads over, he sees a little blind girl with a tin cup extended, asking for donations.

The little boy looks at the dollar bill in his hand, over at the apples, and then at the little girl.

He obviously has a choice here, as do we.

Let's say he goes with choice A:

The little boy nods to himself; he knows what he has to do. He drops the dollar bill into the blind girl's cup, and as he walks away, knowing he's done the right thing, he looks over his shoulder at the girl, and falls into an open manhole.

There's a splash, and some bubbles... then nothing.

He's gone. His unselfish decision led to what kind of an ending?

Tragic, wouldn't you say? And why? Because the boy made the right decision (which is seldom the easy decision, especially when you're hungry), he had our sympathy.

Now let's say we back up just a bit, and have the little boy go with choice B:

The little boy looks at the dollar bill in his hand, over at the apples, and then at the little girl.

This time he makes a different choice. He quietly slips the dollar bill in his pocket, tiptoes past the little girl, and seeing she hasn't heard him pass, he turns around to look over his shoulder at her. As if that wasn't bad enough, he sticks his tongue out at her and places his thumb to his nose, wiggling his fingers at her triumphantly.

While he's looking in her direction, he steps into the open manhole.

There's a splash, and some bubbles... then nothing.

He's gone. His selfish decision (topped off by his downright rude gesture to someone who couldn't even see him) led to what kind of an ending?

Comedic? Don't tell me at least one person in the audience wouldn't find this ending at least mildly amusing... sort of a "cosmic justice," or better yet, a judgment brought on by a "higher power."

An extreme example, perhaps, but done so to stress one of the basic points of drama. So what does that tell us about character development, and not just the difference between tragedy and comedy?

Just like real life, I think we're not judged by what happens to us (the little boy is poor and hungry; a situation that can seldom be the fault of a child), but by how we *react* to what happens to us (giving to someone in a worse situation as opposed to being selfish and/or rude).

Also note one other thing those two different situations had in common. Was there a single line of dialogue spoken during either of those examples? Absolutely not, and you didn't really need it.

In "true animation," you can turn off the sound and still follow the storyline. These stories have a tendency to do rather well overseas. Watch Rowan Atkinson's *Mr. Bean* for some terrific live-action inspiration.

Animation vs. Illustrated Radio

That brings me to another point about animation, which I've heard explained by Chuck Jones, that I'll put in the form of a question:

What's the difference between *animation* and *illustrated radio*?

In animation, the best example is the classic *Roadrunner* cartoons. You can turn off the sound or put it on mute, and though you may miss the terrific sound effects by editor Treg Brown and Carl Stallings' (or later Milt Franklyn's) frantic orchestrations, you still should have no trouble whatsoever following the story.

That's *animation*.

It's a visual medium.

The other example I'll give (though don't get me wrong, I love that silly Great Dane) is *Scooby Doo*. In an event I related to my class, one day after work, I turned on the TV to Cartoon Network (in the days when they played classic cartoons at suppertime) and went into the kitchen to fix supper.

Listening to illustrated radio, you can follow the story without even looking at the picture.

Though I couldn't see the picture I didn't miss a thing from the plotline. It went something like this:

"Man, like there's no way I'm goin' in that crazy haunted house!" (Nervous laughter)

"Oh, no! The monster's got Scooby and he's dragging him inside!"

"Look! The monster's tripped on the stairs and Scooby caught him! Let's take off his mask and see who he really is!"

Do you get the idea? Even though I couldn't see the picture from the kitchen, I could tell everything that was going on in the living room… because they were telling me.

That, my friends, is *illustrated radio*.

Now illustrated radio can be enjoyable, mind you. I still have the complete boxed sets of *Scooby Doo: Where Are You? Seasons 1 and 2* and *The Scooby/ Dynomutt Hour.* I must begrudgingly admit that some of my favorite "illustrated radio shows" besides Scooby are *Jonny Quest, Fat Albert* (just about anything from Filmation during the '70s would have qualified in this category, though very few were favorites), Cosgrove Hall's *Duckula,* Jon Lovitz' lovable loser *The Critic,* and of course, *The Simpsons* (currently the longest-running sitcom in history, animated or live action). I have DVDs of every one of these sets mentioned, so please don't think I'm disdainful of them; I just want to make the distinction between pure animation and illustrated radio. (Heck, I'm guilty of a few illustrated radio TV spots myself!)

Who was everybody's favorite dwarf? (Six times out of seven, anyway.) Who was the most mischievously lovable Marx Brother? And what was the name of the cuddly little elephant, the only title character from a Disney feature that never uttered a single syllable?

That's right. Dopey, Harpo, and Dumbo. What did all three of these key characters have in common? Their characters never spoke a word, but their expressions said so much more than their still tongues would ever allow.

And that's one of the things that truly fascinates me about this magical art form we call animation. Not one of those characters required voice actors or scriptwriters trying to prove to us how terribly clever they were at dialogue. (Not to downplay the contributions of those talented individuals where applicable... ahem!)

With just the correct flick of our pencil or brush, in applying those little bits of carbon to animation paper or ink and paint to clear acetate cels, or placing those pixels on just the right spot at just the right time on a computer screen, we can make people laugh, listen, sometimes even cry when we do it particularly well.

With these lines and forms (or illusion of form) that we create, we can elicit an emotional response from a viewer.

That to me is the true magic of animation, if there is such a thing.

Suspension of Disbelief

And speaking of "such a thing" and "no such things," that's another key element that animation, puppetry, radio, and for that matter any drama on stage or screen has in common. It's called *suspension of disbelief.*

Suspension of disbelief is something that we all do when we sit down in a theatre seat, wait for the lights to go down, and then watch people dressed up in costumes in a living room that (oddly enough) has all its furniture facing an invisible wall.

If we really thought about the fact that these people are just actors in a make-believe living room, regardless of whether we were watching the most amateur of high school dramas or least professional of Broadway comedies, we wouldn't be able to follow what's supposed to be a *story*, an imaginary episode in an imaginary family's life. Yet from the youngest member of the audience who understands "just pretending" to the oldest seasoned drama professor, we "suspend" or *put on hold* our disbelief, and allow ourselves to briefly believe for the next hour or two (at least until intermission) that these people in costumes are real-life characters and their problems and challenges are true experiences that we all collectively share.

That's something we really need to do when we're putting together these little screen stories we call cartoons. As a matter of fact, I think that's one of the great strengths of animation in particular.

The very act of watching animation requires immediate dependence on the suspension of disbelief. We're viewing a series of drawings, each slightly different from the one preceding it, that our eyes (and soon thereafter our mind) accept as a motion sequence... which eventually (when done properly) builds into some form of story.

The very ability to "read" animation is based on a quirk in our visual perception ability called *persistence of vision*, which allows our retina (or some would say the brain) to retain an image for a brief moment, thus giving a sequence of still images (one slightly different from its predecessor) the illusion of movement.

So if you look at it with that approach, it's easier to "pull off" an animated fantasy than a live-action drama... or at best, just as easy. What I mean by that is having Mr. Everyday Executive Business Suit walk from the door of his office and set down the morning paper on his desk beside his computer takes every bit as much effort to draw or believe as a two-headed dragon flapping its wings to a halt as it lands in an empty battlefield wasteland. (I dare say that it's easier to draw the dragon, since *reality* is so much tougher to pull off!) If both scenes are animated drawings, it takes every bit as much effort to believe that the executive and his office is "real" as it does to believe that the dragon and the wasteland is "real."

I hope this is helping you to appreciate the potential of this art form that is quite literally at our fingertips. When used properly, we can use this art not just to entertain, but to educate, enlighten, and inform as well.

Both the Disney and Warner Bros. studios had this figured out as early as World War II (admittedly even earlier than that), when they used animated films to educate soldiers in various survival techniques that would have been (and were) extremely dull, boring, and downright difficult to understand when presented in live action… not to mention life-threatening to the actors who were displaying the importance of these very survival techniques.

Disney's animated propaganda films for the war effort on the subject of patriotism and taxes and the Warner Bros. films produced regarding soldier training could get audiences to laugh and therefore pay attention, so they could deliver the golden nuggets of information that followed.

Line of Action and Silhouettes

All right, perhaps that's enough theory on acting for now. How do we translate all this into our own personal working methods and approach to this wonderful art form?

When animation got its start in the early years of the twentieth century, a lot of its cues were taken from its live-action counterpart, vaudeville. Vaudeville was a sort of traveling live-theatre circuit, where early comedians like George Burns and Gracie Allen, Jack Benny, and the Marx Brothers would travel from town to town, performing at local theatres. It was a lot like *The Muppet Show* pretended to be, a variety show, and a valuable training ground for those skilled performers who would later become legendary stars in radio, film, and finally television.

As a matter of fact, I daresay a lot of animation's conventions, not to mention routines and old jokes, were translated, "borrowed," and/or downright stolen from vaudeville.

Perhaps the reason for that is that these performances taking place on a stage in a crowded concert hall, with a tiny little five-to-six-foot-tall person at one end, had to be seen by people sitting on the back row at the other end, perhaps hundreds of feet away. You couldn't be terribly subtle in those acting conditions without the electronic microphones and gigantic video screens that are present at our modern concerts.

Perhaps that's why animation is so much like vaudeville. Those broad actions that carried across that crowded concert hall to the back row translate rather nicely into these characters that have to be reduced to their most simple outlines.

A *line of action* is an imaginary line that runs through the figure that is acting. I truly believe it's one of the most important ingredients, if not the precise key ingredient, to making a dynamic, action-based, storytelling drawing.

Although his friend on the upper left doesn't seem terribly interested, is there any doubt which direction the character on the upper right is looking? Even though we're giving this example with "gingerbread figures," you can still tell the direction this figure's action is taking.

A line of action gives a drawing direction. Just like the layout drawings we discussed earlier (in the painfully obvious camera shot examples in Chapter 3), a line of action can subtly (or less so) lead the viewer's eye to where it should be.

It goes almost hand in hand with the importance of a silhouette drawing. If you can still "read" what a character is doing in silhouette, or if you were to see the character's shadow cast on the wall, chances are that's a rather powerful (and quite likely successful) animation drawing.

If you can "read" what's going on in silhouette, chances are it's a successful animation drawing. Which of these drawings are perfectly clear and which aren't? How would you fix them?

There's a saying in animation: "When in doubt, act it out."

If you're having trouble coming up with a pose, then read the lines as you act through them. And don't act so much with your mouth, but use your arms and hands... maybe even your eyes as well. (We'll cover that in more depth shortly.) And invest in a full-length mirror if you don't have one already. A camcorder or even a camera (if you don't have room for any of these other suggestions) might provide a useful reference guide. And if all else fails, don't forget the three Rs of animation when you hit a creative block: *research*, *reference*, and *resource* materials.

(Okay, sorry, but I slipped an M in there as well... and they're all strikingly similar, but it's usually easier to remember these things in threes, so we'll stick with that theory.)

Whenever you do get to the point where you realize your 2D acting skills need work, or any time you find yourself in a creative slump, there's only one thing you can do to overcome these psychological brick walls... Seek inspiration!

And how do you do that? Those three Rs of animation I just mentioned, remember?

- Research. Investigate what you're animating. If you're animating some characters dancing, then rent a video of ballet or an old Hollywood musical. If more current dance moves are required for your scene, then go to where they're doing the kinds of dances you'd like to use. Take some reference footage if you have or can borrow or rent a camcorder. (And if it takes any money to do so, then save your receipts for next April 15. Chances are if you're working on a project for profit the related expenses are tax deductible... if they're genuine, of course!)

- Reference. For something as deceptively simple as an everyday walk cycle, you might find a book like Eadweard Muybridge's *The Human Figure in Motion*, or any of his other series of photographic books that provide a useful reference for animators, helpful. Legend has it that Muybridge, prior even to the creation of the motion picture camera, made a bet with a politician that all four of a racehorse's legs were indeed off the ground during the course of a run. The only way to settle the bet was to set up a series of cameras along the course of the horse's run that were activated by a series of trip wires. As the horse ran past each camera, the photo was snapped, and a series of photographs, precursors to motion picture film, were the result. The bet was won, incidentally, because the photos proved that all four legs of the horse did leave the ground during its run.

    Muybridge's work continued to develop toward human motion, and undoubtedly had an influence on Thomas Edison's invention of the aforementioned motion picture camera.

You can also purchase these same plates today, in book format. Besides *The Human Figure in Motion*, you can also get his *Animals in Motion*, which shows everything from the cycles of parakeets flapping their wings to camels, elephants, and dogs walking. I do want to emphasize again that it's not necessary to become an obsessive book collector (as some might call me, and not altogether without reason), but just start out with a few basic titles that can get you moving. (A book collecting dust on your shelf isn't doing you any good... you have to complete the process by actually opening and reading the book in order to apply the knowledge therein.)

■ Resources. Yeah, yeah, the Internet is great and all, but let's face it. Like most technology, the darn thing just offers way too many dangerous distractions. The temptation to read seemingly interesting tangents that might come up (not directly relevant to your search) is easily categorized as procrastination. And if you're not careful typing in just the right search words, you're going to come up with a whole bunch of trash you have to filter through just to get to the useful bits.

Instead, try your local library. There are books there on just about any subject imaginable, there are nice people there who make a career out of helping people find just the information they need for free, and (as I no doubt mentioned already) if they don't have the exact book you need, they may even order it for you. Then when you're done reading it, you don't have to leave it on your own shelf, taking up space and collecting dust. (When it comes time to pack up and move, you'll thank yourself for not buying every single book title that popped into your head!)

All in the Eyes... Eyelids... or Eyebrows?

As you've no doubt heard, the eyes are the windows to the soul.

When it comes to a character's emotions, that's very true. While other facial features help (the mouth in particular), the eyes are the key to visual interpretation of a character's mood.

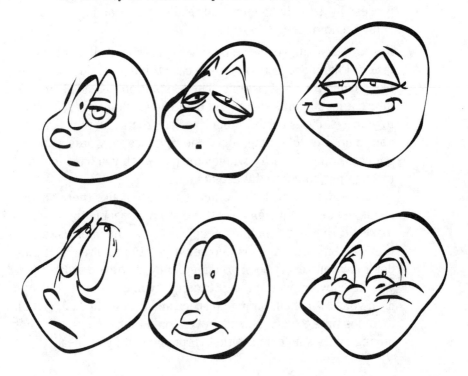

Notice how the direction and position of the eyelids influence the appearance of a character's mood, attentiveness, and state of consciousness.

When you think about it, though, it's really the eye*lids* that are doing most of the work. What we think of as the eye — the direction a character is looking — is determined by the iris and pupil. And depending on your budget/style, often just the pupil, that little black dot at the center of the eyeball, is showing us *where* they're looking.

I think Glen Keane's work on Ariel in 1989's *The Little Mermaid* was one of the more dramatic uses of the lower eyelid to showcase a character's emotional state. I think it was part of what made Ariel just so darn cute and endearing. Up till that point, most characters were essentially animated as though they didn't even possess a lower eyelid (except maybe when they were closed).

The eye*brows* also hold a lot of influence on a character's facial expression. Look at how different these two drawings are even though all aspects of their facial features are exactly alike except for the direction of the eyebrows.

BaaBraw © Mark S. Smith/MarkToonery.com

Notice what a tremendous difference the direction of the eyebrows has on the character's facial expression. Is there any doubt about which one of these characters is thinking pleasant thoughts and which one is hatching a mischievous plot? Which one would you trust?

Many animators keep a small hand mirror right beside their drawing desk so they can watch themselves create expressions. In fact, I recommend that you pick one up at your local dollar store (just don't forget to pay for it) and set it up so that you can study your eyebrows and other facial expressions.

That mirror will be particularly handy in another aspect of drawing animation...

Read My Lips... The Importance of Lip Synch

Lip synch (short for synchronization) is quite simply the act of matching up a character's mouth and lip positions with spoken lines of dialogue. If you've ever laughed at one of those old Saturday afternoon karate movies that was poorly dubbed, I don't have to explain the importance of synchronizing dialogue to the positions of a character's mouth. Woody Allen carried this example to the extreme by making it the basis of his film *What's Up, Tiger Lily?* when he used the whole premise of lip synch purposely not matching original dialogue by turning a former Japanese spy thriller into a search for an exclusive egg salad recipe.

Another example of poor lip synch is in some anime. I've watched some anime where I've counted two mouth positions per character... open and closed! (Now I understand pinching pennies and limited budgets, but I think that's carrying it a *bit* too far.)

A public service announcement from Tangent Man:

Please let me take this opportunity to kindly request anime fans to resist the temptation to ask author-illustrator Mark S. Smith precisely which series that was where he noticed the two mouth positions per character. It was a long time ago, and Mr. Smith is nearing his late 30s, so naturally, senility isn't far behind. Please save your time and energy and ask other, more pertinent questions about the fine art of classic-style, hand-drawn animation. Specifically, why did Daffy suffer a severe shift in personality during the early '50s, beginning drastically with *The Scarlet Pumpernickel*? Yes, we do know the answer to that one, but sorry, for legal reasons we can't go into the details in print. Besides, your poor, pure innocent minds couldn't handle the deep, dark cartoon conspiracy underlying that dreaded tale.

As you'll notice in the following illustration there are a number of different mouth positions, many thankfully similar to one another, that make our work just a bit easier. For instance, the mouth positions for m, b, and p are pretty much identical. (Although I did notice that John K. had Stimpy's cheeks puff out a bit on one instance of the letter p, which I thought was a rather clever touch.) Another good reason to mention that position in particular is that while most of the other positions may last only one or two frames (depending on your actor's dialogue track), that m-b-p position should really be held for a minimum of two frames... three frames perhaps when you can spare the extra frame. But as always, these so-called rules are merely recommended suggestions, to be used with judgment and with each unique circumstance.

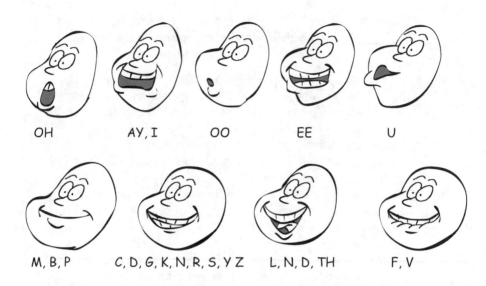

OH   AY, I   OO   EE   U

M, B, P   C, D, G, K, N, R, S, Y Z   L, N, D, TH   F, V

CONSONANTS

And make sure you don't ee-nun-cee-ayyt evv-urr-ee seen-gull syll-uh-bull. Did you get that? Believe me, it looks just as silly if you do enunciate every single syllable as I just did. We don't enunciate, or carefully pronounce, every single syllable of every single word we utter. I'm glad we don't because it would get profoundly irritating if we did. The best thing you can do is listen carefully to the dialogue track for that *one* word that people have a tendency to emphasize in every sentence, and accent that syllable, either with that carefully chosen mouth position or a gesture.

For a good example of using gestures for emphasis, watch Madame Medusa in Disney's *The Rescuers*. Milt Kahl's animation on this aging villainess just blows me away (almost as much as his animation on Shere Kahn in *The Jungle Book*). There's one scene in which Medusa is taking off her makeup, and she scoots her chair across the room while she's talking. She bounces her chair on the key words in her dialogue. In other words, she *hits… every… accent*. (And yes, admittedly sometimes you will have those rare occasions when more than one word per sentence is accented. Therefore, you may find the flamboyant villain is your exception to the rule.)

If you have trouble deciding which words to emphasize in a line of dialogue, try getting someone else to read the line and watch that person's lips in action. You may be thinking about it too hard. (And you've probably figured that it's best not to let them know what you're up to, so they're not thinking too hard about it either.) Sometimes, as you can guess, what is supposed to come naturally is one of the most difficult things to fake. (Or to draw!)

While I'm on the subject of animating dialogue, another animation director whose work I find especially entertaining to watch is Robert McKimson. Again, perhaps not a household name like the other Looney Tunes directors, but he can perhaps be credited as the proud papa of longtime Looney favorite, the Tasmanian Devil. (My favorite childhood character, of which my mom made me a custom stuffed doll years before they became so readily available.)

McKimson's first Taz cartoon was *Devil May Hare*, and my personal favorite was when Taz costarred with Daffy in *Ducking the Devil*. Though Bugs easily outwitted Taz on numerous occasions, Daffy was the only character to physically overpower the seemingly unstoppable brute. (It seems Daffy's unadulterated greed is just as effective as Popeye's spinach.) Both these cartoons and all the original Taz shorts were released years ago on VHS in *Stars of Space Jam: Tasmanian Devil*. Undoubtedly, I could credit this as the most overdue Looney Tunes DVD title to date.

With most of McKimson's other more, well, *verbally* versatile characters, if you watch his cartoons, you might notice that they often make grand gestures during their lines. Some of them, particularly Foghorn Leghorn, almost seem like ham Shakespearean actors, placing one hand emphatically on their chest and/or raising the other hand in the air to point during a key word. Because it's animation, it *works*.

We have an artistic license to overact. Take that license firmly in one hand and a pencil in the other. You're about as ready as you're going to get to start animating.

Three Methods of Animation

When it comes down to it, there are three methods to animate, as stated in Richard Williams' book *The Animator's Survival Kit*. (He goes into the advantages and disadvantages of each method in far better detail.) Allow me just to highlight the main points (because I don't want to be accused of preventing you from buying *his* terrific book), which fall into three tidy categories by approach:

■ Straight-ahead

■ Pose-to-pose

■ The best method

Thurman © Mark S. Smith/MarkToonery.com

Memo pads, Post-it notes, and even index cards clipped together are great ways to practice animation without a computer. I did a Roger Rabbit cartoon on a memo pad while I was working at the radio station, and to prove how exciting things were at that job on the weekend, I hand-colored every drawing with colored pencils.

Straight-ahead

This was the first way I started animating when I was about 10 years old, making those fun little flip-books. (This was just before adolescence and '80s Saturday morning cartoons soured me toward animation.) My mother would buy me these packs of memo pads, and I'd start my first drawing on the last page of the book. I'd turn the page, and trace the previous drawing, keeping anything I wanted to stay *still* in the same position as its predecessor, and anything I wanted to *move* adjusted and repositioned just a bit. When I was done, I flipped the pages, and *voilà*! I was an amateur animator. Without a camera or computer, it's arguably the cheapest method of character animation and the most straightforward, by definition.

In straight-ahead animation, you do all your drawings consecutively, from start to finish. You make drawing number one, drawing number two, drawing number three, and so on. The primary advantage is it's a more spontaneous approach and almost like improvisation. It's fun to watch because surprises happen that even you, the artist, may not have expected.

The disadvantage is a related problem... things unexpected start to happen that aren't so much fun. The scene may go on too long (we're given very specific lengths of time for our action to take place in the soundtrack), the size or proportions of the character may change, or she might not "hit her mark" on the stage at the right time. That same unpredictability that was so fascinating beforehand can just as easily work against us.

As usual, let me provide an unpleasant "straight-ahead" animation experience. I was doing an animated public service announcement for Frazer Methodist Church's Singles Ministry with a little character named Mothley. He was sitting on a phone, which rang, and he jumped up with surprise in midair. For whatever reason (I can't recall specifically), the soundtrack was not yet available, and I was itching to make some progress on the project. (Yep, boredom is a dangerous thing in our branch of the Smith family.) So I went ahead and started animating the character, and though I was fairly new to professional independent animation at the time (I think about three or four years at that point), I was rather pleased with the results.

Unfortunately, after I did get the soundtrack put together and examined the number of frames that were to be filled within that brief shot of the 30-second PSA, I found I had almost twice as many drawings as necessary. What choice did I have? I had to scrap some of the drawings. And again, when you're talking as many as 30 drawings per second of finished video, that's a lot of wasted work.

Fortunately, there's another method.

Pose-to-Pose

The pose-to-pose method introduces us to another term in animation that you'll hear used (and improperly at that, if we're not careful)... key drawings. Pose-to-pose animation often starts out with the director doing the most important storytelling drawings in the scene called the *key drawings*. The director (or another animator) may do drawings number 1, 12, 24, and 36 in the scene. He hands the scene over to his assistant animator, who may fill in drawings number 6 and 9, 14 and 18, 28 and 32. The assistant animator will then quite likely hand the animation drawings over to the inbetweener to fill in the remaining drawings.

Or, if you're working as an independent animator (like yours truly), congratulations, you're responsible for every one of those drawings, from keys to inbetweens.

Those key drawings that the director (or animator) is responsible for are *storytelling* drawings, as we just said. That means don't be surprised if you see slightly more cleaned-up versions of those poses originally from the storyboards. A key drawing is one of the most important drawings in a scene. It has to be there. Without it, the scene would fall apart and the audience wouldn't be able to tell what's going on.

Often (but not always) a key drawing may actually be a drawing you hold on-camera for a whole second or more, so the audience can "read" what's going on and is allowed time for the information to sink in before the story proceeds.

A key drawing is slightly different from an *extreme* drawing, which usually means contact drawing, where the character first comes into contact with something or someone, like the floor, the wall, or a prop. A scene may contain very few key drawings, but several more extreme drawings. If a character is about to pick something up and look at it, the first key drawing in the scene might be when he turns around and sees the object lying on the table. The first extreme drawing might be his first step, when his right foot hits the floor as he walks toward it, and the next extreme drawing might be when his left foot hits the floor. The second key

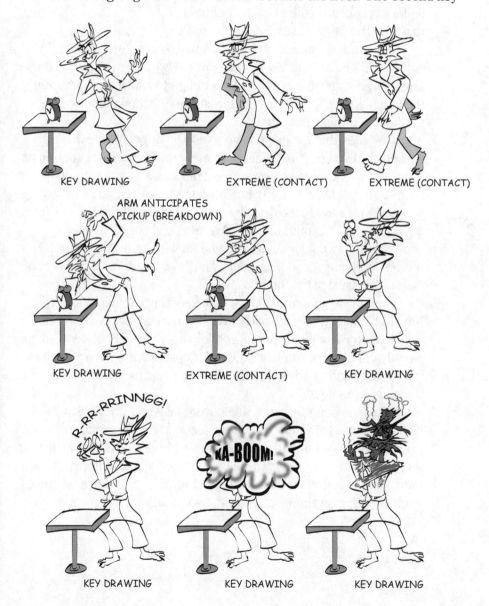

KEY DRAWING   EXTREME (CONTACT)   EXTREME (CONTACT)

ARM ANTICIPATES
PICKUP (BREAKDOWN)

KEY DRAWING   EXTREME (CONTACT)   KEY DRAWING

KEY DRAWING   KEY DRAWING   KEY DRAWING

drawing would be when he pauses before trying to pick it up, and the third extreme would be when he places his hand on the object. The next drawing might be the key drawing when he stops to look at it in his hand.

The eighth and ninth drawings I just added for fun.

So we've only got nine beginning drawings here, but that might be for six seconds (the average length of an animated scene). And that's 30 frames for every *second*, people.

Now do those nine drawings complete our scene? Absolutely *not*! We still need to do *breakdown drawings* (the drawings for the assistant, if your budget is blessed enough to afford one) between the completed *key* drawings, and then the remaining inbetweens left between the breakdowns.

Now does that mean we have to do 180 drawings for these six seconds? Absolutely *not*. This is where a method called shooting on ones, twos, or threes comes in. We'll discuss it in more depth in Chapter 6, but here's briefly how that works: When you're shooting on ones, you shoot each drawing once, giving you 30 drawings for 30 frames (one second) of video. When you shoot on twos, you shoot each drawing twice, so you end up with 15 drawings for 30 frames (still one second) of video. The rule of thumb is: fast action on ones, normal action on twos.

You may be able to get away with shooting each drawing twice (on twos) since these are fairly average, normal, everyday actions the character is going through, at a leisurely pace. Therefore, we've already cut our work in half for every department (animators' drawings, inking and/or scanning each drawing, and painting each drawing, even digitally).

However, don't forget, if these were fast-paced actions, especially say two characters in a chase scene against a panning background (say, I dunno, a certain desert highway), then the action *must* be shot on ones. That rule of thumb once more: normal action on twos, fast action on ones. And don't forget, sometimes on video, even shooting on threes can work... sometimes.

Shooting on twos (left) is fine for normal, everyday actions like opening a jar of peanut butter. Shooting on ones (right) is best for fast actions, like trying *wayyy* too hard to open a jar of peanut butter.

In my case, I had a character carrying a Volkswagen through a doorway in one of my earliest TV commercials (is it any wonder I love animation?), and on ones, he just moved way too fast. He didn't act like that Volkswagen weighed anything, even though his back was arched and his legs were bent.

I reshot the scene so that he was moving through the doorway on twos. Better, but it still didn't look heavy enough. I mean, it may very well have been a cartoon Volkswagen, but cartoon cars, ocean liners, and hippos should have weight, just like any ungainly sized object.

Finally, I shot it on threes. Did it work? As I said, *finally*. That was enough. The character still managed to get through the door and out of the shot in the available time remaining, while still looking as though he had to exhibit just enough effort to move across the sidewalk.

Just judge carefully when determining whether to shoot on ones, twos, or threes. Simply put, it's a financial answer to an artistic question. (As usual, in the words of Richard Williams.)

Don't ever forget that nine times out of 10, animation will always look better when it's shot on ones, because real life is on ones. Perhaps that's why it's so captivating to watch Richard Williams' *Who Framed Roger Rabbit* and *The Thief and the Cobbler.* Both films were shot primarily on ones.

Another major advantage (aside from the fact that our scenes now run just the right amount of allowed time) to the pose-to-pose method is it's easier to assist and therefore do more drawings in the same amount of time, with more artists working simultaneously.

All right, while we're still discussing the pose-to-pose method of animation, are there any disadvantages to it, like the straight-ahead method had its drawbacks?

Sadly, yes.

In fact, that very fascinating aspect of drawing on ones also applies to the straight-ahead method. Straight-ahead animation is more interesting to watch, and by using the pose-to-pose method, we lose some of that "magic" if we're not carcful.

As I usually ask my students at this point... isn't it too bad there's not a third method, where we, I dunno... take the strengths of both of these methods, and somehow... maybe... (are you thinking what I'm thinking?) combine these two methods into one... and we could call this resulting method —

The Best Method

Hey, what a swell idea! We'll combine the advantages of straight-ahead animation and pose-to-pose. That way, the scenes don't run too long, the character proportions are more likely to stay consistent, and yet they still maintain some of that "straight-ahead magic" that makes it more fascinating to watch our finished results.

But how do we apply that to our working method?

Here's what I do: I start by animating the first, most important thing in the scene first. Naturally, when we do first things first, and if you only concentrate on one thing at a time (which is just barely within our capabilities with all of today's technological distractions), you'll be far more able to calm down and focus on completing the task at hand.

If we've got a character walking across the screen, I'll start by animating his legs. Once I'm given (or end up with) the key drawings, naturally I'll continue with those extreme drawings, notably those drawings where his legs contact the ground for each step. (Extremes come next in precedence right after key drawings.) Next, I'll tackle those breakdown drawings; in the example on page 176, this is where the midair leg passes the leg touching the ground, called the *passing position* or *breakdown position*.

Once you get those done, it's just a matter of simple inbetweening. But we'll touch on that more just a bit later.

As far as this method goes, once the legs are done, I'll go back and animate the arms. Then, depending on which actions are important, greatest to least, I'll animate them in order. I'll save for the very last long, flowing objects like hair, a loose dress, baggy trousers, long floppy dog ears, etc. You get the idea. And these last few items I'm mentioning, the loose or floppy bits, will be animated straight-ahead, after all the other pieces are in place.

SECONDARY ACTION

FOLLOW-THROUGH

Secondary Action and Follow-Through

The act of animating these flowing bits we just discussed lead into secondary action and follow-through. A *secondary action* is a motion that results from a previous action, like a long-eared bunny that's hopping along. His ears bounce just a moment after his feet hit the ground, and even his little cotton-tail might do so to a lesser degree. A secondary action is usually delayed a beat behind the previous action by a frame or two.

Directly related to secondary action is *follow-through*. Say you've got a jogging brunette who comes to a stop. Though her legs and arms are capable of coming to a complete stop quickly, her long, flowing hair continues to sway forward past her face (in the same direction as she was running), it sways back momentarily, and then settles straight down. How many times it sways back and forth, and how far, will naturally vary depending on the speed of the run she just completed, wind force (if any), etc.

Details like this are what set apart feature animation from Saturday morning cartoon budgets. Secondary action and follow-through are a large part of what make truly great animation so captivating to the eye. I believe it may have been this very aspect of animation that enthralled me when I saw that scene of Roger counting on his fingers almost 20 years ago. The way his ears just seemed to wobble so perfectly as he bobbed back and forth, and how that red cowlick of his just slightly fluctuated as he swayed in one direction, or shimmered ever so slightly even when he stood still.

It's usually details like secondary action and follow-through that are the first to fly out the window when an animated feature is translated into a Saturday morning or (worse yet) weekday syndicated cartoon. Though I didn't know it at the time, it was magical details like these that went missing from *Dragon's Lair* as it made the transition to stilted Saturday morning from smooth-flowing, feature animation-quality arcade game.

Mechanical Inbetweening vs. "Slowing In" and "Slowing Out"

If you have a character's arm moving from straight up to straight out, and you want it to move at a smooth, uniform speed in the space of five drawings, then you'll need what's referred to as a series of *mechanical inbetweens*. As simply as I can put it, each inbetween is approximately the same distance apart from the others.

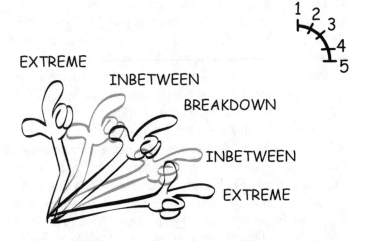

Now all this works fine if you're working with a robot that moves in even, mechanical bursts. But how often does that occur in the natural world, with say, 80% of the characters we'll be animating? (Hmm! I guess I just answered my own question there.)

Right. More often, people and animals (and the machines we drive, according to our guidance) have a strong tendency to speed up or slow down as we move, thanks to the laws of physics that guide us along.

It's what we refer to in the animation industry as *slowing in* and *slowing out*. Or, if you prefer, the terms *cushioning in* and *cushioning out* seem to be easier to remember, and more descriptive.

Take a look at the following example of a character moving his arm from straight up to straight out.

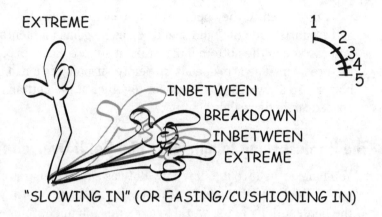

EXTREME

INBETWEEN
BREAKDOWN
INBETWEEN
EXTREME

1
2
3
4
5

"SLOWING IN" (OR EASING/CUSHIONING IN)

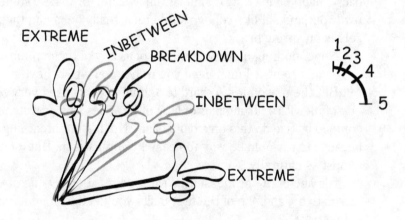

EXTREME   INBETWEEN
BREAKDOWN

INBETWEEN

EXTREME

1
2
3
4
5

"SLOWING OUT" (OR EASING/CUSHIONING OUT)

We've got the same number of drawings, but you can see in the top figure that he starts moving his arm faster from the top of his swing, and slows down, or slows into, the stop at the bottom. The little "tic marks" you see in the example are referred to as an animation chart, which an animator will doodle along the edge of his animation paper so his assistant can see how far apart to space the action in the remaining drawings that are assigned to him.

Consequently, the opposite of slowing in is *slowing out*. A character "starts out slow" and speeds up as he gains momentum. As you can see in the bottom illustration, it's more easily explained in picture form. The arm speeds up before snapping to a halt at the bottom, so drawings cluster closer together at the bottom and are spaced farther apart at the top.

The Hardest Thing to Animate... So Get It Over with First!

You'll never believe it, but it's my duty as author/illustrator of this book, which I really hope you're enjoying so far, to inform you of the hardest thing in the world to animate. You might think it would be something in science fiction, like an alien laser battle, or a pterodactyl flapping its wings, a midair fairy ballet, or maybe something *really* outlandish, like college students actually behaving themselves on spring break.

Nope, nothing quite so unheard of as any of these things.

That's right... I just *know* you're not going to believe me.

But the reason it's so hard to animate is because every single one of us with a strong pair of legs either does this or watches somebody else do this on a daily basis. No, it's not breathing, because that would be way too easy by comparison. But it comes almost as naturally.

It's one of the first essential things almost every one of us learns to do, and one of the first tasks you need to conquer as an animator.

You ready for this?

The hardest thing in the world to animate is a character walking across the room.

See? I told you that you wouldn't believe me.

I'm serious, though. The reason it's so much more difficult to animate than any of those science fiction or fantasy situations I mentioned earlier is because those are unfamiliar scenes to the average viewer. If we slip up, not many people will pick up on it.

However, if it's something everybody does every day, and we slip up on one animation drawing, some nerd in the first row is going to raise his hand (like that annoying Mr. Knowitall in Chapter 2, remember him?) and say, "Oh now, you've really messed that up, haven't you?" (Insert a smug chuckle here.) "Now if I had animated that scene, *I* would have done it *properly!*"

So we've got to make sure we practice and get this absolutely right, if not for reasons of personal satisfaction and accomplishment, then just to keep that guy quiet.

Like any oversized sandwich, if we just take it in small bites we can actually handle, and take one step... in this case quite literally... at a time, then we'll animate characters walking naturally in no time.

First off, we've got to realize that there's no such thing as an average walk, because a character's age, health, personality, self-image, and a long list of other influential factors (not to mention their current emotional disposition, perhaps most of all) are all factors to be taken into consideration that will be displayed in the attitude of this walk we're about to undertake.

All that being said, we're going to start out with a beginner's walk cycle (since there is no average), and take it from there.

As a matter of fact, I'll strongly recommend that you make this your first personal animation assignment to be scanned into Flash.

Before you get started, though, I'd best mention something here called *registration marks*. Registration marks are little crosshairs placed beneath the character that are used as reference points around which your character moves. Even though the character may move left or right above it, the registration mark stays in place.

Though some traditional animators suggest having the character actually walk across the page, I prefer to have the character "walk in place." Why? Because though I consider myself an animator with traditional training, I just happen to know that it's going to be much easier to have your character "walk in place" over that registration mark, and then move him later across the screen as necessary in the computer.

You'll probably come to understand the advantages of that later, especially when we start to cover the process Flash calls "tweening."

If you're drawing this character on paper, it is best not to forget those registration marks on every drawing. Don't forget to ink them; they'll come in handy when lining up your characters in

Flash, and you can erase them later after doing so. Be aware that it's unlikely that your scanner will pick up those registration marks in black-and-white mode unless you ink them.

With as many drawings as you'll be dealing with, I try my best to make sure you have as few headaches as possible. (With all the money you're spending on software, hardware, and art supplies, I'm just trying to save you some money on ibuprofen, okay?)

We'll start off with those contact positions.

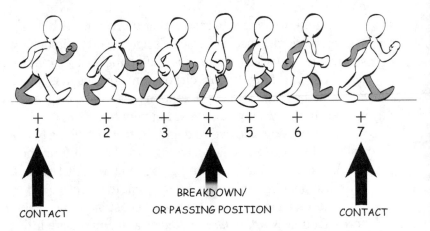

1 2 3 4 5 6 7

CONTACT   BREAKDOWN/
OR PASSING POSITION   CONTACT

Here are drawings number one through seven. If you were to place that first and last drawing (numbers one and seven) on top of one another on a light table, what do you think you'd notice?

If you guessed that these drawings share a common silhouette, then you guessed right. If you were to view the character's shadow on the wall, drawings one and seven would appear similar if not downright identical. So if you were to follow that line of logic, you might have already figured out that in essence, you only need to animate *half* a walk cycle, and then trace over those positions.

But what is the primary difference between those two drawings, before we get too cocky? If you'll notice, the arms and legs are reversed on drawings one and seven.

And that leads us right to another important note regarding opposites on a walk cycle. If you can walk without noticing what you're doing (because once you start thinking about it too hard, what was once effortless becomes immediately difficult), or better yet study someone else who's walking without them noticing your observation, you'll see that the arms and legs move in the opposite direction of each side. Or to look at it another way, the right arm moves in sync (forward and backward) with the left leg, and vice versa.

Why is that? Because each arm is acting as a counterbalance for each leg so we can keep our balance during a walk. Our act of walking has been described as a series of controlled falls. The leg catches our weight just to prevent each fall as we lean slightly forward with every step.

With these extremes taken care of, for the drawings where both feet contact the ground, we can turn our attention to the breakdown drawing, which in a walk cycle is referred to as the *passing position*.

And why, you may well ask with every nuance of justification, is that?

Because in a walk cycle, the breakdown position is where the midair leg passes the opposite leg that is planted on the ground. The leg must be lifted up so that its foot can clear the ground without the character stumbling and falling flat on his face.

Study the drawings on the previous page. Since it would be difficult (if not downright impossible) to cover every sort of character type stepping through every known attitude during a walk cycle, use the guide as a "jumping-off" point for your own explorations for your particular characters. Start to ask yourself questions like, "How would this character hold his head if he were walking to the library, about to explain to his favorite librarian that he lost their most valuable book?" He might hold his hands in his pockets as he shuffled forward, then remove a hand, placing his finger to his chin as he considers the best method to explain the disastrous events that led to the loss.

Or maybe he's about to go on a prom date with that girl he's had a secret crush on since the eighth grade. Maybe he starts out exuberant, even cocky... and then he rounds the corner to her mailbox. Doubt starts to set in... maybe he's not so sure about this date. Maybe she won't like him. Fear overtakes doubt. "Dating is too much stress!" he thinks, and cowers behind the mailbox, petrified with dread. "Maybe single life won't be so tough."

That's what acting is all about. You've gotta get inside the head of your character, whether you're a stage and screen performer or an actor with a pencil... or pixel. Well... you get the idea.

If all goes well with your first beginner's walk cycle and some of your other experiments, then you might want to start asking yourself, "How would this very same character move if he were coming down with something?" Isn't it strange how people who know us can automatically tell when we're not feeling well? Even without red eyes or a drippy nose, when we're getting sick, it reflects in our disposition and our posture. Try to notice those details and apply those toward your work.

Now try to draw that same character walking away after he's just won the lottery. Then draw that character walking on the way to the mailbox when he's paying his income taxes.

This reminds me of one of my favorite character walk cycles of all time. Not surprisingly, it comes from a Disney movie, their first animated feature. There's a scene where Snow White has suggested that Grumpy join the others to wash his hands before supper, and the archetypal woman-hater, insulted, doesn't watch where he's going and bumps nose-first into a wall. Enraged, he storms out the door, swinging his arms violently, and slams the door shut. *Wham!*

You can just feel his rage from that scene.

Watch how other people have animated other character scenes. With the advent of (and ready access to) video and DVD, especially with the frame-by-frame advance features, we can now easily study works of the previous animation masters one picture at a time.

Just remember when you're working on a project to *only* watch the scene you're looking for (another advantage of DVD), and try not to get yourself sidetracked. If you're watching on a break, set a timer. Time is precious in animation, and you can't afford to go off on extended tangents.

The world's first animated feature was not Disney's *Snow White and the Seven Dwarfs*, as so many coffee-table books on animation often suggest. Many sources instead give the credit to *The Adventures of Prince Achmed*, a unique adventure from the silent days of film that was inspired by the Arabian Nights stories. Animated by Lotte Reiniger, this 1926 feature predates *Snow White* by more than a decade. It was made by an intricate technique of silhouette animation by painstakingly cutting out dazzling figures from paper and then placing them over a background. They were positioned, photographed, repositioned minutely, and photographed again, frame-by-frame, in a technique called *stop-motion animation*.

Stop-motion animation, though more popular through 3D model approaches like Wil Vinton's Claymation series (*The California Raisins*), Phil Tippett's kangaroo-like Tauntaun from *The Empire Strikes Back*, and notably in Disney's *The Nightmare Before Christmas*, can just as readily be achieved with 2D methods. Perhaps the most familiar approach to 2D stop-motion animation is a form of "moving collage" made popular by American animator Terry Gilliam's contributions to *Monty Python's Flying Circus*. Gilliam would airbrush and cut apart reproductions of old photographs and works of fine art, and then alternate photographing and repositioning them as described above. Instead of an Arabian wonderland, Gilliam would use his surreal technique chiefly to amuse audiences and provide an entertaining segue between otherwise seemingly unrelated sketches.

We can achieve surprisingly similar results with Macromedia Flash, which we'll soon discuss.

For additional resources on various walk cycles, check out Preston Blair's *Cartoon Animation*, Eadweard Muybridge's *The Human Figure in Motion*, and naturally, Richard Williams' *The Animator's Survival Kit*.

Closing Thoughts on Acting with Pencils and Pixels

When it comes down to it, there's only so much you can say, or read, or research about acting and animation theories. At some point, you're going to have to turn off that DVD player, exit out of those QuickTime movies on the Internet, shut that useful book of Muybridge reference photographic plates, and start drawing.

Practice is where it all comes out.

As I've stated before, no single book could possibly cover all the necessary aspects to succeed in an animation career. Acting is one of the most difficult crafts to master.

Too many people see actors and actresses on screen and think, "Oh, anyone can do that." Oddly enough, if an actor is really quite good at their craft, one of the most difficult things in the world is to make everyday bits of dialogue or even walking across a room in character seem natural. I'm sure if you were to ask some of my live-action favorites like Jennifer Connelly, Phoebe Cates, Christopher Lee, Ian Holm, or Kevin Kline about their theories or suggestions in regard to acting out a particular scene, they would undoubtedly have some helpful advice, and might even give you a brief demonstration. But then hand them a pencil and tell them to act out the scene with that as their only mode of expression, and what might they say?

Ahem…

(Sorry, I don't use that kind of language.)

Section II

Sezquatch, Thurman, and Deadbeat
© Mark S. Smith/MarkToonery.com

USING FLASH TO ANIMATE YOUR DRAWINGS

Chapter 6

First Peek inside Flash

Sezquatch, Thurman, and Deadbeat
© Mark S. Smith/MarkToonery.com

All right, kiddies. It's the moment we've all been waiting for. You've got the basics under your belt, and you know how to build characters with… well, character! Now it's time to roll up your sleeves and get some dirt under your fingernails with your first look inside Flash! Don't worry; don't feel intimidated. We'll get through this thing together!

Installing and Creating a Shortcut

If you're on a Mac, locate and open your Applications folder on your hard drive, then scroll down to Flash. If you've actually installed Flash (which is a pretty simple process of double-clicking the CD that came with it, conveniently named, "Install Flash 8"), you should see it sitting there, comfortably awaiting your permission to begin.

Once you've installed Flash and located your Flash icon, you might wish to make it a bit simpler to get to Flash next time, rather than opening up folder after folder within other folders just to get that one program you want. Have you noticed the Dock (if you're on the Mac), which is that area at the bottom of your screen (or at the top or one side, depending on your personal preference)? You probably have, because that's where all your program icons are set up. Of course, those icons are just shortcuts to your favorite programs. (It's not all that different a concept on the PC; it's just set up somewhat differently.)

Now if you haven't put your favorite icons down there, maybe this is a convenient time to do exactly that. Rather than double-clicking on your Flash 8 icon from its place in the Applications folder, simply drag it down into the Dock. Now clicking on it once in the Dock serves the same purpose as double-clicking on the original icon.

Now the next time you'd like to go straight into Flash, you shouldn't have to locate the Applications folder on your hard drive; you should be able to slide over to your Dock, or Shortcut list, and zip straight into Flash.

Creating a New Flash Document

Like with most Adobe programs, a start screen comes up when you enter Flash. I'm not too crazy about this new standard (I think you can get a little *too* user friendly), but since they didn't ask me, we're stuck with it for now.

Anyhow, your best bet is to start by creating a new Flash document, your first choice in the list in the middle.

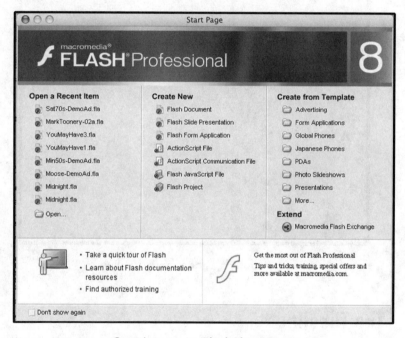

Creating a new Flash document

Overview of Flash

Now that we're inside Flash, let's take a quick look around.

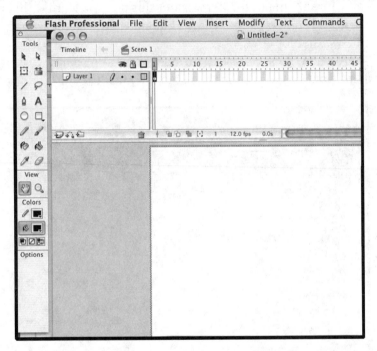

The Toolbox, Stage, and Timeline

The Timeline

You may notice that you've got a numbered "grid" sitting there in front of you, toward the top of the screen. That grid is referred to as the *Timeline*, and serves a similar purpose as timelines in other programs like Adobe AfterFX, Final Cut, and so on. As you move your cursor horizontally, left to right, you should notice that the grid that makes up your Timeline is composed of a number of tiny little boxes called cells (much like the individual blocks within a table in Microsoft Word). Think of each one of those cells as an individual frame within your movie. They're conveniently ticked off in five-frame increments, which makes it fairly easy to tell which frame you're in.

The Toolbox

To the left, you'll see a toolbox that is chock full of handy tools that will make your coming weekend spent within Flash a welcome one. We'll talk more about that later, but if you just can't stand it any longer, and want to know what each and every one of those groovy tools do, just turn to Appendix C for a sneak peek.

Otherwise, we'll take one step at a time, and hopefully cover those most important items first.

The Stage

Sitting right in front of you is a white, blank block. That's an empty stage, which is like an empty sheet of drawing paper. Each and every one of us has the potential to make the greatest story ever told in a blank work area... it just takes some practice.

Let's start by filling that stage with some drawings, okay?

Go to **File | Import**. You'll then have the option to drag over to either Import to Stage or Import to Library, whichever you like. But for now, let's start out with **Import to Stage**.

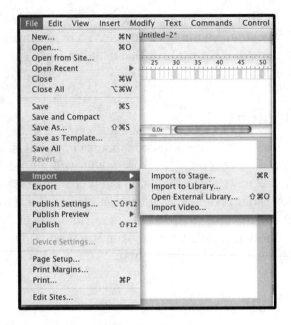

Import to Stage

I'm a big fan of keyboard shortcuts, so if you want to be a little lazy (or *efficient*; call it what you like), go ahead and learn the Flash shortcut for Import to Stage, which is listed (like each shortcut) right next to the command, just to the right of the text. In this case, the shortcut on the Mac is **Cmd+8**. (Cmd is short for Command. The **Command** key is what some people call the **Apple** key, which is a little more descriptive. You'll find it located directly to the left and right of your Spacebar key.) Cmd+8 means press and hold the **Command** key and then press the **8** on your keyboard before releasing the Command key. You'll quickly discover how much time these keyboard shortcuts save you. And as time-consuming as the process of animation is (albeit a *rewarding* process, mind you), any time saved is good time.

If you're on a PC, most likely you'll find that the shortcut is **Ctrl+8**. (Now, see? I may be Mac-centric, but I try to look out for you PC types, too, don't I?)

Creating Your Movie

The following sections take you through the various steps for creating your first movie.

Importing Files

All right. Now locate the artwork file that you want to import. In my case, I scanned in all my thumbnail storyboards at 300 dpi, which almost fills the size of my Stage. (Remember, if you're scanning in significantly larger, full-screen size storyboard drawings, you may want to scan them in at a mere 72 dpi.) I threw in some basic, fairly flat colors with the airbrush in Photoshop, and then I saved each thumbnail panel as its own file.

No matter how many drawings you've saved, please, please, once again... keep your numbering systems *simple*. I would strongly suggest that you name your folders however you like, but make sure your numbering and naming systems make your files show up in chronological order. You could name your folders "Scene 1," Scene 2," etc. But just a quick note on computer numbering. If you know you'll have more than two digits in your file or folder number, don't forget to throw in a zero in front of those first nine digits.

Here's what I mean, and why...

If you have a lot of files or folders (and in animation I can almost guarantee you will), you should name your scanned images along the lines of 01.pct, 02.pct, 03.pct, and so on down the line. (I have a habit of scanning and saving in pict format, primarily a Mac format, but naturally your format depends on your preference.)

Those files will show up in order just fine until I hit number 100. Then the computer may decide that number 100 (in its tiny little mind) should go right after drawing number 10. That could lead to some complications (like a drawing in a long list of files is imported in the wrong order), so just be aware of computer numbering systems and configurations to avoid headaches whenever possible. If you've got more than 100 drawings in a particular scene

(I haven't hit that yet; mine are pretty short), you'll probably need to number your files like 001.pct, 002.pct, etc.

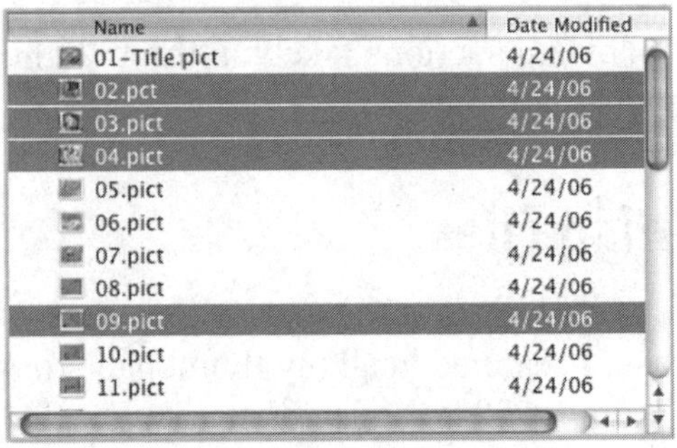

Name		Date Modified
01-Title.pict		4/24/06
02.pct		4/24/06
03.pict		4/24/06
04.pict		4/24/06
05.pict		4/24/06
06.pict		4/24/06
07.pict		4/24/06
08.pict		4/24/06
09.pict		4/24/06
10.pict		4/24/06
11.pict		4/24/06

File numbering nitpickery

If you've got no more than 99 files, it's a good idea to put a zero in front of your first nine numbers, as shown here. If you've got more than a hundred drawings in a scene, place two zeros in front of numbers 1 through 9 (making them 001.pct up through 009.pct) and one zero in front of the next group up through 99 (making them 010.pct through 099.pct).

Also, put each scene in an individual folder. For drawings and scene folders alike, always keep your numbering simple! As many drawings as you may be dealing with, you're quite likely to make life unnecessarily complicated by naming a drawing 0ZQ15-X4-002. (Is that a zero or the letter "O" at the beginning of that sequence?) Instead, stick to simplicity. Folders named *001 Scene* and *002 Scene* and so forth will be much easier to manage.

With those nagging details out of the way, let's get back to importing your artwork.

Notice that your file placed itself smack-dab on the center of the Stage. For now, that should work, because this animatic or pose test we're creating is, as I've said before, simply a planning tool.

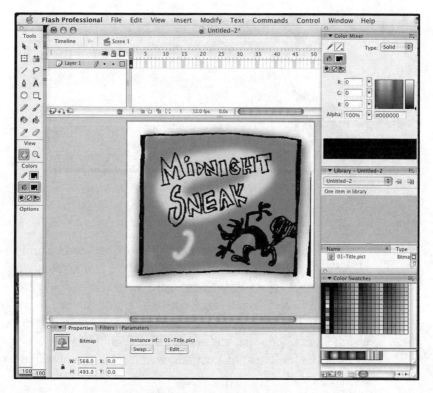

The result of using Import to Stage

If you'd like to reposition your artwork (or resize it), grab the **Selection tool** (shaped like an arrow), which is the first tool in the upper-left corner of your Toolbox. Place the cursor over your artwork on the Stage and **drag** it to a better spot.

Working with Layers

Okay, now that we've got our first piece of artwork on the Stage, let's tidy things up a bit by getting into a good habit of naming our layers in a way that makes them easier to keep up with. A *layer*, just like in Photoshop and Illustrator, is a level of artwork. It's surprisingly like a real animation *cel* from the old days — a piece of artwork painted on a transparent sheet of plastic that can be moved or rotated independently of other layers above or below it.

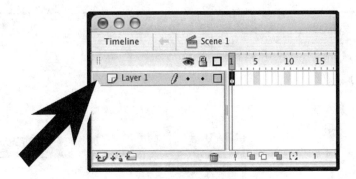

Flash layers

To give this new layer a specific name, double-click on the word "Layer 1" in your Timeline to highlight it. Then just start typing; whatever you type will automatically replace the highlighted word. (You don't have to waste time clicking behind the last letter and deleting the word, space by space. That's a pet peeve of mine, to watch students do that and waste time. Ughh! It's like being forced to sit in the back seat of a car and watch someone else fold a road map... *wrong!*)

Okay, now name the storyboard something nice and simple, like, oh, I dunno... Storyboard!

Next, let's make a new layer on which we can place our soundtrack.

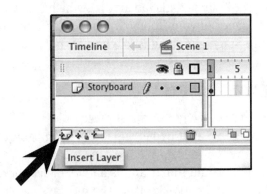

The Insert Layer icon and tool tip

Right now, you should be looking for the Insert Layer icon, which is located directly to the lower left of your Timeline. It looks sort of like a turned page with a plus sign superimposed on its left side. That's what you want to do, so click the Insert Layer icon to insert a new layer.

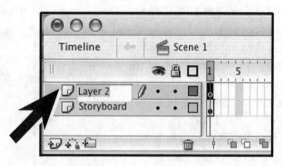

Creating a new layer

Note:

On the Mac, by default, you should have something called "Tool Tips" set up for you. If not, check your system preferences. If you float over a tool, icon, or any specific area within your Stage or Timeline, if that area has a name, it will pop up.

Just like you did last time, double-click on the name Layer 2, which should have appeared just above your Storyboard layer, and rename it Sound. As you can probably guess, this is where we're going to place the second element of our animatic/pose test, the soundtrack.

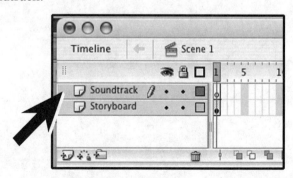

Renamed layer

Importing the Soundtrack

Now let's bring in that soundtrack. This time, just to prove to your-self that you can do it (which is reason enough in this case), go up to your menu bar at the top of the screen, and choose **File | Import | Import to Library**.

Look over to the right side of your screen. Among the several windows you'll probably see floating there, the one of immediate concern is the one most likely down toward the middle right, called, you guessed it, the Library.

The Library is a window that holds all the assets of your Flash movie: scanned artwork, sound effects, and any other sym-bols. (Yeah, I know... hang on; we'll get to symbols soon enough.)

You can either hide or show your movie's Library by pressing **Cmd+L** (or **Ctrl+L** on the PC). Right now, go ahead and drag your soundtrack over into your Timeline. Make sure that you have the Sound layer of your movie selected.

The Library

Otherwise, you'll find things can get unnec-essarily complicated if you try to place things that are better left apart (in separate layers) into the same layer. I'll explain that in a bit.

Working with Frames

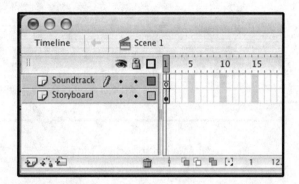

One frame does not an exciting movie make.

As you can probably see, we've now got one frame. While nothing's changed in our Storyboard layer (at least it shouldn't have yet), you should now see a small line showing up in your Soundtrack layer in that single frame.

Of course, it doesn't make a whole lot of sense right now, since our movie is only one frame long. If you pressed **Return** on the Mac (or **Enter** on the PC), which is exactly how you get a movie to start playing in Flash, you'd find that this particular movie lacked one thing… time! Until we tell it how many frames it needs to be, our movie isn't going to be terribly exciting to watch… it'll just be that one frame.

Aha! Why not add more frames, you say? Why not indeed!

The quickest way to add a frame is to use another keyboard shortcut. In this case, it's as simple as pointing to the layer and the frame to which you want it to be added. And how long is your soundtrack? Hmm… Let's see if we can figure that out. In my case, my soundtrack was roughly 51 seconds long. But I can already foresee one problem. Notice at the bottom of the screen a window called Movie Properties. You'll find that it, like most other windows, can be moved around (grab them by the menu or title bar and drag, then release).

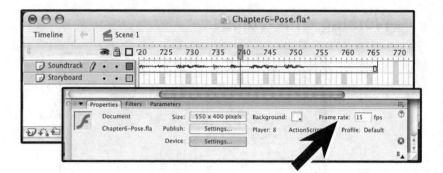

Movie Properties window

Toward the upper-right corner of the Movie Properties window you'll see a box for the Frame rate setting. If your number is set to 12 fps (or frames per second, as you probably guessed), that's fine for playback on the Internet.

I just happen to know that this movie I'm creating will be eventually burned to DVD, so I'd like to stay within the frame numbering conventions of video. In video, as you may know, there are 30 frames per second. If I were to draw my characters one drawing per frame, then I would be "shooting on ones" as it's known in the industry.

"Shooting on twos" means that you're essentially "shooting" (or in our case *using*) each single drawing for two frames, like we're stretching it out over two frames instead of the conventional one frame. You can even (to a degree) "shoot on threes" on video... sometimes... and still achieve an acceptable result. But that depends on the action.

Shooting on ones is what looks best. One of the main reasons the animation in *Roger Rabbit* looks so good is that everything was shot on ones. It pretty much had to be! Every time the camera was moving, which was in almost every given shot, the perspective changed just the slightest bit. So if you left the character standing in the exact same position, when the camera moved the feet would appear to be slipping, which would naturally ruin the illusion immediately.

The reason I bring that up now is that it's best to have an idea what you're shooting on before you start to set up your movie. Otherwise, you'll run into some problems with timing, and may have to reset your scenes — a time-consuming process, if ever there was one — especially if you thought you were done!

Just keep the following rules in mind.

If you're shooting on *ones*, then:

Film: 24 frames per second
Video: 30 frames per second

Of course, if you're in the United States, or anywhere Region 1 DVDs are used, these video rates are true for NTSC (USA's standard of video, National Television Standards Committee).

If you're shooting on *twos*, then:

Film: 12 frames per second
Video: 15 frames per second

And of course, should you decide to shoot on *threes*, then:

Film: 8 frames per second
Video: 10 frames per second

Notice these first sets of numbers both divide up nicely into twos and threes. (Anything after that, and you're on your own, pal!) Beyond this, your animation will definitely start to look jerky and unnatural. Beware... That's one of the differences between the smoothness of classic-style animation like *Roger Rabbit* and the jittery, stilted action of Saturday-morning anime.

For my purposes, I'll shoot this cartoon mainly "on twos," and therefore set my frame rate to 15 fps. So if I'm shooting this on twos, and I just happened to have noticed that my cartoon soundtrack is 51 seconds long, then multiply 51 x 15 = 765. Does that make sense? Simply put, 51 frames times 15 frames per second equals 765 frames.

Before my snobby teenage attitude about animation ("being for children") had fully set in (no doubt a nasty side effect of adolescence), former Disney animators Don Bluth and Gary Goldman had created the animation for the world's first LaserDisc video game, a terrific adventure called *Dragon's Lair*. (Fortunately, you can now get it via Amazon.com and other outlets as a DVD, which you can either play with your remote or choose a "Play All Animation" feature, for those of us who just never had all the quarters necessary to become any good at that game when it first came out!)

I think I was about 12 at that time, and this was roughly 1982. Then I heard they were going to make *Dragon's Lair* into a Saturday morning cartoon!

I had seen the spectacular animation of the video game, and though I didn't know then the details of why feature animation was better than original Saturday morning cartoons, I thought to myself, "At last! They're finally going to produce some *decent* animation for original Saturday morning cartoons!"

And of course, it ended up looking like most of the other limited animation produced on limited budgets for Saturday morning in those days... limited.

One of the reasons was because lots of *Dragon's Lair*'s animation was done on ones. I dare say it went with one of the best rules you can arrive at, as far as what to shoot your drawings on: "Fast action on ones, and normal action on twos."

In other words, if your character is in a high-speed chase, better shoot that on ones. If your character is standing still in the kitchen, struggling with the lid on a jar of peanut butter, feel perfectly justified shooting it on twos. (Now that's if the peanut butter is creamy. If it's crunchy peanut butter, you might choose to shoot it on threes! Heh-heh... just kidding.)

(You should've seen the disappointed looks on the faces of a group of fifth-graders when I was asked to speak at my hometown Jemison Elementary School. I told them that I made cartoons for a living, which absolutely *thrilled* the little darlings. *Then* I told them that even cartoonists still had to use math, and the room was filled with a collective "Awww…" as their faces fell into sunken frowns. Sorry, kids, but it's true.)

So with that theory in mind, then I scroll over in my Timeline by dragging that blue slider bar (it looks slightly different for PC users, but please don't let that be a source of panic) at the bottom of the screen until I can read frame #765 on my Timeline counter.

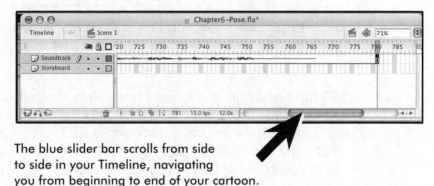

The blue slider bar scrolls from side to side in your Timeline, navigating you from beginning to end of your cartoon.

I'll hit the **F5** key at the top of my keyboard while I have selected frame 780, just to be safe. As soon as I hit that, it extends my Soundtrack layer to the cell of frame 780. You can also see that our calculations were correct. The line in the middle of the Sound-track layer ends right at frame 765.

"All right, Wise Guy," I'm sure you're saying to me by this time. "You just stuck me with 15 extra frames that I don't need. Now what do I do?" Don't worry… it's easy to trim back those frames and, believe it or not, it's something else you need to know about Flash… how to extend and trim frames.

One of the easiest ways to trim your frames is simply to place your pointer over the "offensive" or last extra frame, and hold down your **Command/Apple key** (use the **Ctrl** key on the PC). Then drag your *playback head* (that little red marker that shows where you are in the Timeline) forward or backward, depending on whether you want to extend or trim your frames.

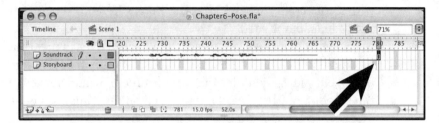

The playback head shows you "where it's at..." literally. It shows you the current frame in your Flash movie.

With that done, your next impulse might be to simply place your playback head in the Storyboard layer and hit the F5 key, just to insert a frame, and thus extend that drawing all the way into the last frame of the movie. *Wait...* not yet!

If at all possible (at least if you haven't already), please resist that impulse. Here's why. The point of your animatic isn't to show that first storyboard for the entire movie. The point of your animatic is to show each storyboard onscreen *in time* with its corresponding line of dialogue, music, or sound effect.

So in preparation for this next step, you'll need to set something on your Movie Properties window, if it's not already set.

Your Sync options (short for synchronization) give you different choices. The most useful for our cartoons is probably Stream, which enables you to play back the exact moment of sound within each frame. That way you can ensure your animation will match your soundtrack precisely during playback.

As you can see in the previous figure, make sure your Sync sound option is set to Stream. Setting this to Stream has two advantages: First of all, when you play back your movie (by hitting the Return or Enter key, remember?), it will only play the sound back once. Better yet, it will play the sound back from wherever it happens to be in the soundtrack... not from the beginning of the soundtrack.

Secondly, it also allows you to "scrub" (as it's called in the video production industry) through the soundtrack as you drag the playback head. That means whether you drag backward or forward, fast or slow, through the Timeline, you should get a pretty good idea of how your drawings are matching up to your soundtrack. That's pretty hard to beat.

Now find out where your next storyboard will play through, and we'll extend it to that frame number. Since your soundtrack is extended through its duration, you can simply play through or scrub back and forth until you find the exact frame where the first storyboard will end and the next will begin. In my case, I think that's in frame 70, just before there's a sound effect that Deadbeat is about to zip into hiding atop Sezquatch's mailbox. So I'll place my playback head at frame 70, select that cell in the Storyboard layer, and hit F5 to insert a frame there.

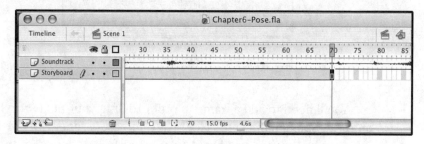

Inserting a frame

Next, let's go ahead and import your second storyboard. You may have figured out by this time that you can import more than one item at a time. In the following figure, you'll see that if I hold down the Shift key while selecting 02.pct and 04.pct, I can also select any or all files in between my selected items. (That should save some time!) Also notice that if I hold down my Mac's Command key (or your PC's Ctrl key) while selecting 09.pct, it will keep 02.pct, 03.pct, and 04.pct selected, and in addition, it will also select 09.pct. That comes in mighty handy if you want to select some oddly numbered files. (But better yet, keep your files tidy and named appropriately, and you'll continue to save yourself a few bucks on aspirin later!)

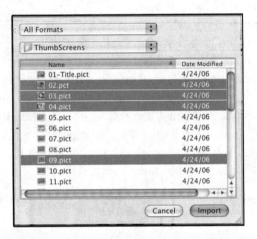

Importing multiple files

You'll need to add a frame in order to drag your next storyboard onto the Stage, but again, "Hold your horses, pardner!"

A quick thing or two about frames in Flash. If you were to simply hit F5 again, it would only extend your current frame of Storyboard 1 into frame 71. Obviously, that's not what we want here. Instead, we want a new blank keyframe, so we can start anew in frame 71 with Storyboard 2.

Go to **Insert | Timeline** and choose **Blank Keyframe,** as shown below. This, naturally, will give you that blank keyframe in which we can place Storyboard 2.

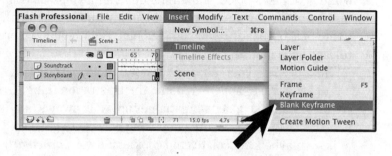

Inserting a blank keyframe

Now, just like last time, simply use your mouse to drag your Storyboard 2 (in my case, 02.pct) into that blank keyframe you've created.

Moving frames

Here's where it can get a little tricky, especially to someone relatively new to Flash (like I was not too terribly long ago). If you try to drag your frame forward to, say, frame 85, where the next storyboard shot takes place, something quite annoying will happen. Instead of staying put (as it should, in my humble opinion), the last frame of Storyboard 1 will come zipping right behind wherever you release your mouse.

Just prepare yourself, and try not to get frustrated.

(That's what happened to me, the frustration thing! *Grrr!* All I could do was take a deep breath, get up, walk away from the computer for about five minutes, just long enough to get a cold glass of milk — maybe a chocolate chip cookie, if I was *particularly* perturbed — calm down, and try it again. If you can get past this, you'll be on your way to creating some great cartoons; just keep that in mind as you practice.)

Instead, try this approach. Click in frame 85, without dragging or anything. Just click there... and just once.

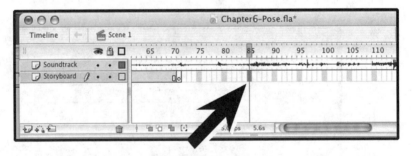

Click only once (we're about to place a blank keyframe).

Now go to **Insert | Timeline** and choose **Blank Keyframe**, just like you did before. There. Your screen should look pretty much like the following figure now.

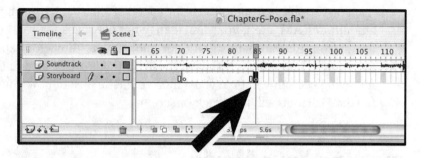

Inserting a blank keyframe

Okay, did you get that? Whew! Great! Now what exactly did you do?

Basically, if your screen looks like the example above, you inserted a range of blank keyframes, from frame 71 to frame 84 or 85, depending on where you clicked. In this case, I've got a new blank keyframe starting at frame 85.

Now, with your cursor still nestled snugly within frame 71 (if it's not there, put it there), then *drag* your next storyboard up into place. It should then extend from frame 71 to frame 84, depending on how your particular movie is set up.

Continue to do this until your entire animatic is set up. Whenever you get ready, you can simply hit Return, and your movie will play through once. If you want to watch it again (and I'm sure you will, because this is when your movie is just beginning to take shape, and hopefully on the path to making some sort of sense, even to a first-time viewer), just click back in the first frame and hit Return again.

Next, you might want to get an idea of how the movie will play back without all those little windows and panels stuck all over the place. In other words, you might want to export your movie to get a better idea of how it's going to run in "real time."

For various reasons (processor speed of a particular machine, amount of RAM, etc.), your movie may not play back in "real time" speed from Flash. It's best to either publish your movie or export it as a QuickTime movie. Either of these methods, discussed in the following section will give you a more realistic idea of how your finished cartoon will play back onscreen.

Exporting Your Movie

You've actually got a couple of options for exporting, and I'll explore both of those. One option, if your final output will be to video, would be to export your movie. In that case, go to **File | Export** and choose **Export Movie**.

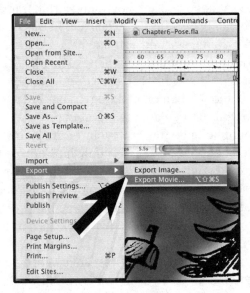

Exporting a movie

That will bring you to the following screen, if you slow down enough to review your possible choices.

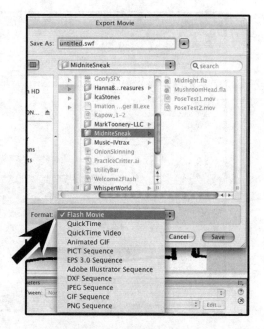

Export Movie format options

The first choice you see highlighted here is Flash Movie, which will give your movie the extension of .swf. That's the most common way to export, or essentially share, a Flash movie. Even someone who doesn't have Flash Professional 8 installed on their computer should be able to view this film once you're done exporting it. However, they must have Flash Player installed on their computer in order to watch it. We'll get into that a little deeper once we start the discussion about distributing your work, in the last chapter.

For right now, if you're interested in displaying your movie on the Internet, exporting it as an SWF file is the route of choice. If that is the case, you could also simply choose to publish your file by going to **File | Publish Preview** and choosing **Default - (HTML)**, which will "temporarily publish" your file to whatever your default web browser is. In my case it's Mac Safari, and with you PC folks, it might very well be Internet Explorer. Obviously that will vary per your computer.

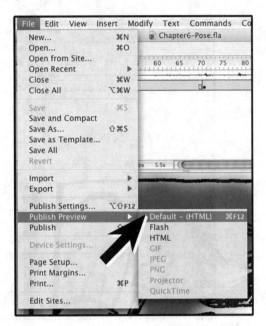

Publish for web preview

Whichever the case, it will open your web browser, and you'll see what your animation (or work in progress, at this point) will look like so far.

However, if you want to export it for distribution via DVD or video duplication, you might best export the file as a QuickTime movie. Once you export a file as a QuickTime movie, then you can burn it directly onto a DVD via iDVD (a program that comes installed on any Mac with a DVD-burner capable drive), or import it into editing programs like Final Cut, or even into image manipulation and special effects programs like Adobe AfterEffects.

As you can guess, you've got a wide variety of options. Myself being a video enthusiast, I like the QuickTime Video route.

Once you click Save, you'll find *another* list of options comes up.

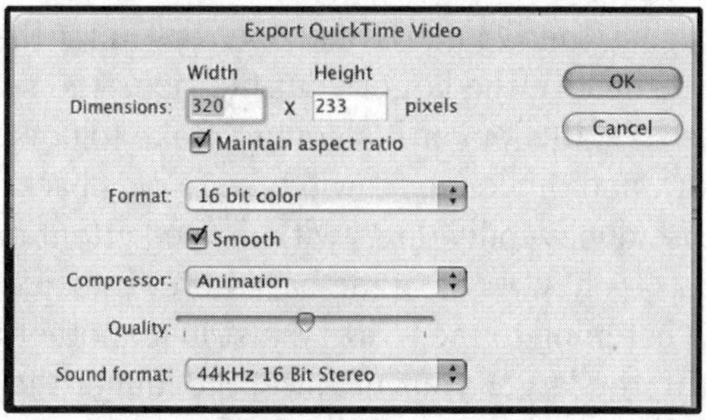

```
                    Export QuickTime Video
             Width        Height
Dimensions:  320     x   233         pixels         ┌─── OK ───┐
             ☑ Maintain aspect ratio                ├─ Cancel ─┤

    Format:  [ 16 bit color            ↕ ]
             ☑ Smooth
Compressor:  [ Animation               ↕ ]
   Quality:  [          ○              ]
Sound format: [ 44kHz 16 Bit Stereo    ↕ ]
```

QuickTime save options

As far as your options here go, you can probably go with the default dimensions of 320 x 233 (as mine just happened to be set up). However, if you decided to have your movie screen set up to the NTSC DVD standards of 720 x 486, you might want to shrink it down for the purposes of a preview (mainly because of varying playback speed, which depends largely on your computer's particular processor). As you can see in the above figure, the check box next to Maintain aspect ratio is checked. What that means is that if you were to type in half of 720 (which is 360) for the width, the height would automatically also cut itself in half, from 486 down to 243. Does that make sense? It's because you don't want your picture to be squashed too wide or stretched too tall. You want your *aspect ratio*, or ratio of width to height, to remain consistent.

Other choices are 16 bit color (which is fine in this example), the Compressor option (I usually leave it at the default of Animation), and finally, your Quality option. Now here's another item where personal preference and final output comes into play.

It's tempting, I'll admit, to those few perfectionists of us in the audience to crank the Quality meter all the way to the right for the highest possible quality. If you're about to burn that perfect and pre-tested file directly to DVD or take it into AfterEffects for some tweaking, you go right ahead, pardner. However, if you're merely at the testing stage (as you probably are at this point), and/or you're burning this QuickTime movie to play on your website, out of consideration for those couple dozen folks with slow processors on their computers (and believe me, they're out there) you might want to leave the Quality setting somewhere in the middle.

As usual, there's more than one reason for that. First, the better the quality, the larger your file size. And second, the larger your file size, the longer it's going to take to download from a website... and the longer it will take to play back. And you know how those dopey individuals with limited attention spans are, they just won't — hey, wait! Come back here, I wasn't finished talking! Are you listening to me? (Sorry, just lost another one. Oh well...)

Right, the larger your file size, the longer the download time.

The last option you have is the Sound format setting. The default setting is 44kHz 16 Bit Stereo. For now, since we're just doing this for our own benefit of previewing the work, that should work fine. But if you're planning to have this QuickTime movie posted on your website, the same rule for QuickTime quality applies to sound. How low can you get this setting without adversely affecting the quality of the sound?

That may be something you have to try for yourself to find out. Now is the time when (hopefully) you've got some time to sit back and enjoy learning the software. Play with these settings now, and not when you've got a client breathing down the back of your neck, wanting their work yesterday.

Which reminds me of a funny story, actually. Oh, is that Tangent Man I hear?

If you've ever worked in an office, and ideas for cartoons like this have never occurred to you effortlessly... well, there may be no help for you!

I Need It Yesterday Machine artwork © Mark S. Smith/MarkToonery.com

All right, Tangent Man, that's enough out of you for today, buddy.

Once you click **OK**, it will begin to export your file. Depending on the length, size, and complexity of your movie, this may be one of those moments when you decide to go grab yourself a cup of cocoa or a nice bag of cashews.

If you exported it as a QuickTime movie (always make sure you know where you're saving those files, kids!), you'll need to locate the file on your external drive or hard drive, and open it up by either double-clicking on it or dragging it onto the QuickTime icon in your Dock (Mac).

Otherwise, if you published your file via your local disk HTML settings, once it was done processing, it would open your file immediately and begin to play your movie.

Critiquing Your Movie

You'll probably want to watch your movie a few times before you go on. No, seriously *watch* it, and *honestly* ask yourself that vital question, "Can first-time viewers tell what's going on without me personally explaining it to them?"

If you can't answer that question, get a second opinion from a friend, family member, coworker… anyone's opinion you honestly respect. Either way, one, both, or several of your viewers will most likely notice some things that can use some tweaking at this point. Right now, you'll likely notice things like:

"Maybe that shot goes on a bit too long."

"This shot doesn't last nearly long enough for that line of dialogue."

"I really need to cut to a close-up on that character's face at this point, so his surprise can really register with the audience."

"I can't tell what's going on during that fight sequence… who just punched who out?"

These are just a few possible examples of things that might not be happening quite as clearly as they should, even if you're dealing with thumbnails or storyboards. But remember, that's exactly why we're not jumping feet first into animation.

As much time as you're going to be investing in this project, even if it's no more than a 15-second cartoon, you need to know ahead of time what scenes need revision and which ones are working fine enough to be further developed.

When I showed my wife the Georgia Library PSA pose test, she said something to the effect of, "It's really kind of hard to tell what the narrator is saying. Can you maybe bring the music track down, and also perhaps lower the volume of the dragon's laughter?" She almost immediately followed those questions up with the statement, "I'm *really* sorry to tell you this."

To which I replied, "Absolutely not, honey! Don't apologize, please. These are *exactly* the kinds of things I need to hear now... *before* I show this to my client."

As a matter of fact, I often tell my clients (and as usual, make sure you have everything spelled out in writing ahead of time) that if they do want to make changes to a cartoon, we need to spell those things out during the pose test.

Once a scene is animated, it's extremely frustrating, time-consuming, and therefore expensive (especially if you're charging by the hour, which you should be for revisions) to have to reanimate it.

For instance, if you're working in the traditional, hand-drawn method (Flash or not), let's say you've got a scene. Let's say it's even a relatively short scene, like 48 drawings (on ones). You've done the storyboards, they've been approved, you do the pose test (preferably in color), and that's been approved. Your client has signed off that it's okay to proceed with animation. You pencil-animate and test the 48 drawings, you ink the scene of 48 drawings, and scan each one of those 48 drawings in. Those 48 drawings are painted, placed, and set up in Flash.

You show it to the client.

The client says, "Well, that really looks great and all, but last night I was watching this television special about bats, and now I am really 'liking the bats.' Is there any way we could have a bat somewhere in this film?"

I wish I was making this story up. But I'm not.

My reply was as diplomatic as I could muster (without laughing, crying, or some tragic cross in between), "Well, bats are definitely fascinating creatures, I'll grant you that, but the thing here is that this film takes place beneath the ocean. If we were to randomly place a bat somewhere in there, the first thing the viewer would say is, 'Hey, what's that bat doing underwater?'"

("Oh, drowning," I wanted so badly to answer my own question, but didn't.)

Gladiola, the squid candystriper vs. the drowning bat

Fortunately, that soft answer was enough to satisfy this particular client, but believe it or not, the people with control of the purse strings aren't always this "reasonable" (for lack of a better term) or easily debated with. Since the graphic design center director (who had recruited me as animation director on the film) had foreseen such last-minute decisions from this rather unusual client, he had made certain that she signed her approval on every stage, including the pose test.

She had made this "creative suggestion" *after* the final animation was done. If we had not had her sign off on the pose test/animatic, and she had made this suggestion, and we had come to an actual disagreement, she could have feasibly withheld the next check until she got her way. It could have happened.

And she could have made suggestions far worse and far more time-consuming than inserting a "random bat shot." What if she suddenly decided one of the main characters would look better if we removed his moustache? What if she wanted to make changes to the backgrounds after they had been approved and painted?

Even digitally, there are instances in which we would have to redraw, reink, rescan, repaint, and resetup each one of those scenes in which the character or background made an appearance. And that's bad enough if it was a scene with only 48 drawings required... a relatively short scene, right? What if you've got a longer animation scene, shot on ones, that lasts 15 seconds? 15 seconds x 30 frames per second equals 450 drawings you'd have to discard, and possibly do all over again.

Not a pleasant thought.

So get the client's approval on the animatic/pose test, and get it in writing that any changes made after that stage will be charged at an hourly rate. If you are unable to come to a mutually beneficial agreement, it's a tough thing to say, but perhaps you might consider passing on that project. I'm not telling you to turn down work, but just proceed with *caution*.

All right, well, you've obviously got a few things to think about while you make the necessary changes to your animatic. All these things being said, please do try to remember to have some *fun* with it!

Again, frustration is all part of the learning process, and we shouldn't let temporary frustration keep us from learning some valuable software skills... or keep us from having some *serious* fun.

Chapter 7

Inking, Scanning, and Tablets

Sezquatch, Thurman, and Deadbeat
© Mark S. Smith/MarkToonery.com

Drawing with the... Mouse?

All right. I may not agree with everything written by some of the other Flash authors I've read, but there is one thing in particular we all seem to agree on.

If you're serious about being a Flash animator, you had best do us all a favor (*yourself*, primarily). If you don't have a Wacom digitizing tablet by the time you're reading the end of this paragraph, there's something clinically wrong with your head (and/or wallet). If it's a matter of your head, get help; that's well beyond the scope of this book. If it's a matter of expense, do what it takes to follow the advice in Chapter 11, "Jobs, Colleges, and Film Festivals," and get a job that will *pay* for a digitizing tablet. (At least that's been my experience. *Usually* you can get an advance for putting together a TV commercial. Ask for something to cover the startup expenses

Artwork © Mark S. Smith/MarkToonery.com

like animation paper, a royalty-free music CD, and such… especially if it's with a client without much experience in animation. Just tell them how much *quicker* you can produce the TV spot with a digitizing tablet.) Trying to draw with a computer mouse is almost as productive as trying to take a live mouse, dip its pointy little nose in ink, and write the great American novel.

Do I make myself clear?

I'm not kidding. When I got my first graphics computer (yes, that good ol' Amiga 2000, back in 1990), I picked up the first piece of animation software I could find at the local mall's software shop, MovieSetter. It wasn't bad, quite honestly. It was low-resolution, but it enabled me to put together custom-animated characters, backgrounds, and sound effects. Back then, I paid about $70 for it (if memory serves).

Regrettably, though, my digitizing tablet, one of the first "pressure sensitive models," which enabled me to trace my paper drawings on its surface with an everyday pencil, had not arrived. I had just paid over $2,000 for this setup, and I wanted to get started. I wanted to *animate*. I didn't want to wait. So I did the only thing I could while I waited almost two weeks for the tablet to arrive — I learned to draw with the mouse.

How well did I do?

Well, I was told by family members that I did pretty well for drawing with a *mouse*, but family members (bless them) have a tendency to shield our feelings from being hurt. Whatever the case, I was more than thrilled when my digitizing tablet finally did arrive.

It had adhesive pegs so I could keep my drawings in registration with one another by sticking them on the tablet frame in alignment just below the active digitization area.

I even managed to get good enough with it so that I was able to make my first freelance animation sale a year or two later, to WCOV-TV, our local Fox affiliate, with a character called Farley. Somehow I introduced myself to the station owner, David Woods (I don't remember the particulars), and he asked me to come up with sort of an "animated emcee" (master of ceremonies, kinda like Kermit the Frog on *The Muppet Show*) for their syndicated afternoon cartoons like *Goof Troop*, *Darkwing Duck*, and *Tiny Toons*. I came up with a list of good fox names, all starting with the letter *f*. You ever notice how so many characters have alliterated names, like Droopy Dog, Screwy Squirrel, and Barney Bear? Well, the only other name I remember being on the list besides the one we chose was Franklin. I'm glad that wasn't chosen, because I had another fox character named Franklin, sort of a modernized version of the Tex Avery wolves. In any case, he chose the name that I was secretly hoping he'd pick... Farley Fox. I got the name off my favorite brand of chocolate-covered raisins.

HE, UH... SAYS HIS NAME'S THURMAN, DOLLFACE... AND WHAT'S YOURS?

I get ideas for character names from the craziest places. Sometimes the name is the result of a typo, like when I was learning to type (making plenty of mistakes); back in 1986 I tried to type "guard," and came up with "gurad." I was sort of looking for a sinister "guru" character. You know, those wise old men in cartoons who sit on top of a mountain and impart knowledge to mountaineers. In this case I was creating an evil version, still tall and ancient with a flowing beard... but with talon-like hands, catlike eyes, and tusks protruding from his lower jaw. Gurad just seemed to fit.

On a more pleasant note, when I wanted to come up with a name for a formerly generic porcupine character (one I had streamlined from a cartoon I'd done for AUM's college paper), I settled on the name Thurman Q. Porcupine. Although Porcupine is obvious, I'm not quite sure where the Q came from, except maybe something to do with quills. His first name, though, comes from one of my three favorite actresses: Phoebe Cates, Jennifer Connelly, and Uma Thurman.

Guess which one?

Since it's a name from the phonebook, I'm not terribly worried about getting sued for using it. If Thurman ever has siblings come to visit his hollow log home, guess what their names will be? (Probably Cates and Connelly!)

Oh, for Crying Out Loud... Buy a Wacom Already!

My point is, of course, get yourself a digitizing tablet as soon as you can afford it. Ask for it for Christmas or for graduation, buy it on a layaway plan, just do what it takes within whatever legal means necessary to acquire it. You won't regret it.

Here is another place where I'll suggest going to a student discount website for those of you who are students, teachers, or otherwise academically entangled. Myself, I like Academic-Superstore.com. Though I paid almost $400 for my 9 x 12-inch tablet (I have to draw *big*... that's just how I am), right after my purchase, they began to sell a "wide-screen" 6 x 11 tablet for just over $300. I probably could have learned to live with that. And if you don't mind drawing a bit smaller, you can get a 6 x 8 for just over $200. And if you really don't mind doodling really tiny-like, you might want to consider the 4 x 5 model, at just under $100. (All prices were effective at the time of this writing, and naturally subject to change with or without notice. Offer is void in the city of Tebunkle, Idaho. Operators are standing by!)

Deadbeat © Mark S. Smith/MarkToonery.com

Don't forget, you might be able to find a used model on Amazon.com or somewhere that sells factory refurbished equipment. That means that a company bought the equipment used, sent it back to the factory to have it checked out and have any glitches fixed, and is selling it back to the consumer crowd at a discounted price. I bought my first actual Mac computer, a PowerMac 6500, factory refurbished, and ended up selling it to one of my computer students years later when I bought my current iMac. Last I heard, she hadn't had any problems with it, either. As always, buy with caution.

When you do get one of these delightful little toys, it will likely come with a CD to install the driver software and instructions. You might even get one that comes with a free accompanying software package. Mine came with a version of Photoshop Elements; if you can only afford one piece of software in addition to Flash, get Photoshop or Photoshop Elements. You can touch up (or create entirely from scratch, for that matter) your backgrounds, and import them into Flash as JPGs. (One of the semi-minor differences between Photoshop and Photoshop Elements is that Photoshop Elements only allows you to work in RGB mode, which is fine if you're only working for web, video, and multimedia presentations. If you want to have the work printed professionally in CMYK mode, with color separations and such, you may be stuck shelling out the extra few hundred bucks for Photoshop itself.)

One of the things I like best about my digitizing tablet is that in Flash, I can set it to an oval-shaped brush (I use the vertical one), which gives me a nice line width variation on my characters. But we'll get to that directly, when we discuss the Flash Toolbox.

Once installed, the tablet will naturally work with Flash, Photoshop, and Illustrator. Experiment with activating the Pressure Sensitive function. Pressure sensitive means that the harder you press down, the thicker your resulting line will be. The lighter you apply pressure with the stylus (that pen tool the digitizing tablet comes with), the thinner your line.

Another fun thing about the digitizing stylus (in Flash, anyway) is that if you turn it around and rub the opposite end over your drawing, just like a real pencil, it acts as an eraser. How cool is that!?

All right, hopefully I've done my job of convincing you of the importance of getting a digitizing tablet. And once you have a tablet, you may decide you no longer need to draw your animation on paper anymore. You'll be saving time and money by not buying animation paper and avoiding the need to scan your drawings.

The Inking and Scanning Approach

If I haven't totally alienated those of you who don't have a digitizing tablet yet, for whatever reason, all is not lost. I've produced freelance animation for almost 11 years on the Mac (not counting those first three years on my Amiga), and did so without the aid of a digitizing tablet for quite some time.

That's one of the reasons I discovered that blue-line pencil technique you probably recall from Chapter 2. Using a light blue pencil, you can produce your animation drawings as messily as you like and even without erasing all those extra lines if time doesn't allow.

Then you can ink your drawings with a thin brush and waterproof ink or a Pilot Precise V7 black ink pen (my preference).

Inking with a Pen

After I bought my first scanner, I stopped using my digitizing tablet. Honestly, I can't recall why. I had bought it to use with my old Amiga computer and need some sort of adaptor because it was designed to work with the Mac or PC. I don't remember using it with my new RadiusMac, which I bought when Apple briefly allowed other companies to produce Mac-compatible computers before they decided that wasn't the best idea.

In any case, that first Wacom tablet I bought was huge; 12 x 12, I think. And incidentally, the word Wacom is pronounced "WHA-com," like the "wa" in "walk," according to the owner's manual that came with it, that book that so few of us seem to read. So if you want to impress people and make yourself seem like a *real* know-it-all (like that guy sitting in the front row), you can correct all those folks out there who pronounce the name "way-com."

As I said, I have a tendency to ink with the Pilot Precise V7 pen. You can buy them in packs of a dozen at stores like Office Max and Office Depot, or at Wal-Mart in packs of three. At first, I inked with the V5. It was a habit I started while working at KinderCare. It wasn't really a specific choice; it was just the pen they happened to have there. But I discovered a couple of points in its superior performance as I worked with it over time: It had real ink, and if it started to die, it didn't slowly turn gray before dying; it just sputtered out and died.

What do I mean by those points?

First, if it has real, genuine ink in it (unlike trying to use a felt-tip pen), the ink will *stay* pure black, regardless of age. Some of my older pieces that I did draw or "ink" with felt-tip pens have a nasty tendency to turn blue with age, especially around the edges. Felt-tip pens also have a tendency to bleed around the edges and get fuzzy. That may be nitpickery, again, but there you are.

The Pilot Precise doesn't bleed with most papers I've tested it on, from plain typing paper (which I tried animating with at one point, because it was thinner than copier paper for tracing advantages) to the all-purpose copy paper available today.

On the other hand, I also tried inking with technical pens. Naturally, you've got the pure black ink that works delightfully well, but

Inks that fade, bleed, or leave gaps

when they go dry you have to refill them, and you have to keep cleaning them or they get clogged up and won't ink. I'd rather spend my time inking than cleaning.

I also tried inking with some artist's "disposable" technical pens. They usually started out well enough, with the pure black ink, but when they started to run out they didn't have the decency to sputter briefly and die. Instead, the ink slowly... but ever so slowly... started to turn... gray.

And that's a major pet peeve; actually it's beyond a pet peeve, because it slows down your working process. Why? Because when you start to scan that somewhat gray drawing in black-and-white mode (or photocopy it), your characters will start getting gaps in their outlines. And when you get gaps in your outlines, that means that in many paint programs (like Macromedia Director's built-in paint window, or at least the older version I used) if your outlines aren't closed, if you've got so much as a one-pixel opening, your Paintbucket tool will "spill" the paint to the surrounding areas. If you're painting 15 to 30 characters per finished second of screen time, that's a serious drawback, and a potential bottleneck in your production line output. I need my lines to be solid, without gaps and holes.

Sadly, I ran into a similar problem with what had been my favorite ink pen of choice, the beloved Pilot Precise V5.

It was one of those rare, wonderful projects I speak of with great nostalgia. It was a project for which I actually had a budget and I could afford to pay assistants! Most of the projects I've worked on have been 30- and 60-second TV spots, but on a couple of occasions, I've had the good fortune to be able to hire help. The first time was on a 13-minute children's film on which, because of the comparatively limited budget, everyone working on the film was working part-time (myself included) and most were student interns. In that fashion, it took us nine months to complete that project.

On the next occasion, we had a five-minute budget with a much tighter production deadline. We were producing a sales video (which eventually won us an Addy Award, the equivalent of an Emmy for television commercials and commercially themed video productions) that had to be ready in roughly half of our previous production schedule, so I knew I'd need assistants to meet the deadline. The video would need to be ready for our client to show at a forthcoming trade show, so there was little time for production-related delays. Time was short.

And it was in this project that we discovered a problem with my formerly favorite V5 pen. My friend Shawn was helping me by scanning and painting the animation drawings that the other artists were bringing him. But he told me several times that he was having to spend his time zooming in on the artwork and trying to fix the gaps that resulted from scanning in thin pen lines. Instead of spending his time just painting, he was practically having to spend the same amount of time on each drawing trying to fix a problem before he could *start* painting.

Again, if you multiply the time each one of these drawings took to paint times 15 to 30 drawings per second, you can see we had a serious problem indeed.

I didn't want to give up the Pilot Precise pen, because I knew that the ink was the best quality I had found, and I didn't have a whole lot of time to experiment with other ink options.

I went to one of the office supply stores and found a three-pack of Pilot Precise V7 pens. I inked a drawing or two and gave it to Shawn to scan and paint. Shawn gave it a try, and thankfully (pause briefly for melodramatic effect) … No gaps. (Whew!)

I don't know what we would have done otherwise. I might have had to try inking with a brush. And though I liked inking with a brush, there would have been a serious difference between the inking styles of the drawings that we had already completed and the new brush-inked drawings. We didn't have time to reink, rescan, and repaint those previously finished drawings. Our schedule was too tight, so gladly I changed over to the V7 pen from that day forward, and used whatever V5s I had left over for taking notes and writing checks.

Inking with a Brush

If you have the time (and patience), inking with a brush has the best look to it. I really like the line width variation created by inking with a brush. I look at the old newspaper comic strips that were inked with a brush like Al Capp's *Lil' Abner* (on which legendary fantasy illustrator Frank Frazetta was a "ghost artist") and Walt Kelly's *Pogo* as perhaps the primary examples of how the "beauty of brushwork" can be best exemplified. A more modern example of some terrific brush inking is Jeff Smith's *Bone* series. Look for reprints of these great stories on the Internet or buy them from Amazon.com, but don't forget you might want to try your local library first. (Again, they'll often order books by request. Then you don't have to keep up with them after you're done reading.)

When I'm going to ink with a brush, I use the following supplies:

- A #4 brush or smaller
- Waterproof India ink
- A small jar of water, about half full
- A jar lid that I can use as an inkwell
- A 100% cotton cloth that I can use to dry my brush after washing

An X-Acto knife is not a toy. Its blade is designed to be sharp and to cut things with almost savage precision. I don't say that lightly. At the art department where I designed T-shirts, one of the guys from the screen department came to visit and was chatting with us while he awaited some artwork. They would burn our line art designs onto screens from the vellum sheet printouts we provided them, before being transferred to the shirts.

He had picked up an X-Acto knife while leaning against the large light table, and begun to at first casually tap the sharp tip against his finger. Before we knew it, he was letting it drop about an inch or two from one hand and into the finger of the other.

Not a particularly bright example of behavior, for on the next drop, the blade went in one side of his finger… and came out the other side.

Unless I'm much mistaken, he had to have stitches.

Again, some art tools are not to be treated lightly. So above all, treat the X-Acto knife with respect. It's sharp. *Real* sharp.

As for the brush, don't even *dare* think of using one of those packets of so-called "art brushes" you buy at the local dollar store, usually in the kid's section. They generally have about 10 to 12 brushes in a pack, and they look like someone stuck the exploded end of a spider onto a fluorescent plastic handle with superglue. The bristles stick out like a porcupine with one finger in a light socket. I don't even trust those things to stay within the lines of a five-year-old's paint-by-number. You need a small, reliable brush that will "behave itself" on small, sharp turns. It needs to come to a sharp point that will give you consistently precise twists and strokes as needed. Eventually, with age, certain bristles may start to poke out on even the best brushes, which can lead to unwanted extra lines on your inking. But the life of the brush can easily be extended by carefully trimming off the offensive, odd bristle with an X-Acto blade.

A brush gone bad. This is not a character you want to run into late at night, when you're working on a deadline. His wild bristles are an inking disaster, and will cause you much grief.

It's best to spend a little more money on a brush (roughly $4 or more) that will actually last you longer than a month. As one of my art teachers informed me, if you invest in a good brush and take good care of it, it can literally last you a lifetime. Winsor & Newton is just one brand of many worthwhile brushes you can get at an actual art supply store... not a craft store (where they sell baskets, mind you).

Make sure you wash your brush out after each use, before the ink (or paint, for that matter) dries, and wash it gently with *plain* cold water. Hot water can loosen the glue that's keeping the bristles attached to the brush, which might allow them to fall out. When you set the brush out to dry, set it on the handle end, not the end with the bristles. If you let a brush sit on the bristle end, it will bend those bristles and ruin your brush. Then you'll have to buy another brush prematurely. Please avoid eating into your own profit margin whenever possible, and just take sensible care of your tools.

My technique is something like this. If you've used the blue-line technique as I suggested, you can simply ink directly on top of your drawings. If you mess up, no worries; there's always Liquid Paper, or you can simply trace the drawings onto another sheet of paper and start over. But I'd really suggest practicing for a while on some drawings you're not too nostalgic about, because you probably won't get it right the first time.

I'll take a few drops of ink out of the ink bottle, and I do mean a *very* few drops (they'll go a lot further than you expect), and place them on an overturned jar lid, which I use as an inkwell. (Sure, if you want to get fancy, you can use one of those plastic paint wells with multiple indentations that work well with acrylic paint. They're pretty easy to wash out when you're done.)

I'll dip my brush first in water (a half-full jar, and your average jelly jar works fine) to make sure the tips of the bristles are sticking together in a fine point. Then I'll use that cotton cloth (which absorbs water better than polyester) to lightly dry off the brush, just enough so that it doesn't water down the ink and make it gray.

Next, I'll dip just the tip of my brush in the ink drops and start brushing. One of the best things to practice is making a line that starts out small and thin, and then gets nice and thick around a curve, and then ends up small and thin again. Probably the best example of this is those aforementioned comic strips of *Pogo* and Jeff Smith's *Bone*, especially the large, bulbous noses of the title characters in each case. That's the best example I've seen. Or you can take a look at the character I've drawn in the following illustration. The arrow points to one of those thin/thick lines. Though inking with a pen can certainly get you by, inking with a brush just gives the character drawings a little more weight, a little more personality, and frankly, a little more *depth*.

That may sound odd in a discussion about two-dimensional artwork, but I find it true. It is a matter of personal preference, but please try it yourself both ways before making a hasty decision. You might just find out you're a pretty good brush inker before you know it!

Jayle © Mark S. Smith/MarkToonery.com

Look carefully at Jayle's ear and eyebrows. You'll see what I mean by "line width variation." This is why I like inking with either a real-world brush and scanning it, or using one of the paintbrush tools in Flash that simulates this effect. In my humble opinion, lines that vary between thick and thin have more depth, more elegance... and more *character*.

One of my students from Auburn University Montgomery at one point even reminded me of my own advice that came in handy in his ink brushwork. If you move your brush quickly, with practice, you'll keep a cleaner line. If you move your brush slowly, the ink, being a liquid, has time to seep into the surrounding fibers of the paper and "bleed" or give you a messy and ragged edge rather than a nice *clean* edge to your line.

So practice brushing quickly as you get more comfortable with the feel of it. Like anything else, you'll improve with practice.

As a matter of fact, when I had just started at the T-shirt company, a comic book editor told me that though he liked my artwork, my inking needed some practice. He liked it so much (thankfully), he sent me some comic books of a guy's inking style that he thought would suit my drawings (I think it was Chuck Fiala, on a comic book named *Bullet Crow*). I wanted to practice inking to get better, so since my drawings would have to be scanned in black and white, I figured here was a chance to practice and get better... on someone else's time clock. I did, and after a few weeks, I felt comfortable enough with the brush to apply the new practice to my own drawings.

And one more quick thing. If you have especially large areas of black to be filled in on your drawing (like a certain little black duck, for instance), I wouldn't bother brush inking more than his outlines. You'd be waiting and waiting for the ink to dry before you put it on your scan bed, and waiting for drawings to dry (especially needlessly so) is something to be avoided. If it's a simple outline that you're waiting to dry, it won't take so long. Also, if you're inking a large, flat area of black, you'll find that when it dries your paper will be nice and wrinkly.

The point is, it's much easier (and way quicker) to later fill in that large area of black (or any color for that matter) with one click once you've imported your artwork into Flash.

Any way you look at it, your drawings will need to be dry when you scan them. Otherwise, if they're still wet when you put them on the scan bed, they'll naturally rub off on the glass, mess up the current scan, and you may not notice until after you've scanned a dozen drawings or so that you've got to clean your glass and start scanning all over again.

Whether you use the brush to ink your drawings or a pen, there is one advantage to having real artwork once you're done. You can frame it... and just possibly sell it, once you're done with your cartoon.

But I'll talk more about selling your work in the last chapter.

Scanning Your Inked Drawings

You'll probably be very happy to hear that this is going to be a *very* short section, because so many things depend on the different brand of scanner you have.

I was quite thrilled when they came up with the brilliant innovation of combining a scanner and printer into one device, particularly when you have limited desk space. As a beginning freelance artist, most of us have to start out with limited space (apartments, parents' attics or basements, etc.), at least until we get on our feet. If you don't have either (scanner or printer), I would highly recommend one of these combo devices. My particular model is the Hewlett-Packard PSC 750xi, but that's not to say there aren't many other great models out there. There certainly are. The particular model I have scans, prints, and even makes color or black-and-white copies at the touch of a button.

But there's one thing you have to make absolutely sure that your printer has: a black-and-white and/or line art scanning mode. Unfortunately, I bought a scanner years ago that for whatever reason couldn't. The closest it came was grayscale scanning.

For what I do, it simply wouldn't work. I had to return it. It was a hassle, but it would have been a *bigger* hassle to take each one of those grayscale scans into Photoshop, adjust the brightness and contrast until it looked like line art, and then take each one of those into Flash only to find out they *still* hadn't been cleaned up enough to start painting... only to scan all over again.

If your scan turns out like the example on the left, it's quite likely that you've accidentally scanned in grayscale mode rather than line art/black-and-white mode. Your life will be much, much easier if your scan looks more like the example on the right. See all those gray lines in the grayscale scan? They might not look so bad now, but just wait till you get into Flash and try to convert this grayscale scan to vector art. Look at the close-up in the next section and you'll see what I mean.

Scanning Tips

I have just a few tips for scanning your character artwork for Flash:

1. **Scan in black-and-white** (or **line art**) mode...*only*! It's easier to paint. Don't even *try* to scan in grayscale, because I've seen students spend close to an hour trying to clean up bad lines on one drawing before even starting to paint. Yes, one drawing. If I caught someone doing that on my time clock (especially after warning them several times to go ahead and rescan the art, which I've done in class), I'd have to let them go. Why? We're working on a deadline, and I need to find someone who can follow directions to bring a project in on budget. It may sound cold, but facts can be that way.

Remember that *nasty* grayscale scan from the previous section? On the left is a close-up of what it looks like once it's been converted into vector art. See all those nasty gray lumps? It irks me *deeply* to catch a student trying to clean up a mess like this. When I ask him how long he's spent on cleanup so far, he'll mutter, "Only forty-five minutes." "Forty-five minutes? To clean up one drawing? And how many more drawings do you have in this shot? Twenty-six, huh? How long do you think it would take you to rescan all twenty-seven of those drawings in line art mode, as I suggested in the first place? Twenty minutes, maybe, if that long. And then how long would you have to spend on each one of these line art drawings, cleaning them up? No time, probably. Right. Go rescan them, and save yourself some sweat in the first place."

I haven't really used words quite so intense in the classroom, but after you see people making the same mistakes repeatedly, it gets mighty tempting to go off like that. Especially after your warnings go unheeded.

The moral of the story is, scan your inked drawings in line art mode in the first place, and you should get a nice clean image like the one on the right. You'll find yourself far less stressed out, and far more likely to meet or beat those deadlines!

2. **Scan at no greater than 72 dpi** (if you can help it). You're
   scanning for the web or video, and scanning at 300 dpi or
   greater (recommended for print) only wastes time and disk
   space. It slows down your computer to scan at almost three
   times the resolution necessary (yup, 72 dpi is *all* that's necessary), and wastes roughly three times the disk space for each
   one of those drawings you're saving. Again, multiply time
   wasted scanning and space wasted at extra resolution for each
   drawing times 15 to 30 frames per second, depending on
   whether you're working on ones or twos.

3. **Keep your numbering system simple**, and make sure you
   realize *where* you're saving files. Try to avoid saving files to the
   desktop, as I've noticed some Mac students developing a nasty
   habit of doing. (Do you PC folks have trouble with this?)
   Because when you're saving stuff to the desktop (so I've
   heard), you've only chosen to steal from your own RAM,
   slowing down your computer.

   Is that what you're *meaning* to do... on purpose?

Importing Art into Flash

All right, that magical moment has arrived! You've done all your
animation drawings, and scanned them, and now you're ready to
bring them into Flash! Hooray!

Now you may remember some of this from way back in
Chapter 4, when we talked about putting together your pose
test/animatic. But the subtle difference here is that most of the artwork that we were bringing in before was merely for *preview*, or
planning purposes. The artwork was just for our own benefit and
viewing.

Now we're getting to the point where the actual artwork we're
bringing into Flash is going to be the finished art the audience will
actually see, whether we're putting together a cartoon for web
download, a multimedia CD-ROM presentation, or my personal
favorite, video production.

Open up Flash, just like you did last time.

Setting Your Stage

We didn't go into a whole lot of detail last time, because as I've already said, that was mostly for our own benefit, for purposes of timing and layout with your animatic. Now that we're setting the stage for the real deal, we have to be a little more persnickety about our details.

I will say up front that it's not altogether disastrous if you accidentally set up your web cartoon for video preferences. Sure, such problems can be fixed, but isn't it just easier to do the job right the first time?

For Video

As I mentioned briefly in Chapter 4, you have a number of different choices when setting up your cartoon for a video production. In the old days (well, the days when I got into video, anyhow), you just had to set your screen to 640 x 480 resolution, and you were pretty much set. Nowadays with the advent of digital video, things have changed considerably with many more choices such as wide-screen, HDTV, and all, but since I know that most of my presentations will be burned to DVD, I almost routinely set my screen to 720 x 480. If there is any cause for question, it's always best to ask someone directly involved with your video production. It is quite possible for the setup to change on a case-by-case basis, because there are so many variables involved.

I remember once asking a teacher (before I started my first algebra class), "So what does this x stand for, anyway?"

"That's just it; it's a variable," came the reply. "It changes from one equation to another."

"You mean it's never the same?"

"It's seldom the same. You'll understand later why it's important to have variables for different circumstances." She was right.

Every time you do a TV spot or web banner, different clients will have different needs and therefore different screen setups will be necessary.

If you're doing the work for a TV station or video production facility, ask either the creative services director or the production manager their preferred screen resolution/size. If all else fails, ask the station manager, and he or she should be able to direct you to someone who knows for certain.

For Web and Multimedia

If you're doing the work for a website, ask the webmaster. He or she probably already has a preference for you to work in. If you're putting the project together for a CD-ROM presentation, ask the creative director, project manager, or coordinator. Most of the time — I dare say 100% of the time — people much prefer that you ask what you think is a dumb question rather than make a stupid mistake and run the project late trying to fix it.

Go ahead and ask up front.

Document Properties

When you go into Flash to set up your movie, the Start page comes up.

You'll notice you've got three major groups of choices: Open Recent, Create New, and Create from Template.

As you'll soon learn, you may very well find yourself using the same setup regularly, and like most of these other steps, they'll soon become habit.

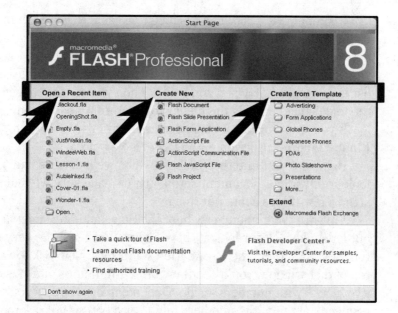

Your three main choices when opening a document are: Open a
Recent Item, Create New, and Create from Template.

After you've been working for some time in Flash, you'll notice
that the **Open a Recent Item** section becomes particularly handy.
Naturally, you'll seldom finish a Flash project in one sitting...
although it *can* happen. I finished a presentation for an animation
workshop one weekend in less than three hours (thankfully just
before midnight), but don't count on them all to be that quick.
Chances are, in the midst of some of your projects, you'll want to
sleep, or go out to lunch, or possibly go bang your head on the
refrigerator, in which case you might end up going to sleep (for a
few weeks if you're not careful — so I strongly recommend resist-
ing the temptation to do this).

Though I try my best to remember to keep my projects in sensible folders in sensible locations, occasionally my mind slips into
the second dimension, and I forget or don't notice where I'm saving
something. When you're working on a deadline and can't find your
file, that can be beyond frustrating... it can be downright
maddening.

It's times like that when it's nice to be able to go to **Open a Recent Item** and see your list of the last nine or so projects. Also notice that if you happen not to see the file you're looking for, and you happen to know where it is anyway, down at the bottom of the list is just a plain ol' Open command. Then you can just navigate to the folder that contains the file and open it from its location.

If you want to start a Flash document from scratch, go to the **Flash Document** option in the **Create New** area.

Before we get into the Toolbox (which we'll discuss later), let's look briefly at our document setup, just to make sure we understand a few things about our movie.

I'm sure you remember where the Stage and the Timeline are, but let's take a closer look at that window floating at the very bottom of your screen, the **Properties window**. If you look toward the top of that window, you'll see the word **Dimensions**, and beside it two blocks with numbers inside. Depending on whether you've changed anything, the numbers might read 550 x 400 or some other number. In my case, the number is set to 720 x 480, a sort of custom default that we'll set in just a moment.

Whatever the number reads next to the word Size, click on that number. (Don't bother clicking on the word Size; it won't do you any good.)

You should see a screen similar to the one shown here. This new window is the Document Properties window. You'll notice there's a place where you can enter text for a title and a description. I usually skip past this and head straight down to the Dimensions area.

Document Properties		
Title:		
Description:		
Dimensions:	550 px (width) x	400 px (height)
Match:	○ Printer ○ Contents ● Default	
Background color:		
Frame rate:	12 fps	
Ruler units:	Pixels	
Make Default	Cancel	OK

Light Blue Skies in Flash

If your movie is a daytime scene, you may have tried finding a nice blue marker for drawing a custom background. You may also have found, like I did, that even with the greatest range of otherwise beautiful Prismacolor markers at your fingertips, it's virtually impossible to find a convincing daytime light blue sky color.

You'll find it's quite easy to leave your sky blank in such cases when a sky-blue marker (or pencil) is unavailable or downright nonexistent. In such a case, import your background, as described in this chapter, select the instance of your JPG background (or however you brought it in), and then go to the Modify menu and drag down to Break Apart.

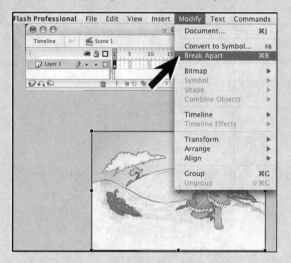

Now that your background image is "broken apart" (broken down into its elements), we can erase edges that will be invisible when placed over other objects, much like the Photoshop layers. As you probably know, Photoshop's layers work like artwork painted on sheets of glass (or old-fashioned animation cels, which are transparent) rather than artwork painted on a white sheet (being translucent), which we otherwise can't remove.

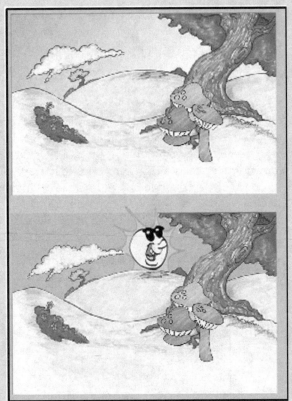

If you import a hand-drawn background or one
created in Photoshop, you may decide that you want
animated elements to appear *behind* it. In this case,
you may need to "break apart" your artwork in
order to delete elements like the blue sky gradient
over the hills, so Mr. Sun can shine through the
background and over the hilltop.

I'll select the Eraser tool in Flash and begin to erase that
blue sky, which may not quite be working for me here. That
way my light blue background color, chosen directly in Flash,
or a Gradient fill (which I can also choose in Flash and which
will be investigated in the forthcoming Toolbox section) that I've
placed on a layer below can show through. Or I can even have

a cartoon sun come up from behind the hillside between the clouds! Like the other drawing and painting tools, you can select the size and shape of your brush. And as always, I'll serenely suggest activating the Pressure Sensitive option if you have your digitizing tablet set up (which I hope you do).

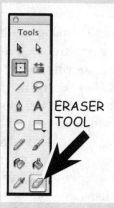

Hint: You can also use this approach to do Terry Gilliam's *Monty Python*-style "cutout animation" by cutting out bits and pieces of photographs. You can cut out people's jaws, paste them on a separate layer, paint the resulting mouth hole in the face layer black, and start using these old photos like ventriloquist dummies, marionettes, and so on.

As I just mentioned, I tend to set up my movies for DVD, so for my width I'll type in **720**, and for my height I'll type in **480**. Under Match, I'll click **Default** (if it's not already selected).

And then there's your Background color, which is set to white by default. That may very well suit you as is, or if you've scanned hand-painted backgrounds or created them all in Photoshop, it may simply not matter what your background color is set to. (In those last two cases, any background color would be covered by custom backgrounds.) Is your scene set in outer space or, like my *Midnight Sneak* cartoon, does it take place at night? If so, you might want to set your background color to black and create your animated, twinkling stars right here in Flash.

Of course, you can choose any color you like to be your background color. Maybe green, purple, or fuchsia if your cartoon takes place on an alien world... or in a 1960s car dealership, for that matter.

Frame Rate

As you no doubt recall from our pose test discussion earlier, the frame rate is largely a matter of preference (how fast you want your characters capable of moving) and the destination output of your final movie. The default is usually set for 12 frames per second, which is fine for most multimedia applications (web, CD-ROM).

Since I have a tendency to work mostly on twos (and ones when I can afford to, which is a budget issue), that would reduce 30 fps (the video standard) by half, which, for all you math buffs that already figured it out, gives us **15 fps**. If you think you want to move your video characters faster, on ones (like a roadrunner chase against a moving background, or a similarly paced action), then it's best to set your frame rate to 30 fps. In the event that this is a project for a theatrical feature (lucky you!), then set your frame rate to the film standard of 24 fps.

I'll leave my Ruler units setting as **Pixels**.

Now if this is a setup you think you might use repeatedly, or more often than any other setup, you're certainly welcome to click the **Make Default** button, and every time hereafter when you go into Flash (you may have to quit the program for the changes in the Default settings to take effect this first time), it will choose all these same settings for your document properties.

Not bad, huh?

The next option for getting started in your Flash movie is equally impressive (and a real time-saver).

Create from Template

As I just said, the Create from Template feature is a nice time-saver. Especially for those of you who are using Flash to come up with web banners. As you've no doubt realized already, there are quite a few variations on the sizes for "standard" web banners. Notice in the figure below that they've already got setups you can choose for skyscraper ads, rectangle, those pop-ups we all... just... (sorry, I can't finish that sentence diplomatically), and your traditional banner sizes. If you're putting one together for yourself or for a client, you're in pretty good shape.

And naturally, if another size is needed, you know how to set up custom screens anyway, so all is well.

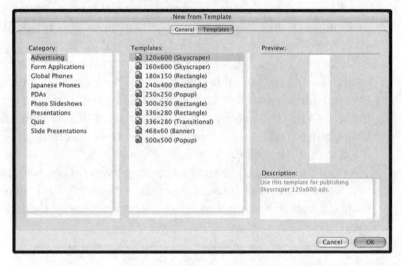

Whew! Now that your Stage is finally set, we can begin to bring in those characters we want.

Just as with your pose test, go to **File | Import**. You have two choices. You can either import to the Stage, which will place your art immediately center stage, or you can import to the Library. (Incidentally, either way a copy of your art will end up in the Library.) The Library is pretty much what it sounds like. It is simply an area, like a bookshelf, where you're keeping all your artwork, sound effects, buttons, and anything else you import into or create directly in Flash. Once your files are imported into Flash, you can create folders and put similar files together to keep better track of them. For example, you can make a folder for all your sound effects, a folder for your backgrounds, and a folder for each character. You can even make folders within folders. For instance, you could have a folder for your character, like a Sezquatch folder. Then inside that folder, you might have a folder for Sezquatch faces, one for Sezquatch legs, and so on. There's a much better way to organize your character's mouth positions, though, and we'll get to that later. In fact, that was the coolest thing Les Harper (a Turner Studios animator) was kind enough to show me.

Since we chose Import to Stage last time, let's try the Import to Library option this go-round. Go to **File | Import to Library**. You'll see that your artwork is brought into the Library.

There is a slim chance, however, that before continuing, you'll get a message like the following: Cannot Import this Image/Would you like to import this image via QuickTime? As a matter of fact, since I'm a Mac guy and have a tendency to save in PICT format (which seems to take up less space than those enormous uncompressed TIF files and are cleaner than JPG files), I used to see this message a lot. But since I upgraded to Flash 8 (from Flash MX), I thankfully haven't seen it lately. It seems to be something they fixed with the upgrade.

Another bit of good news: If the image you choose to import is in a folder with a bunch of other similarly named images (like 01.pct, 02.pct, 03.pct, and so on), Flash will show you the following message:

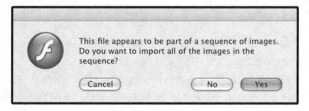

Therefore, if you followed my advice from earlier (keeping your file numbering system simple and sequential), you can import a whole bunch of drawings at once... in order.

Think of the time that will save you!

Regardless of whether you're importing one image or a sequence of images, the process is essentially the same. Let's start with one image that we've imported into our Library.

Let's say I have a figure named 01.pct, just as I suggested. I happen to know it's my wacky wildcat, OldMane of the Mountains. Not just by sight, but because I'd saved him in a folder that read "OldMane." If I like, I can go ahead and start a folder in my Library before or after I place him on the Stage. (Don't you love how versatile Flash is in letting you do certain things however you like? But tread carefully; it's not always this straightforward.)

"Just for giggles," as my dad often said, I tried something just to confirm a theory.

I scanned in the aforementioned OldMane picture, which is roughly seven inches tall, cropped off the edges in Photoshop, and saved it in three different formats. (I didn't want you guys to think I was stuck in a rut, as far as my image formats go… and besides, it's been so long since I started the habit of saving in PICT format, I wanted to make sure it still held true.)

Of the three most common formats, two are common on both the Mac and the PC (TIF and JPG), and one is common to the Mac format (PICT — and it will work either way if you've got Photoshop, which is one of the most reliable programs for opening almost any conceivable graphic image format).

Anyway, the same image in the different file formats ended up as:

OldMane.pct   112K
OldMane.jpg   168K
OldMane.tif   468K

As you can see, my longstanding theory held true… at least this time, with a fairly straightforward, black-and-white image scanned at 75 dpi. (Ahem! Apparently, my scanner won't do an "even" 72.) The fact that the PICT format is the smallest file size is somewhat reassuring. Though it's a Mac format (sorry, PC folks), it's also uncompressed. A compressed image is less likely to be perfectly black and white, which is essential here. (A compressed image is like stuffing a shirt in a crowded suitcase. When you unpack the suitcase, it's possible that when you remove the shirt, you may have a few noticeable wrinkles in it; in computer terms, these wrinkles are the occasional little gray or off-color pixels, which might later make painting a pain.) I saved the JPG sample file at a compression rate of 8 (High) when asked in Photoshop, and you can see it came out at 168K. You PC folks might want to settle for JPG then, because the TIF file weighs in the heaviest at 468K. That extra 356K of disk space might not sound like a lot, but if you take into consideration that you're doing as many as 15 to 30 drawings per second of film, you can see how that would add up really quick.

Trace Bitmap

All right now. Let's say that I want to start coloring OldMane. I could grab one of those handy paint tools like the Paintbucket and pick a color to paint with, but if I click the image, nothing happens. Why not?

Well, we've got to remember that Flash is a vector-based program, and therein lies its strength. But the image we've just brought in is a bitmap, or raster-based image, based on pixels (basically a mosaic composed of tiny little squares). Vector images are like dot-to-dots in that they compute the line information and angles between one another; no matter how much you enlarge, skew, or rotate them, the angles keep nice, crisp-edged lines and the curves stay curvy.

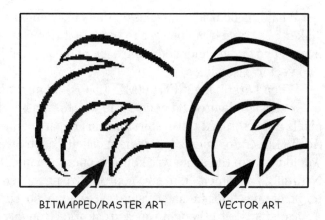

BITMAPPED/RASTER ART   VECTOR ART

You'll soon see how handy that is.

But in the meantime, we've got to somehow transform this pixel-based image (which we can't paint or manipulate particularly well... or at all, for that matter) into a vector-based image. To do this, go up to **Modify** and choose **Bitmap | Trace Bitmap**.

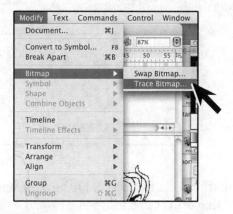

Note:

After buying my first three Flash manuals (not counting the one that came with the program), not one of them had the decency to come right out and tell me this handy little tip, which was a personal epiphany of how useful this program is. (If they did mention this anywhere, I couldn't find it in their index, which is just as bad as not telling me.)

What this does for you is essentially like sending a tiny robotic "inker," or "tracer" if you care to think of it that way, around every line you've drawn, and modifying each of these pixel-based lines into vector-based lines.

When I first bought Flash (MX, that is), I knew that it was vector-based, so I figured I'd need some way to transfer my lines from pixels to vectors. At the T-shirt shop art department, we used Adobe Illustrator and had a program called Adobe Streamline that would perform the same trace bitmap operation just described. Naturally, I assumed I'd need a copy of Streamline, so I was quite proud of myself for finding this now seemingly obscure software on Amazon for what I thought was a great price (roughly $60 or so, I guess).

But when I discovered this handy little feature was built right into Flash, well... maybe I better sell Streamline right back to Amazon (if I can still get my money back...)!

All right, back to the subject at hand.

After choosing Trace Bitmap, you'll get a window that prompts you for several pieces of information.

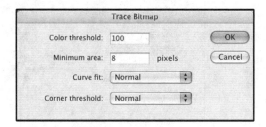

The first is Color threshold. I have a tendency to leave it at its default setting of 100, and for the black-and-white images I've used it on, it's worked just fine.

(Just keep in mind that as you increase the Color threshold value, you'll *decrease* the number of resulting colors. Chances are for line art you only want two resulting colors: black and white.)

Minimum area is asking you to enter a value (from 1 to 1000) that sets the number of surrounding pixels to take into consideration when it assigns a color to each pixel. Again, I leave it at the default setting of 8.

Curve fit is something you're more likely to adjust. Though I normally also leave it at the default setting (Normal), you need to take into consideration (once again) whether you're going to be outputting your final cartoon to video/DVD or posting it on a website as an ad or Flash SWF file.

The reason I say that is this: Although we are talking about vector files here, which naturally download faster than bitmap files, the more points and curves you have in an image, the more memory/space it takes up, and therefore, the slower it will eventually play.

So in other words, I'm saying that if your cartoon is destined for the web, you might want to set your curves to Smooth. The downside of this, of course, is the closer you are to a setting of Smooth, the less accurate, looser, and further away from your original drawing your image will become. Though the Smooth setting creates files that take up less memory, it also results in more "holes," or lines that don't connect.

On the other hand, my experiments with setting Corner threshold on anything but Normal weren't terribly better. Your choices are Many Corners, Normal, and Few Corners. Feel free to experiment as you like, but Normal worked best for my sample line art.

Look at the following examples I've done here, comparing the Corner threshold setting. When allowing the computer to "trace" all your artwork for use in Flash, keep in mind that Flash will "simplify" or streamline your art by removing points.

As I mentioned earlier in this chapter, you do have to contend with the "problem of gaps." Remember when I spoke of my digital painter named Shawn? Because of his advice, I switched over from Pilot Precise V5 to V7 ink pens because there were disconnected lines with the V5s, causing the paint to run out between the gaps in the scanned drawings. It was costing our limited budget money, so we had to make a change that saved time and therefore those aforementioned greenbacks.

BEFORE TRACE BITMAP

MANY CORNERS

NORMAL

FEW CORNERS

Fortunately, in Flash, there has been some advance with technology (an option called Gap Size) that enables you to set the width of "gaps" or "holes" that the computer will "fill in" for you. (But we'll discuss that later, when we talk about the Toolbox.)

All right, hopefully now that you have some idea of how these different settings will affect the overall look of your artwork, you can proceed, by clicking OK.

You'll notice straightaway that it looks as though your artwork has acquired a hideous grid of tiny little dots. Don't worry; that's just showing you that the item, now traced, is still selected.

GAP FROM
LINES NOT
TOUCHING

DOTTED GRID
RESULTING AFTER
TRACE BITMAP

If you'd like to deselect the artwork, just click anywhere else on the screen (or Stage) off the selected art. The grid should disappear and you can see how your artwork has been traced. You can zoom in on it (by either clicking on the Zoom tool (the magnifying glass) or simply by pressing Cmd+plus (+) on the Mac or Ctrl+plus (+) on the PC), and see if it looks okay, or if perhaps you should try experimenting with different settings or even retrace the art.

One of the first things I do (having settled the issue of Trace Bitmap settings) is delete that unused white area that surrounds your traced artwork. It's there, whether you see it or not. If you have your background color set to white, you naturally won't see it. However, if you were to set your background color to anything other than white, you'll see it quite clearly. Go to the Properties

window at the bottom of the screen. Deselect your character artwork (if you haven't already) by clicking anywhere else on the
screen. The reason I tell you to do this is because the Properties
window is context sensitive, meaning it depends a lot on what is
currently selected. If you have a piece of artwork or button
selected, the Properties window will reflect options you have with
that artwork or button. If you don't have anything selected, the
Properties window will reflect the movie properties.

I set the background color to a color, as mentioned, and can
clearly see the area I need to delete. I select the area, and if it just
so happens that there are *still* some of those infuriating little gaps
left, you'll notice that it selects some of those as well. In this case,
the character's mane, his right leg, and the tip of his tail have gaps
that will need to be fixed. We'll get to that soon enough, but let's
start with what we know.

I've gone almost a whole chapter now without mentioning Richard Williams, but he quotes Rembrandt (1606-1669) by saying,
"Start with the things that you know, and the things that are
unknown will be revealed to you."

For now, I'll continue by throwing in some colors with my
Paintbucket tool set to Close Small Gaps onto my character.

Toolbox Basics

The following sections focus on some of the Flash Toolbox tools
used to create our character.

The Paintbucket Tool

To select a color, I simply click on the small Fill Color box. The
Eyedropper will come up, and I can then drag it over to the color in
the color palette that also pops into view. When I release the mouse
over my selected color, that color hops into the Fill Color box, and
whatever I paint (by clicking on its area, obviously) will instantly
become that color.

Animation Cels vs. Acetate, and the Lost Art of Cel Painting

In the old days, animation cels were actually painted on clear sheets of celluloid. But as was soon discovered, the celluloid was extremely flammable, and studios very wisely switched over to using clear sheets of plastic acetate (which a dwindling number of animation studios still use). Although they've been made of acetate for decades, the name "cel" remains in use.

The last Disney animated feature to use physical animation "cels" was *The Little Mermaid* (1989).

The reason I mention animation cels here is to help you appreciate how comparatively easy we have it today. In the old days, each animation drawing was traced onto one of these clear cels by one of the "pretty girls" in the ink and paint department. (Walt Disney married a girl from his own ink and paint department in the early days of his studio.) After the ink dried, the cel was turned over, and color by color was filled in with opaque paint in each specific area of the character. The reason they turned the cel over was so that it was a little more "forgiving" to stay between the lines, and also you could paint "under" details like freckles on a dog's snout or individual black lines of hair, eyelashes, and such.

Just out of curiosity, I tried painting a couple of animation cels that I drew myself on acetate. Besides a pad of acetate being expensive (for a curious college student), I also found out how difficult it is to stay between the lines and get the paint thick enough to be opaque! The reason the paint needs to be opaque is because when it's dry, each cel is placed over the painted background, with the clear, unpainted areas of the cel showing the scene behind it. The character needs to look solid (unless, of course, you're painting a ghost).

Nowadays, we just click once per enclosed area, and it's filled instantly with the correct color of paint. We don't even have to worry if the paint has been "mixed" properly. If we forget which color we just used, we simply use the Eyedropper tool to click on the color we need (from a previous drawing), and it's automatically selected.

I was probably seven or eight when I first saw a special on making animated cartoons. I think it was a picture of Bugs Bunny sitting in front of a campfire outside a tent. Somehow, I thought they had cut the drawing of Bugs from a piece of paper and pasted it on the clear sheet of plastic. All I can remember thinking was, "How did they manage to cut that picture of Bugs Bunny out without slicing his whiskers off?"

You'll see that, once again, you have several options, starting with **Don't Close Gaps**, which will not paint an area if it has so much as a one-pixel gap. (I don't think that's the one you want it set at. That's putting us back pretty much where I started from with the version of Director I used before!) The next setting, **Close Small Gaps**, seems to work best for me. Naturally, you can try **Close Medium Gaps** or even **Close Large Gaps**, but pretty soon it might stop filling areas you prefer to be colored if you set it too high.

I rather like the "loose" style this now allows us. You're no longer restricted to those perfectly enclosed lines, like old kindergarten coloring books. You may decide to paint your characters in a style that *allows* gaps. It makes me think of some of those old

Sesame Street cartoons where they had a variety of animation styles, some with thick, enclosed lines, others with purposely open lines of gaps, almost like dotted lines. It's quite liberating, really, to no longer be so restricted. Oddly enough, despite all this, my personal style seems to be those perfectly enclosed lines. But it's nice to have the option.

After several tries with this artwork we've been using, I wasn't terribly happy with the results. I finally figured that it wasn't the fault of any of these particular Trace Bitmap settings, but rather the resolution at which I originally scanned my character.

This particular example was something that I inked with a brush, mind you! That means there were some pretty thick lines that were losing the "integrity" of their original look, and I readily admit I can be pretty nitpicky. Therefore, as an experiment, I rescanned the artwork at 150 dpi (rather than the original 75 dpi).

Here are the results so you can judge for yourself.

As you can see, the example on the far left is the original, untraced artwork, scanned in at 75 dpi. (If you look closely, you'll notice the pixels.) I tried several levels of detail for the Trace Bitmap settings, but finally settled on those shown in the Trace Bitmap box above. Both the middle and right examples resulted from the same settings, but as you can see, the center example has less detail and turned out a little too "angular" for my liking, without the original rounded curves I preferred from the original. The center and the original were scanned in at 75 dpi. However, when I rescanned the artwork at 150 dpi and applied the same settings, then scaled it down to match its predecessor in size, I arrived at a far more satisfactory result. The new one is at the far right... and with fewer gaps, no less.

The only possible downside is that you're ending up with more points. But of course, that may be the only way you can maintain the look of your original lines.

The first thing I suggest is to experiment with different settings on a single piece of art to better make the comparison. Make sure you're satisfied with the look of one drawing before you import 45 or more drawings into a scene.

Keep in mind though, that if you use the higher resolution setting, the artwork will essentially be "twice as large" (if scanned in at 150 dpi vs. 75 dpi), which means that you'll have to scale it down to fit onto a Stage that's designed for 72 dpi. If that's the case, and you've scanned in all your characters at this size, hold your horses *before* scaling them down. It will be much easier to paint them first, then scale them all down at once *after* you've made them into symbols. Remember that tasks such as scaling, rotating, and resizing are much easier after turning a character or paint object into a symbol.

What is a symbol? you ask. A symbol is a graphic, button, or animation. You create a symbol by selecting an image, sound effect, sequence of images, text, etc., and telling Flash to make it into a symbol. The quickest way to do so is to select the item and press the F8 key; then you'll be asked to name the symbol. Chapter 8 covers this in more detail.

An instance, on the other hand, is simply a copy of that symbol as it appears onstage. You can make modifications to the instance of that symbol such as size, skewing, color, alpha channel, etc., without affecting the original symbol. That, in itself, is truly one of Flash's innate strengths and selling points. You can make multiple copies and alterations of a symbol, and Flash only needs to load the original symbol into memory once. That keeps things moving faster.

The Paintbrush Tool

All right, back to the painting process. Let's say, for instance, that none of the Close Gaps options on your Paintbucket tool is doing you any good. You might actually have to fill in that open gap and be done with it already! Okay, go over to your Paintbrush tool.

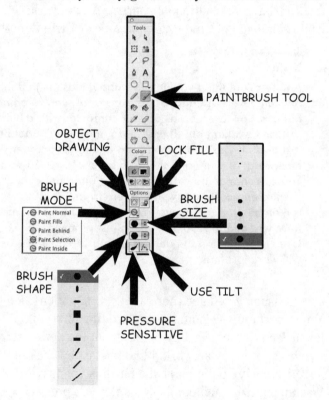

I'll go ahead and tell you up front that my favorite tool in the Toolbox is undoubtedly the Paintbrush tool. Why is that? Because I can ink my artwork directly in Flash with the look of a brush — that line width variation you may have heard me mention before. Thanks to the different sizes and shapes of brushes available, especially when you team that up with the Pressure Sensitive option available through a Wacom digitizing tablet, my real-world paintbrush is for the first time in decades gathering dust. As a matter of fact, I think I misplaced that brush sometime last term and haven't even looked for it.

First things first, though. Let's select the Paintbrush tool. Like a lot of these tools (especially if you're using a Wacom for the first time), I would suggest that you try playing around with it in some blank space on the screen before you start touching up your actual art... just as a precaution, of course. (Although there's always the Undo command of Cmd+Z on the Mac or Ctrl+Z on the PC.)

Note:

Another cool thing you'll notice about Flash is that it has *multiple* levels of undo. Say, for instance, you've painted about six or seven areas of your character with a blue that just isn't working out. If you Undo once, it will unpaint your last area. If you Undo *again*, it will take yet *another* step backward, and unpaint the area before last, and so on. You can change how many levels of undo are available in the Preferences window, anywhere from 2 to 300. Just remember, the more levels of undo you have, the more RAM you might be taking up, so just proceed with caution. Usually, you'll find the default setting of 100 levels of Undo will work just fine.

As usual, you'll see there are several options tied to this tool. You're certainly welcome to explore the different options at your leisure, but let me start by pointing out my personal favorites. Once I've brought in my artwork, I like to start by clicking on the **Pressure Sensitive** option. (That's for those of us with those lovely Wacom digitizing tablets.) The harder you press down with your digitizing stylus (and it is quite sensitive; you don't have to press hard at all), the wider your brush stroke will be. The lighter your touch, the thinner your brush stroke. And of course, as you practice, you'll notice that you can go from thick to thin in one stroke.

The next thing you might want to set is the Brush Shape. Although your first instinct might be to select a traditional round shape, let me encourage you to try out one of the diagonal-shaped options instead. It ties in with the pressure sensitivity quite nicely. As you'll soon see, you can get some almost calligraphic-quality brush strokes. You can easily help return the forgotten art form of inking to its former glory with a little practice. I really think those variations in line width on a character's outlines helps them stand out from the backgrounds.

Brush Size is another option to play around with, and its role is fairly obvious without a wealth of explanation. Again, I would just suggest toying with the different options available to you, in various combinations.

Allow me to mention one little thing in relation to Brush Size, however.

Look at the following illustration. It looks like roughly the same squiggly line drawn three times with three different brush sizes, right? Actually, yes and no. The first time I drew the squiggle (starting at the left) I used an average-sized brush. With that same brush size selected, I zoomed in on the picture by clicking once on the Zoom tool. I drew another squiggle at the new magnification, zoomed in again, and drew a third squiggle, never changing the actual *size* of my brush tool. I just kept zooming in larger, and painting my line again. Do you see what I mean?

Even though these three squiggles were drawn by the same size brush, the amount of magnification I was zoomed in affected the brush size "appearance" on the Stage. Just try to keep that in mind. In other words, if you'd like to keep your brush *size*

Keep in mind that even though you may use the same *size* brush, if you zoom in and draw again, the finished brush size will yield a smaller result onscreen. All three of these squiggles were created with the same size brush, and simply zooming in on the image.

consistent, then try to use the Paintbrush tool at a consistent *screen* size.

Use Tilt is a pretty nifty option to have, but personally, I didn't find it made a whole lot of difference in my own inking efforts. It varies the angle of your brush stroke according to the angle you're holding your stylus. I'll admit, it's pretty neat that the tablet can actually measure the angle between the top (the eraser end of your stylus) and the drawing tip. As an example, if you were to hold the stylus at a perfectly vertical relationship to the tablet, that is, straight up, the tilt would be 90 degrees.

Brush Mode, on the other hand, has a far more impressive set of options to tinker with. **Paint Normal** is pretty much self-explanatory. If you paint on empty white space, it becomes a stroke of your color of choice. You paint on something else, it gets covered with that color, and so on. You may notice that in Paint Normal mode, once you're done with a paint stroke, it's surrounded by a blue outline to designate that it is selected. When an item is selected, you can rotate, resize, or use any of the choices under Free Transform. Those choices are easily accessed by either right-clicking on the selected item (for you PC folks) or Ctrl-clicking with the Mac. (Actually, you can use a multi-button mouse with a Mac too.)

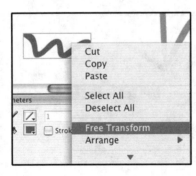

If you right-click on a selected object (PC) or Ctrl+click (Mac), you'll notice an array of options appears, perhaps the most useful of which is Free Transform. This allows you to rotate, resize, and modify your artwork.

Paint Fills may at first seem to operate in pretty much the same way as Paint Normal, but there is a subtle difference. In Paint Normal mode, once you release an object, it can be selected separately from other objects in the same layer. Not so in Paint Fills mode.

I should now explain how Flash treats objects on the same layer, depending on the paint mode you're in. You might be familiar with other drawing programs like Adobe Illustrator, and how it treats objects on a single layer. When you finish drawing something and "let go of it," or deselect it, if it so happens to land directly on top of another piece of artwork on that same layer, no worries. They're separate objects, and you can pick up either one individually from the other.

Not so in Flash... at least not in Paint Fills mode. (It works pretty much like that in Paint Normal mode, however.)

Admittedly, I found it a little vexing at first, but like any new piece of software, I've just learned to deal with it. Flash's strengths far outweigh its drawbacks, and once you know it's there, like a mucky mire of quicksand, you'll learn to avoid complications... and it will seem like less of a drawback.

What I'm talking about is that Flash's Paint Fills mode treats objects drawn on the same layer, particularly once they touch or overlap, as one object. So be careful. For instance, if I were to draw a blue circle and then a blue square on top of it in the same layer, once I let go, Flash treats those two shapes as if they've been glued on top of each other. And if I try to move one without the other, it will "tear a hole" in the shape of the object you just moved.

However, like any drawback, you can use this to your advantage. Let's say that I have an object that I want to cut a hole through. Like a lamppost with some ornate, frilly holes at the top.

The "lumpy lamppost" on the far left was my first drawing, to which I added some scrolls. Removing the scrolls created an almost "cookie-cutter" effect by opening a hole the exact shape of the design, leaving a window to the background beyond. I moved the shapes all the way to the far right so you can see what I "pulled." If you ever need to have a crazy rabbit tear through a wall and leave a rabbit-size opening in his wake, well... now you know how to do it!

As you can see in the example, I drew a lumpy lamppost in one color, and then made some frilly little squiggles at the top. Just for safety (as I often do), I made a copy of my lamppost and moved it to the right. (If you hold down Option on the Mac and drag something, it makes a copy of the selected item; Alt-dragging serves the same purpose on the PC.)

Then I selected my first squiggle, held down the Shift key (to enable me to select more than one item), and selected the rest of my colored squiggles. When they were all selected, I simply moved them to the right. You can see that the squiggles "tore a hole" that reveals the background behind them.

I'm sure you can probably think of some useful applications for this little trick.

Paint Behind is another straightforward description of what the option actually claims to accomplish. Try as you might to paint in *front* of something, it will avail you not. You can only paint *behind* the objects. How does this come in handy?

Perhaps you'd like to paint your characters in a nontraditional way. Instead of flat color fills, maybe you want to give them a sort of sketchy line fill. It might just look kinda cool. Who knows?

BRUSH MODE

Here's what you do:

1. Make sure you have your **Paintbrush** selected in the Toolbox.
2. Select **Paint Behind** from the Brush Mode options.
3. Draw a character outline in a dark color, like black.
4. Select *another* color by clicking on the **Fill Color** icon (next to the Paintbucket icon, right under Colors) and dragging out to your second color choice.
5. Start scribbling over your character with the second color. When you release the mouse (or remove your stylus from the drawing tablet), the colors will show up only *behind* the character's outline. Pretty neat, huh?

Paint Selection works like this: Select an object or an area *within* an object that you've created on the Stage, and when you start painting, your strokes will only affect those *selected* areas.

PAINTBRUSH TOOL

PAINTBUCKET TOOL

FILL COLOR

BRUSH MODE: PAINT SELECTION

Here's what you do:

1. Make sure you have your **Paintbrush** selected in the Toolbox.

2. Select **Paint Selection** from the Brush Mode options.

3. Draw a character outline in a dark color, like black.

4. Select *another* color by clicking on the **Fill Color** icon (next to the Paintbucket icon, right under Colors) and dragging out to your second color choice.

5. Fill an enclosed area of your character with that second color by selecting the **Paintbucket** tool and then clicking on the enclosed area.

6. Now select a *third* color by clicking and dragging out the **Fill Color** again.

7. Select the area of your character you'd like to paint (preferably that fill color you just created) with the Selection tool (the arrow icon at the top of the Toolbox).

8. Click on your **Paintbrush** tool again, and start scribbling over your character with the third color. When you release the mouse (or remove your stylus from the drawing tablet), the colors will show up only *inside* the area that you selected.

Paint Inside may seem vaguely like Paint Behind at first, but with one key exception: It makes a world of difference *where* you start painting. Look at the following illustration.

PAINTBRUSH TOOL

PAINTBUCKET TOOL

FILL COLOR

BRUSH MODE: PAINT INSIDE

I had already painted the character on the far left with some fairly straightforward fills, notably a pinkish flesh color for his face and a red fill for his turtleneck collar. With Paint Inside selected for the Brush Mode, I chose a dark purple for the Fill Color and started to "paint inside" the flesh color on his face. Note how even though I obviously scribbled all over and outside his face, the only area that remained changed (after I released the mouse or drawing stylus) was that same flesh color I started painting *inside*.

At first that might not seem terribly useful; and on that particular approach, it might not be. However, note what happens when I'm just a little more careful with what I do with those paint strokes on the figure in the center. When I start painting inside that flesh color, I could come up with a tattoo on his head, purple lipstick, eyeliner, and even the shadow *inside* his ear. And perhaps the best part is none of these strokes cover my original outline; when I release my mouse/stylus, my original outline remains clean.

Also note the last example on the far right. Here I start drawing *outside* the outline (on his face, at least), and it acts as though I was drawing with Paint Behind selected. If you look closely at the outline on his chin and neck (on that same last drawing), you may notice that I tried to start drawing *inside* the black outline. The result? It covered the black outline with purple, but left the red color of his turtleneck collar intact.

The Pencil Tool

The Pencil tool has its advantages and disadvantages, but I'll start by saying the folks at Cartoon Network use it with good reason. Just remember, everyone has his own personal preference, and although mine is the Paintbrush tool for drawing vs. the Pencil tool, don't let my personal tool predispositions steer you away from something that might prove terribly useful.

The reason I prefer the Paintbrush tool (generally speaking) is that it affords me the line width variation you've heard me talk about so often. I guess it comes from that comment a comic book editor made long ago about my inking needing work. Once I started using a brush to ink my work, the "character" the line almost instantly inherited won me over. I just didn't care for drawings inked with a flat, uniform-width line.

However, there is a possible disadvantage to the Paintbrush tool. You may notice that when you enlarge your characters (by choosing the Free Transform option under the Modify menu at the top of your screen), in the instance of a drawing generally created for a medium shot that might now be needed for a close-up, lines painted with the Paintbrush tool get *thicker*... and rather quickly at that.

PENCIL TOOL

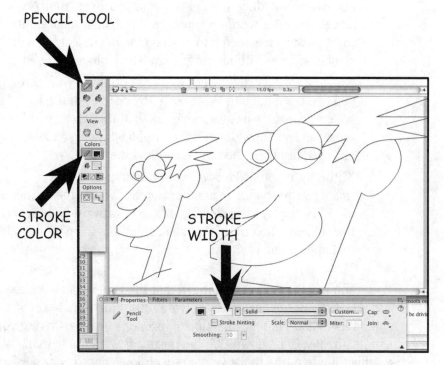

STROKE COLOR

STROKE WIDTH

The main advantage of the Pencil tool is that no matter how large you transform a drawing, the stroke width remains consistent on the character... it doesn't get thicker or thinner.

Here's where the advantage of the Pencil tool is quite helpful.

Try this:

1. Select the **Pencil** tool from your Toolbox.

2. Draw a character's outlined face on the Stage.

3. Select the drawing by dragging over the entire area with the Selection tool. If you miss an area, just drag over the entire drawing again.

4. At the top of your screen, go to the **Modify** menu and choose **Transform | Free Transform**. A small box should appear around your selected drawing.

5. Enlarge your drawing by clicking and dragging on one corner of your box in the direction desired. If you hold down Shift at the same time you drag, it will keep your transformation *proportional*. (In other words, a square will remain a square, rather than getting stretched into a tall rectangle, or a circle will remain a circle without getting squished into a flattened oval.)

6. Notice the Properties window at the bottom of your screen. If you don't see it, go to **Window | Properties** at the top of your screen to make sure it's active. Look at the stroke width setting there, and see how on both the original drawing and the enlarged drawing, the stroke width is the same.

7. Naturally, if you'd like a thicker or thinner line, you can adjust this by either typing in another number where the default width of "1" is displayed or clicking on the downward-pointing arrow that appears next to this number, and then dragging the slider that appears up or down.

You may have already noticed that the Pencil tool has a tendency to "smooth out" your drawings after you release the mouse/stylus. That may be kind of nice, or it may be driving you nuts already. Calm down! We can make adjustments to that. (Well, adjustments to the tool's smoothing options, not to your personal tendency to be so easily driven nuts. Yeah, yeah, I *know* we artists are temperamental, so don't worry. You're among friends here.)

Like the Paintbrush and Paintbucket tools, the Pencil tool also has different options you can modify. You have several choices as to which mode you choose to draw with: Straighten mode (the default), Smooth mode, and Ink mode. They work with varying levels of "cleaning up" your artwork as you draw.

Straighten mode will actually turn lines into perfectly horizontal, vertical, or diagonal lines... sometimes even turning your curves into *corners*. **Smooth** mode will work in a similar fashion, except it will allow your lines to have more curves. You may find that **Ink** mode is the closest to a "natural drawing" style.

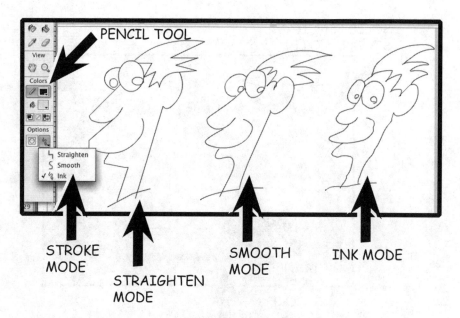

STROKE
MODE

STRAIGHTEN
MODE

SMOOTH
MODE

INK MODE

You can see that I drew basically the same character using the three different pencil stroke modes. Straighten mode, the default, has a tendency to clean up your drawing to the point of perfectly straight lines, leaving you with the ability only to draw a few curves. It did, however, turn the pupil and eyeball shapes I drew into nice circles and ovals. Smooth mode is probably the middle ground, granting you more curves with a few straight lines. Ink mode will probably be the "scribbly" artists' style of choice, because it keeps most of your original stroke intact, wiggles and all.

There is one more modification you can make to your drawing style with the Pencil tool: the stroke style. Up to this point, we've only used the solid line option, which is naturally the default setting for the stroke style. The stroke style modifier is located in the Properties window, right next to the stroke width modifier. Apart from the hairline and solid options, we can choose from a variety of dashed, dotted, and wiggly line strokes.

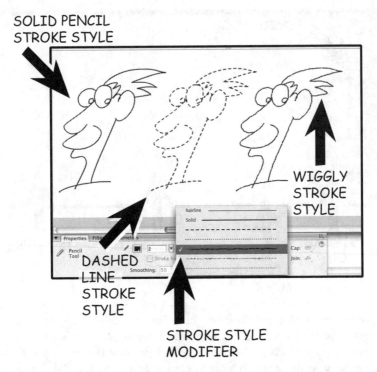

SOLID PENCIL STROKE STYLE

WIGGLY STROKE STYLE

DASHED LINE STROKE STYLE

STROKE STYLE MODIFIER

Here I have duplicated the same character and show him with several different stroke styles. In the far left example is the solid line, in the middle example is a dashed line, and perhaps the most interesting is the last example on the right, which is rendered with a "wiggly line" stroke style. There are several more, and I would encourage you to experiment with each at your leisure.

Object mode is one other thing I should mention in this section on drawing with the Pencil tool. As I mentioned earlier, Flash treats shapes drawn with different tools in different ways, as you might well guess.

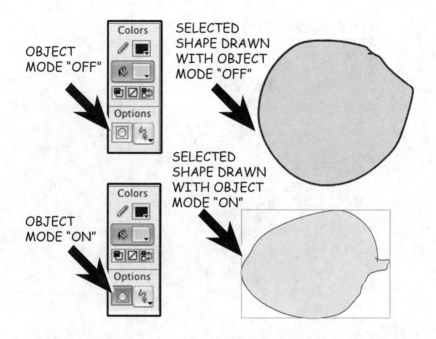

OBJECT
MODE "OFF"

Colors

SELECTED
SHAPE DRAWN
WITH OBJECT
MODE "OFF"

Options

SELECTED
SHAPE DRAWN
WITH OBJECT
MODE "ON"

OBJECT
MODE "ON"

Colors

Options

If I draw with the Pencil tool and Object mode is deselected, and then I try to select my object when done, the resulting shape will be treated as a *line*. What's more, if you try to select that line, you'll probably notice that it treats the shape not even as a full line, but sometimes as line *segments* (depending on how complicated your shape is).

That can get a bit tricky, especially when you're trying to select an entire line that you wish to modify.

Therefore, if you know you'll want your shape treated as an entire object, you've probably already guessed it's best to draw with the Object mode selected.

If I draw with the Pencil tool and Object mode is selected, and then I try to select my object when done, the shape will be treated as an object.

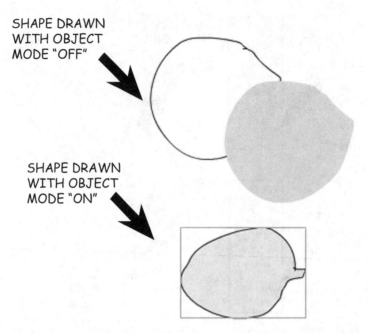

SHAPE DRAWN
WITH OBJECT
MODE "OFF"

SHAPE DRAWN
WITH OBJECT
MODE "ON"

When I selected the filled color in the shape drawn with Object mode off and tried to move my shape, it only wanted to move the fill color and not the outline, which stayed behind. If I wanted to select both shape and outline, I'd either have to drag over everything with one of the selection tools, or I'd have to select the fill color, hold down the Shift key, and then select the outline. Then I could move both.

Or better yet, if I knew this is what I wanted from the outset, I could have just drawn my shape with the Object mode on.

The Ink Bottle Tool

One last thing about drawing options with the Pencil tool, and I'll set you free to start filling your characters with the Paintbucket tool. If you are happily inking along and stumble across another ink style that strikes your fancy when you are almost done with inking (or so you thought), well, here's a possible solution.

1. Select the **Ink Bottle** tool in the Toolbox (see the figure in the next section).

2. Select the new stroke style you'd like to use in the Properties window.

3. Click on the pencil line you wish to modify.

As you'll see, with the click of a button your new stroke style has been applied, thanks to your friendly neighborhood Ink Bottle tool.

Now let's do some painting.

Gradients with the Paintbucket Tool

Okay, now that you've got some ideas about how outlines work in Flash, let's look at some different ways to go about filling those outlines with color. We've touched on it briefly, but there are actually a few choices at your fingertips about filling colors with the Paintbucket tool. By now, you've probably got the routine down:

1. Select your **Paintbucket** tool.

2. Select a fill color.

3. Now click on an enclosed area and try to fill it.

Naturally, that's generally the method you take when you're filling an area with flat colors. But you've probably also noticed that in your color palette, tucked away down toward the bottom, are some color gradients. A color gradient is a multicolor fill that results from the computer starting out with one color, such as red, and gradually working its way to another color, such as black. This might come in handy if you had a fire hydrant character that you wanted to start out red in the side nearest the sun and gradually fade to black on the side in the shade.

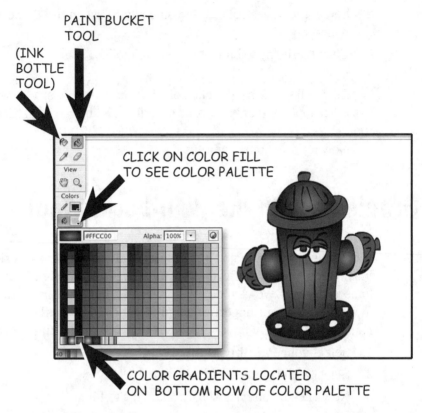

PAINTBUCKET
TOOL

(INK
BOTTLE
TOOL)

CLICK ON COLOR FILL
TO SEE COLOR PALETTE

COLOR GRADIENTS LOCATED
ON BOTTOM ROW OF COLOR PALETTE

I painted the fire hydrant with a red gradient that is pretty standard in the color palette, but you can easily modify the colors used, the number of colors, and the direction of your gradient.

There are actually two kinds of basic gradients that we're dealing with. There is the linear gradient, which moves either horizontally or vertically from one color to another in a standard straight line. Then there is the radial gradient, which starts out bright in the center, and fades to another color along the outer edges. If you look at the above illustration of the fire hydrant character, you'll see that I decided to go with the standard-issue radial gradient of red to black.

"That's fine and dandy," you might well say, "with a pretty standard red-to-black color gradient, but what if I want to come up with my own gradients? I've got characters that aren't necessarily going to be red-to-black fire hydrants and green-to-black bullfrogs, y'know."

(Wow! You're in *another* one of your moods again, aren't you?) All right, don't worry. I was thinking the same thing. My first major project with Flash 8 was a second Georgia Library PSA, and I wanted to fill a turtle character with a blue-to-green gradient. I'm sure you'll notice that no such gradient exists in the color palette, so let's make our own.

Creating Your Own Custom Gradient Fills

And you probably guessed it, there's more than one way to skin a gradient... or create one, or, well... something like that.

First, try this way:

1. Make sure your Color Mixer window is open. (If not, go to the Window menu and choose Color Mixer.)

2. Also make sure your Color Swatches window is open. (If not, yessir, go to the Window menu and choose Color Swatches.)

3. Click on the **Gradient Start Color** icon (see the following figure).

4. Pick a color for your gradient from the multicolor block you see in the center of the Color Mixer window by dragging until you find a color you like.

    The new color should appear in your gradient as soon as you release on the color of choice.

5. Do the same for the Gradient End Color, if you like.

6. When you're pleased with the new gradient color (and this is an important step), click and drag down on the **Add Swatch** icon you see on the upper-right corner of the Color Swatches window. This adds the new gradient swatch to your color palette so you can use it as many times as you like.

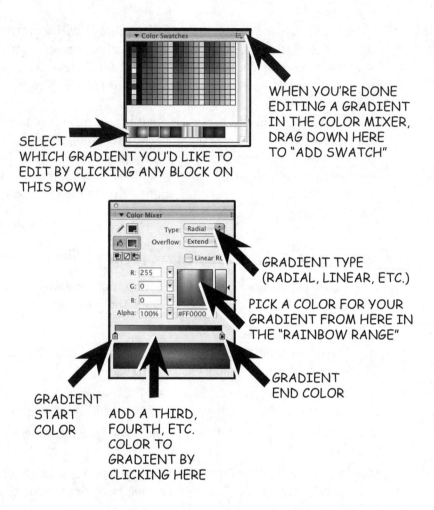

WHEN YOU'RE DONE
EDITING A GRADIENT
IN THE COLOR MIXER,
DRAG DOWN HERE
TO "ADD SWATCH"

SELECT
WHICH GRADIENT YOU'D LIKE TO
EDIT BY CLICKING ANY BLOCK ON
THIS ROW

GRADIENT TYPE
(RADIAL, LINEAR, ETC.)

PICK A COLOR FOR YOUR
GRADIENT FROM HERE IN
THE "RAINBOW RANGE"

GRADIENT
END COLOR

GRADIENT
START
COLOR

ADD A THIRD,
FOURTH, ETC.
COLOR TO
GRADIENT BY
CLICKING HERE

Also notice that you're not limited to two colors in a gradient. By hovering anywhere between Gradient Start Color and Gradient End Color, you'll see that your Selection tool gains a plus (+) sign behind it. That means you can add another gradient (a third, fourth, and so on) to your range of colors.

One other cool thing about gradients. If you look at the Alpha setting you can see that changing it from its default of 100% to anything less makes it start to become transparent. The lower you make that number, the more the grid in the preview area becomes visible. It's almost like the checkerboard pattern you may have seen in Photoshop that denotes a transparent background. We'll talk more about the Alpha setting later (when we discuss special effects), but just know that essentially it controls the level of opacity or transparency of the color or gradient you're painting with.

See where the ghost passes over the fire hydrant character? He's a see-through ghost! I've made a haunted hydrant!

NOTE THE APPEARANCE WHEN LOWERING ALPHA
CHANNEL BELOW 100%...
GIVES "GHOST" EFFECT

CLICK AND DRAG
YOUR ALPHA CHANNEL
DOWN TO CREATE
TRANSPARENCY

Modifying Gradient Direction and Distribution

Now we're down to one last thing I think you really need to know about painting your characters with gradients. Sure, you can change your colors and distribution in the Color Mixer, but I dunno... It all seems to be a little constricted.

Wouldn't it be great if we actually had the freedom to *transform* those gradients, even after we've applied them to our characters?

Would you faint if I told you... there *is* a way?

(Oh dear, someone help that lady in the front row... I think she *has* fainted. That's weird; I'd think she would've expected it. I mean, I *did* put a bold heading at the beginning of this section precisely for those excitable types.)

SELECT THE GRADIENT
TRANSFORM TOOL

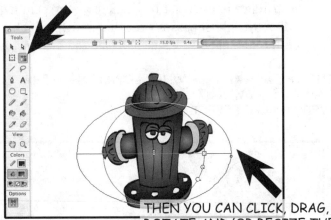

THEN YOU CAN CLICK, DRAG,
ROTATE AND/OR RESIZE THE
DISTRIBUTION OF YOUR GRADIENT
DIRECTLY ON THE STAGE

All you have to do is:

1. Select the area of gradient fill on your character you wish to modify.

2. Select the **Gradient Transform** tool from the Toolbox.

3. Click and drag on your artwork to rotate, resize, and/or scale the distribution of the gradient to your liking.

Drawing in Flash with Onion Skin

One of the last subjects I want to cover in this chapter is directed toward the growing population of Wacom tablet owners who draw directly in Flash. As I mentioned, there are those of us who are hesitant to give up paper altogether (I'm one of them), but Flash makes it just so darn easy, even those dwindling few of us have to admit it saves a lot of trees. (Well, actually, most paper these days has a high content of cotton fiber, the better quality of paper you... oh, never mind.) And that means it also saves us from buying quite so *much* paper.

As a matter of fact, speaking for myself, I've arrived at a happy halfway point, of sorts. I still like doing my thumbnails, rough sketches, character conceptual work, and even my key drawings on good ol' animation paper. But when it comes to inbetweens, breakdowns, and even some of my extreme drawings (contact positions, you may recall from our earlier discussion), it's hard to beat Flash's Onion Skin option for cutting down not only on paper consumption, but the time it takes to clean up, ink, and scan those drawings. Especially if you do those drawings directly in Flash.

Yeah, this onion skinning technique is the next best thing to a light table. Again, I hate to admit it, but since I discovered this fancy little deal in Flash, my "real-world" light table has been collecting dust lately.

Try this technique out for yourself and see what I mean:

1. Create a blank movie in Flash.

2. In your first frame, draw a character of your choice. I drew Mr. Smileyface.

3. Go to the **Insert** menu and choose **Timeline | Blank Keyframe**.

4. Click on the Onion Skin icon in the Timeline (see the following illustration).

5. Your previous drawing (in Frame 1, for example) becomes transparent so you can use it as a guide to trace your second drawing.

CLICK ON ONION SKIN
SO YOU CAN "TRACE" OVER
PREVIOUS DRAWINGS

I will also mention that you have two more choices right after Onion Skin: Onion Skin Outlines and Edit Multiple Frames. **Onion Skin Outlines** performs a similar function as Onion Skin, but instead of a clear transparency of your character, you get only colored outlines. You can even change the color of your outlines by right-clicking on the layer (or Ctrl-clicking, if you don't have a right mouse button), and going down to Properties, then choosing a color that is darker or more easily visible. If you feel more comfortable with this method, feel free to experiment with it. Personally, I find it easier to see the previous drawing using the plain ol' Onion Skin option as though I'm viewing the art through a standard light table.

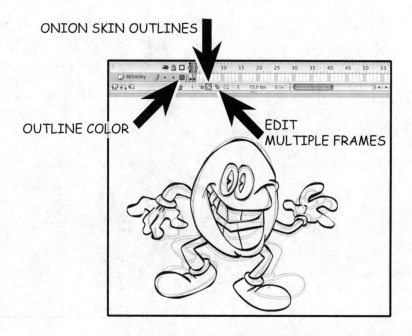

ONION SKIN OUTLINES

OUTLINE COLOR

EDIT MULTIPLE FRAMES

Lastly, you have an **Edit Multiple Frames** option, which I reserve for the bravest of the brave. I can barely focus on one thing at a time, so I don't risk this one very often... if at all. (Again, don't let my personal ruts prevent you from exploring and carving out your own new ruts.) This option enables you to edit all frames between the onion skin markers. Onion skinning normally allows you to edit only your current frame.

On this same subject though is a far more useful option you may select, located right next to the Edit Multiple Frames option, and that's **Modify Onion Markers**. With this, you can extend or reduce the number of frames/drawings that you're viewing at any given time. It's almost like having an adjustable light table, so to speak. The larger the number of frames, the brighter the light, which allows you to see through more drawings. And the fewer frames, the dimmer the light, and therefore the fewer drawings you can see through.

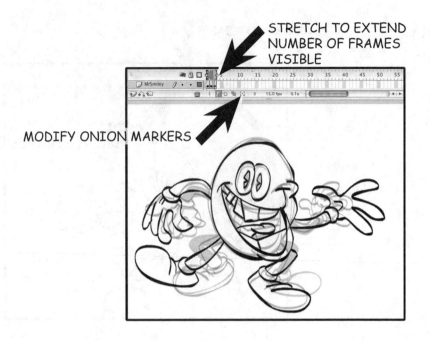

STRETCH TO EXTEND
NUMBER OF FRAMES
VISIBLE

MODIFY ONION MARKERS

Necktie Fashions, Talking Bears, and Character Layers

You're certainly welcome to redraw every detail of your character anew for every new frame, but did you ever think it was peculiar that every single Hanna-Barbera character, from forest ranger to bipedal national forest bear cub, or cotton candy-colored cougar to blueberry basset hound wore a *necktie*? I'll let you in on a little secret: It was more than a fashion statement. It was a time-saving device.

That's right... a budget issue.

If Yogi and Scooby were standing still, and only their heads were moving from side to side or just their mouths were moving, the heads or moving bits would be on a different cel level. In our case, moving objects would be located on a different Flash Timeline layer from the objects or body parts standing still.

The collar, or necktie, or ascot or whatever the character is wearing simply covers up that separation between the shoulders and neck, which are on separate animation cel levels.

Naturally, that's one of the first things we want to use to our advantage.

(To be perfectly blunt, it looks better if even "static parts" are *traced back*, or retraced, when they maintain a constant position. A subtle line wiggle retains that "illusion of life" even when a character is standing still. But to be fair, even the Disney folks will to a degree use this technique, so if it's okay for the Mouse, it's okay for us.)

Here's what I would do:

1a. Draw your character's static body portions on one layer to begin with.

   or

1b. Select and cut the necessary bits that will move, like the head.

2. Create a new layer by clicking on the **Insert New Layer** icon below the Timeline.

3. Name your new layer something like **Head.**

4. Go to the **Edit** menu and choose **Paste in Place**. This should paste your character's head in the exact spot that you cut it from, but just on a different layer. (Naturally, which layer it pastes into depends on which layer you had selected when you told it to Paste in Place.)

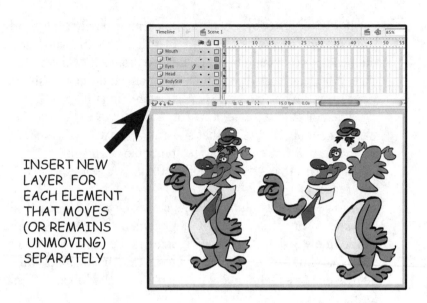

INSERT NEW
LAYER FOR
EACH ELEMENT
THAT MOVES
(OR REMAINS
UNMOVING)
SEPARATELY

Now, on the parts that don't move, let's extend those a few frames.

In this character's example, the most obvious part that isn't moving in this shot is his body layer, which contains his belly and chest, legs, tail, and left arm, which is jutting out at his side. None of these items move in this full shot, so I'll simply extend the static body cel from Frame 1 to Frame 10.

Here's how I'll do that:

1. I'll click in Frame 10 of the BodyStill layer (or however many frames you wish to extend your nonmoving part, or *hold cel*, as it's often referred to in the animation industry).

2. I'll hit F5 on my keyboard, which is the shortcut for Insert Frame. (Sure, you could just as easily go up to the Insert menu and choose Timeline | Frame, but there it tells you the short-cut is F5 anyway, so no, actually I don't guess that *was* just as easy, was it?)

CLICK IN THE NUMBER
OF THE FRAME YOU WISH
TO EXTEND THE "HOLD
CEL," LIKE FRAME 10.
THEN HIT F5 TO "INSERT
FRAMES" THERE.

Uh-oh! I don't know how it happened for you, but suddenly my character's head (not to mention some other vital bits) just disappeared! Not to worry; we've just got to repeat these same steps for each layer. Until we do that, his other features disappear after Frame 1. In my case, I have to insert frames for his tie, eyes, head, and arm layers.

Do notice now that I did *not* extend the frames for his mouth. Again, don't worry. We'll tackle that once you've extended the frames for his nonmoving parts, or hold cels.

DON'T EXTEND THE
MOUTH LAYER JUST YET!

YOU CAN EXTEND
MULTIPLE LAYERS AT
A TIME BY CLICKING ON
THE FIRST LAYER YOU
WISH TO EXTEND, THEN
DRAGGING DOWN TO THE
LAST LAYER. THEN HIT
F5 TO "INSERT FRAMES."

Go ahead and extend those cels now... for everything *except* that mouth layer. Done? Good. Let's move on to moving that mouth.

Mark's Favorite Shortcut: Option-Drag

I'm sure you're probably asking yourself about that heading, "What is *Option-drag*, and why is it Mark's favorite shortcut?"

I'm glad you asked that slightly predictable question. Sometimes, it's easy enough to simply go to Flash's menu bar and select Insert | Timeline | Blank Keyframe. But anybody can do that, right? And we're not just *anybody*... we're aspiring animators, right?

As you may well know, selecting something, say a cel with some artwork in it, then Option-dragging it to another position makes a *copy* of that frame, or art, or whatever, and then you can modify that resulting frame as you like.

Here's how:

1. First, I zoom in on the face so I can get a better look at this mouth I'm about to modify (use the Zoom tool to zoom in or zoom out, or better yet, hit Cmd++ or Cmd+– on the Mac; Ctrl++ or Ctrl+– on the PC).

2. Next (and this part is optional but helpful), I click on the Outline button for each layer I'm not immediately concerned with (all but the Mouth layer). This makes it easier to focus on one thing at a time.

3. I lock each layer I'm not immediately concerned with by clicking in the Padlock column of each layer (again, all but the Mouth layer). That way I can't accidentally select the wrong layer and alter it.

4. With these precautions in place, I click on the cel I want to copy, and then Option-drag it into its new position; in this case, that copied position is to Frame 2 in the same Mouth layer.

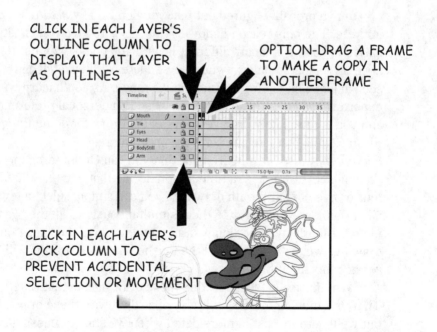

CLICK IN EACH LAYER'S OUTLINE COLUMN TO DISPLAY THAT LAYER AS OUTLINES

OPTION-DRAG A FRAME TO MAKE A COPY IN ANOTHER FRAME

CLICK IN EACH LAYER'S LOCK COLUMN TO PREVENT ACCIDENTAL SELECTION OR MOVEMENT

Now you'll quickly understand why I decided to lock those layers and display them as outlines.

1. Make sure you're in Frame 2 of the Mouth layer.

2. Select the Lasso tool and draw a line around the mouth area, but do not select the nose.

3. Delete everything in the Mouth layer *except* the nose. You should have a nose and perhaps a bit of the character's upper lip left.

4. Turn on Onion Skin (if it's not already).

5. Option-drag that nose into each of the remaining eight frames (or however many frames you like).

6. Starting in Frame 2 (and using the onion skin as a guide), draw the mouth in a different position.

7. Keep drawing the mouth in different positions for each of the remaining frames, using the nose as a starting point.

You've probably figured out that you don't really *need* that nose in there. The only reason I showed you this is to give you an alternative to having so many different layers. You could even put the nose on a separate layer if you like, and later let it stretch and squash just a bit as the character's lips move. As you'll learn with experience, a lot of these things are based on personal preference, and you'll quite likely discover ways of your own for doing things in Flash... well, just like any software program, really.

You may also have figured out that you can Option-drag more than one cel or frame at a time. If you decide that you like the first four or five of your mouth drawings, you can simply select a few or all of them, and Option-drag them simultaneously to fill the "gaps" in your Mouth layer, or simply drag them on top of the "nose-only" drawings we just created, and the finished mouth drawings will replace the "mouthless noses."

We're basically just repeating those drawings, in that case. There's a much more efficient way of dealing with these drawings, but we'll get into that in more detail when we start discussing the management of symbols and scenes in the next chapter.

We're just playing for now, and will learn those more efficient techniques soon enough.

If you'd like to get a preview of what the finished animation will look like, you can just drag the playback head back and forth. It gives the same effect as animators flipping their pages (or rolling them, if you're one of those aforementioned "bottom-peggers" like myself).

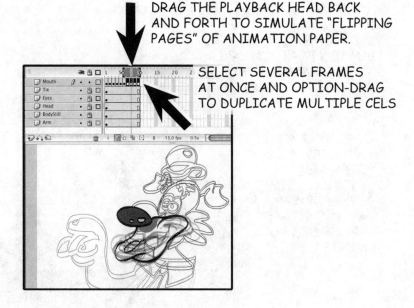

DRAG THE PLAYBACK HEAD BACK AND FORTH TO SIMULATE "FLIPPING PAGES" OF ANIMATION PAPER.

SELECT SEVERAL FRAMES AT ONCE AND OPTION-DRAG TO DUPLICATE MULTIPLE CELS

Playing Your Animation

You've now got some basic movement on your character, but before you play your movie to check out that movement, don't forget a couple of things. First of all, make sure you switch off the Outline mode before you play back your movie by clicking in each one of the layer columns, underneath the Outline button. That way you can get the full effect in full color.

Next, make sure you switch off the Onion Skin mode (at the bottom of the Timeline) so you can get a better preview of what the final animation will look like.

Now let's play your movie and see how it looks so far.

To play your movie, hit Return on your Mac keyboard or Enter if you're on the PC.

Your movie should play through once. If you'd like to have a little more control over your movie, you can open the Control window by going to the Window menu and choosing Toolbar | Controller. That brings up a VCR-type controller with options to Stop, Rewind/Go to First Frame, Step Back (one frame), Play, Step Forward (one frame), and Go to Last Frame.

CLICK BACK ON THE OUTLINE
BUTTON FOR EACH LAYER
TO RETURN ARTWORK
TO NORMAL BEFORE PLAYBACK.

CLICK ON THE
ONION SKIN OPTION
TO DEACTIVATE IT
BEFORE PLAYBACK.

THE CONTROLLER
WINDOW WILL
STOP, REWIND,
STEP BACK, PLAY,
STEP FORWARD,
AND GO TO LAST
FRAME OF YOUR
MOVIE.

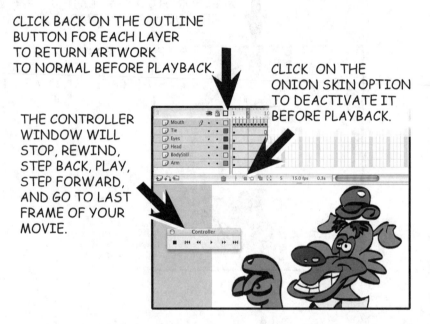

I'm sure you'll want to watch and rewatch your movie a few times to make sure the movement looks right. That's normal! It's a lotta work, but it pays off unlike any other art form.

All right, now you should have a pretty good grasp of creating characters and getting some basic movement on those characters.

But there's more to be learned, believe it or not. In order to understand how a moving character interacts with other elements of the movie, like backgrounds, sounds, and even other characters, we need to start talking about the management of symbols and scenes. Fortunately, that's the subject of our very next chapter.

Chapter 8

Managing Symbols and Scenes

Sezquatch, Thurman, and Deadbeat
© Mark S. Smith/MarkToonery.com

Why Should I Care about Symbols?

At first, as with all the other features of any unfamiliar software program, I was mildly annoyed by the term itself — "symbol." Good grief! I exclaimed to myself. These people are Macromedia, the same ones who created Director, aren't they? Why not just call them Castmembers (their counterparts in Director, naturally), and be done with it?

Once I got past my initial petty annoyance (as usual), I found out that these symbols can be rather useful. Once you've turned a piece of artwork into a symbol, it's resizable, distortable, and, perhaps most importantly of all, *recyclable*.

Artwork © Mark S. Smith/MarkToonery.com

Remember how you'd always see that same stock footage of Scoob and the gang running from the monster in every single episode? It was obviously the same animation cycle of the Great Dane and his pals, but they just switched out the background every episode (a spooky house vs. a spooky museum vs. a spooky forest, etc.) and then switch out the monster chasing them (a creepy Dracula character vs. a creepy Frankenstein monster vs. a creepy werewolf, etc.). Then they'd use the same close-up of Fred as he'd explain to the group how they were about to split up, and how he and Daphne would inevitably end up on the same "team." (*Ahem.*) You may or may not have noticed this act of recycling artwork (not to mention plot devices) as a kid, but now that we're trying to bring in a cartoon on or under budget, we need to pay special attention.

It was because they could use tricks like this that Joe Hanna and Bill Barbera were able to put animators back to work after most of the major studios' animation divisions had closed down (MGM, Warner Bros., Walter Lantz, and even Disney's shorts department).

A theatrical Tom & Jerry "Golden Age" six-minute short might cost $50,000 to make, while an entire half-hour episode of *Ruff & Reddy* cost only $2,800 to produce.

That's thanks to the act of (to quote the wise words of a certain McDuck), "Work[ing] smarter, not harder."

The world of animation is changing. It's not like the old days. You don't need to have a whole studio to produce animation anymore. The technology has brought the cost down to the point so that anyone with a scanner and/or a digitizing tablet and a computer with a DVD burner can make animation.

Yep, one person… one person with knowledge and talent.

And about $3,500 doesn't hurt…

What do I mean by that?

I paid about $2,000 for my G4 iMac (which I'm still using four years later), maybe $125 for my all-in-one HP printer-scanner-copier (which saves on money and desk space), about $420 for my 9 x 12 Wacom digitizing tablet (which came with a free copy of Adobe Photoshop's kid brother), and of course, my copy of Flash 8. Naturally, the cost of that depends on where you buy it, and whether you're able to use a student/educator discount to legally obtain a copy. (There are so many reasons I'm glad to be a teacher, and this is one of them!)

Naturally, we're going to assume you've got most of the items on this digital grocery list (or it's unlikely you would have made it this far, anyway), so we'll continue.

Now, before that irksome Ol' Tangent Man gets me any further off the subject (as usual), let's get back to business.

Okay, So What Is a Symbol, and How Do I Create One?

Oddly enough, that's two questions that are rolled into one answer... sort of. A Flash symbol is anything... any artwork that you've imported (JPG, PICT, etc.) into Flash, artwork you've created directly inside Flash, or sound files that you've imported into Flash. Any of these things that you've told Flash to make into a symbol.

In order to make a symbol, you have to designate which part of your artwork on the Stage you want included in that symbol. You can select the art either by drawing a rectangle around it with the Selection tool, or you can draw a freehand shape around more intricate areas with the Lasso tool.

To make a piece of artwork a symbol:

1. Draw something on the Stage. It could be a circle, a square, a pair of googly eyes, whatever.

2. Select the item you've just created. You can either use the Selection tool and draw a square around the item, or draw a freehand shape around it with the Lasso selection tool (like I did in the previous figure). Use whichever tool you prefer.

3. With the item selected, choose **Modify | Convert to Symbol**. (Or better yet, go ahead and learn the shortcut: F8.)

Once you've selected your artwork, go to Modify | Convert to Symbol, or simply hit F8, the shortcut.

Transforming a Symbol

First, let's just try a few things to modify that one symbol. If you're on a PC or if you have a Mac with a right-click button, then, you guessed it, right-click on the symbol that you created. If you don't have a right-click on your Mac, then Ctrl-click on it.

When you right-click (on a PC) or Ctrl-click (on the Mac) on a symbol, the Free Transform option appears, which enables you to make numerous alterations to your artwork without having to redraw simple transformations (like flip, rotate, etc.) that would otherwise be unnecessarily time-consuming. Better yet, it takes Flash less effort and memory (and in turn, download time) to use this approach.

First of all, once you select the Free Transform option, as directed above, your symbol will be surrounded by a box; and to be precise, a box with a circle in the center. That central circle is the center point around which all your transformations will take place.

If you can imagine sticking a thumbtack in a piece of artwork on a bulletin board, and then spinning it around that tack, you've got a pretty good idea how it works.

You have three choices when you transform artwork in this way, but there are a couple more (and don't worry, we'll get to that shortly). The main three transformations you can make by right-clicking (PC)/Ctrl-clicking (Mac) are:

■ Rotate

■ Resize

■ Skew

When you hover the cursor over a particular edge of a selected symbol (when it's highlighted, and therefore in "Free Transform mode"), the cursor arrow changes shape. When the cursor shape is a **circular arrow**, that means if you were to click and drag you would rotate the symbol. When it becomes a **diagonal arrow**, that means your click and drag will scale the symbol larger or smaller, depending on which direction you drag. An outward drag makes it larger, and an inward drag smaller. The same thing happens with the vertical or horizontal arrows, only now the scale is constricted to one axis at a time (x or y, horizontal or vertical). Finally, a **double arrow** signifies that you can skew the artwork. Skewing means that a square can become a parallelogram, for instance. To place that in terms that might prove more useful to an animator, let's say you want a character to screech to a halt. You could skew the character to the right just a bit to give the impression that he is leaning forward a bit before stopping altogether. If this is the case, you might want to make sure that your center point or registration point is located at the base of the character's feet.

Remember, if you need to change the registration point of a symbol, you can do that at any time by using the Free Transform tool, which is just below the Selection tool. Make sure your symbol is selected, then click on the Free Transform tool and drag that empty circle from its old location (most likely the center of your

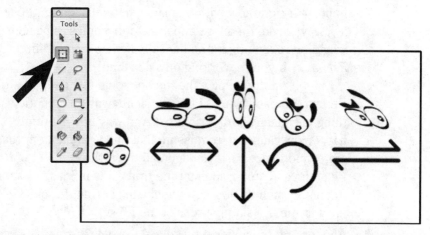

At the far left is the original "google-eye" symbol. If you select it and right-click (PC) or Ctrl-click (Mac), then hover over different corners of the selected artwork, your cursor arrow will change to any of the transform arrows, depending on your location. Starting below the second pair of eyes from the left, the horizontal double arrow will enable you to stretch the selected symbol horizontally. You've probably already guessed that the vertical arrow therefore stretches symbols vertically. The circular arrow will rotate a symbol, and the double arrow at the far right will skew artwork. This last one might be particularly handy if you have a character's high-speed chase come to a screeching halt.

symbol) to its new location (the base of your character's feet, for instance).

The other methods of transforming art are accessed from the Modify | Transform menu option: Flip Horizontal and Flip Vertical. And quite useful options they are.

Let's play around with an animation that makes use of these options.

1. Start by placing the "google-eye" symbol in the center of the Stage. (You should have created this in the previous section.)

2. To keep things neat (or better yet, organized), let's rename our Layer 1 to **Google-eyes**.

    Remember, to rename a layer, you just double-click on it to highlight the name. Then you can simply type in the new name (while it's still highlighted), and that will immediately replace the old name (Layer 1, most likely). This may not seem so important right now with one layer, but believe me, the more layers you add, the more important it becomes to be able to find what you're looking for on logically named, easy-to-find layers. *Especially* if you're working on a deadline!

    If you wanted to play the movie, you'd just need to hit Return (Mac) or Enter (PC), but right away you'd notice something peculiar. *Nothing* happens! And why not? Nothing happens because we're missing that one vital element that separates motionless art from animated art: the element of *time*. Like film and video, adding time translates in Flash to adding frames. Hopefully you remember the shortcut for quickly adding a frame is a simple press of the F5 key.

3. And for that to happen, you select one of the "frameless cells" in your Google-eyes layer. (Let's select Frame 30, because that's one second of video.) Now, if you haven't already, press the **F5** key. That should extend your movie to 30 frames.

Click in the empty Frame 30 and hit F5. That will insert a
frame at 30, which then extends your Google-eyes
symbol from Frame 1 to Frame 30. Note how it begins
with a black dot in Frame 1 and continues along a gray
highlighted line to an empty vertical rectangle denoting
the last frame.

Now we can start animating.

Naturally, if you were to hit Return even now (on the Mac, or
Enter on the PC), sure enough, you'd see your Time Marker (or
playback head, as I generally call it) go puttering forward, but still
nothing appears to happen. We don't have that *second* vital ingredient of animation going for us just yet.

Although we have time, it still looks as though the eyes are sitting still, like a rock. Not terribly interesting.

We may have time, but we now need *change*. That's what makes
animation. Notice I didn't say *good* animation. Change over time
with sound judgment... now *that's* what makes good animation.

Oddly enough, that sound judgment comes... *with* time. (And
generally, lots of that, when accompanied by years of practice and
study. But before ol' Tangent Man takes over once again, let's continue with our Google-eye experiment.)

4. Click in Frame 10 of your Google-eyes layer. From the menu
    bar, choose **Insert | Timeline | Keyframe.**

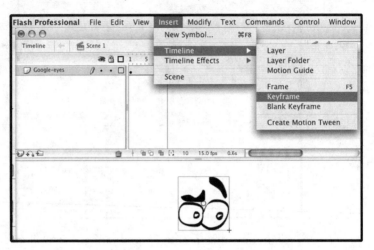

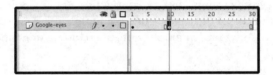

Inserting a keyframe allows change to take place within a
layer, either by changing out artwork or symbols frame by
frame or by modifying a single symbol over a series of frames,
as we'll discuss later in the section on tweening.

Note how (as shown in the above figure) once you insert a
keyframe, what was once an unbroken line of gray stretching from
Frame 1 to Frame 30 is now broken at Frame 10. On Frame 9,
you'll see that vertical rectangle denoting a keyframe sequence has
ended. A new sequence begins at Frame 10, noted by the dark circle, and stretches to Frame 30, which ends with its own vertical
rectangle.

That means that the Google-eyes symbol starts at keyframe 1
and stays in place through Frame 9. Something possibly happens
(which we're about to define) at Frame 10 and lasts until Frame 30.

Now, let's do something to animate that symbol.

5. Go to Frame 10 and click on it. Your Google-eyes symbol in Frame 10 is selected. Now go to **Modify | Transform | Flip Horizontal**.

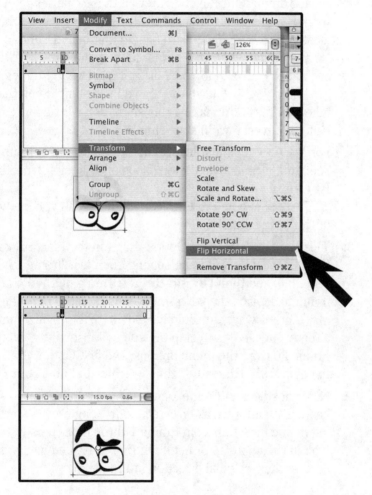

When you flip your artwork horizontally as shown (top), you'll see the change immediately (bottom). In this case, a pair of eyes that suspiciously looked to our right now darts to gaze in the opposite direction. Of course, in this case, the eyebrows also become a mirror image of their former selves; but for now, that's not much of an issue.

6. Okay, now click back in Frame 1 and press **Return** or **Enter.** What happens? If all goes as directed, the eyes look in one direction until Frame 9, and then immediately dart to look in the opposite direction.

    It's animation! Finally! After all these chapters, your artwork is *moving*! It may not be full-fledged magic yet, but at least you're learning how to handle that magic wand.

    If you like, you can also just move your Time Marker/playback head back and forth by dragging between Frames 9 and 10.

    When you've had all the fun you can stand doing that, let's take a step toward making this animation a little more complex. But don't worry, we'll start simple.

7. For starters, let's just insert another keyframe in Frame 20 by selecting Frame 20 and then choosing **Insert | Timeline | Keyframe.**

    Instead of going to Flip Horizontal, which you know how to do, let's try something new.

8. This time, let's try that Option-drag (on the Mac; Alt-drag on the PC) trick I seem to be so fond of. Select Frame 1 in the Timeline, and then **Option-drag** (Alt-drag on the PC) that frame to replace the keyframe we just created in Frame 20.

    Another way you could have done that (which you may have already guessed) is to skip the stage of inserting a keyframe at Frame 20 from the menu options, and just Option-drag/Alt-drag to begin with. Honestly, I think it's nice to know your options.

9. Now click back in Frame 1 and play your animation to see what happens. If all went as directed, your Google-eyes started looking in one direction from Frame 1 through 9, then darted to look in the opposite direction in Frame 10, and finally darted back to their original direction in Frame 20.

Simple animation, surely, but the thing is we're giving the illusion of movement using only *one* symbol instead of two. That means half the drawing work, half the painting time (if you decide to color the eyes, maybe a nice lurid yellow), and half the download time for those of you playing these cartoons over the web. Remember, we need to be using this recycling issue to our advantage, but as always, with judgment.

You've probably already figured that although we may be amused by this simple animation of eyes darting back and forth, it will grow old with our viewer just as quickly as it has with us. Something more interesting needs to happen to keep our viewer watching.

Let's take that slightly more complex step I hinted toward earlier.

10. We'll start by adding another layer. Click on the **Insert Layer** icon on the lower-left corner of your Timeline. Double-click on the new layer name (Layer 2, most likely) and rename it to read **Pupils**.

    Note I said Pupils with an *s*, but we're going to start off by making one symbol we'll double into two. I want to show you the advantage, once again, of minimizing the number of symbols you'll need, and we can't start out more simply than by using one pupil symbol to make two pupils onstage.

11. Double-click on your Google-eyes symbol on the Stage, which should take you into that symbol's Timeline. The reason we do that is so we can edit the symbol. You can't simply edit artwork that has been converted to a symbol on the Stage. You may have already noticed if you click on it once, it gets that bluish square around it, and any attempt to draw on it will only result in a drawing that's not attached to the symbol. (This can be an advantage or a disadvantage. In this case, since we want to remove the pupils from the Google-eyes symbol, and it won't allow us to do that on the Stage, that's something of a disadvantage. However, if we double-click (rather than single-click), we go into the symbol's Timeline, as mentioned.)

Now follow these steps:

12. Select one of the pupils and delete it (either one).

13. Select the remaining pupil and convert it to a symbol by **right-clicking** (PC) or **Ctrl-clicking** (Mac) and dragging down to **Convert to Symbol** (as shown in the above figure).

14. When prompted to name the symbol, type **Pupil-1**.

15. Once you see the Pupil-1 symbol appear in your Library, delete your Pupil-1 symbol from the Stage. (If you don't see your Library window open, go to Window | Library to open it, or press Cmd+L on the Mac or Ctrl+L on the PC.) Now you should see a pair of google-eyes with no pupils on the Stage, like the Lil' Orphan Annie character!

Symbol Timeline vs. Movie Timeline. Double-clicking on a symbol takes you into that symbol's Timeline. You can return to the Movie Timeline by clicking on the Scene icon beside the Symbol Timeline icon at the top of your menu bar.

All righty. Don't bother trying to put the Pupil-1 symbol on the Stage, at least not in your symbol Timeline, yet. Remember, we're within the Google-eyes symbol's Timeline, not the *main* Timeline of the movie. This may seem a bit confusing at first, and trust me, it took some serious getting used to. It comes in somewhat handy, as you'll hopefully soon agree.

16. Click back on your Scene 1 Timeline at the top of the screen (see the figure above), which will take you back into the main Timeline of your movie.

17. Click on your Pupils layer to make sure it's active. (If you like, for safety, you can click the Padlock column of your Google-eyes layer to make it temporarily inactive. That way you can't draw on that layer or modify it accidentally.)

18. Drag one Pupil-1 symbol from your Library onto the Stage, over the empty Google-eyes symbol. Center the pupil in the white of either eye.

19. Drag another Pupil-1 symbol from your Library onto the Stage (in the same layer) on top of the remaining empty eye. Again, center that pupil so it's also in the white of the second eye.

Don't forget that at any time you can lock a layer by simply clicking in the Padlock column of that layer. Using this feature, you can prevent accidentally drawing on or editing that particular layer.

20. Click in the first frame of that Pupils layer to select it. (Both pupils should highlight with blue squares around them.)

21. Go to **Insert | Timeline | Create Motion Tween**.

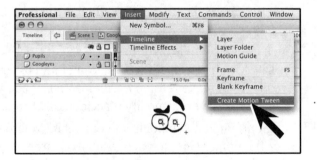

At first, you may not notice much of a change. The only visible change you'll probably notice is that the gray line highlighting your Pupils layer from Frame 1 to Frame 30 now has a dotted line running throughout. That's not much just yet. In fact, if you were to play your movie, you might be slightly concerned that *nothing happens*.

Well, nothing just yet.

That dotted line is just a visual note that although a Motion Tween keyframe has indeed been placed there, it's what would be called a *hold cel* in traditional animation. For instance, it might be like Yogi's body (from the necktie down, anyway) for 90% of a scene… unmoving.

Now let's say we want to change that. After all, we do want change, because that's what animation is all about!

22. Click in Frame 10 of your Pupils Timeline.

23. Click on your Pupils symbol onstage, and drag it anywhere else, but preferably to the outer edge of the eye.

As soon as you insert a Motion Tween at the beginning of a layer in the Timeline, once you change position, size, etc., of any frame after that, Flash automatically assumes you want it to animate, and replaces the dotted line (indicating a motionless "hold cel" or frame) with a directional arrow to indicate the presence of the Motion Tween.

See what happened? Your dotted line got replaced by the directional arrow! As long as there is a difference of position, rotation, size, etc., between those two frames, you've suddenly got animation!

Play it back and see!

Once you've had all the thrills you can stand from watching that repeatedly, let's add some more motion keyframes.

24. Click in Frame 20 and then on the eyes.

25. Move the eyes somewhere else, maybe in the opposite direction.

26. Click in Frame 25, and then on the eyes.

27. Move the eyes somewhere else. Maybe move them looking directly down.

Play it back again. Maybe we'd like to get the eyes looking exactly in the same direction as when they started. Or we might decide to have them loop, in which case they need to be in the exact position as when they started on Frame 1.

Remember that little Option-drag/Alt-drag trick I like so much? Let's use it now.

28. Click on Frame 1 of the Pupils layer.

29. Option-drag that keyframe all the way to Frame 30.

Now play it back again and see what happens. The eyes dart back and forth, and then finally back to the direction from which they started.

And here's where we need to start asking ourselves, "Now is that *really* how a pair of eyes might look around a room?"

The answer is no... or at best, probably not. Drunk eyes might lazily scan the room without pausing (or attempting) to focus (however briefly) on an item before continuing the search. If we were really darting our eyes around the room, searching for something, chances are our eyes would dart in one direction, pause for a fractional second in that direction, and then dart in another, pause, and so on.

Again, we'll go back to Option-drag/Ctrl-drag:

30. Click on Frame 1 and Option-drag to Frame 5.

31. Click on Frame 10 and Option-drag to Frame 15.

32. Click on Frame 20 and Option-drag to Frame 22.

By selecting keyframes in your Timeline and Option-dragging, you can duplicate keyframes and build pauses in your action, or even simple cycles, like eyes darting around a room.

Play that back and see if that's not a little more convincing. I think you'll agree it is.

It always goes back to drawing on what I call the *thinking* aspect of animation. Don't let the computer do your thinking for you. It simply can't. That's *your* job.

We're supposed to be observant. If you want to mimic life, you have to study life. Watch people in their little everyday actions like fumbling in their pocket for change or trying to find the right key on a keychain to open the car door. Where do their eyes go? When they can't find what they're looking for, do they roll their eyes in frustration? Do they clench their fists or drum their fingers? Watching people's everyday habits is a fascinating study.

And more importantly, it's essential to producing convincing, or at least *believable*, animation.

Rotating or Resizing a Symbol

It doesn't take a whole lot of imagination to figure out that once you can reposition a symbol using the tween capabilities of Flash, you can use that same principle for rotating and resizing.

To more fully appreciate these capabilities, we'll start with rotation. First, though, to help this demonstration make more sense, I've drawn a man's body on a new layer I called "Dude."

1. Create a new layer and name it **Dude**. (Or something like it.)

2. Draw a simple character like the one you see in the following figure on that layer.

Note:

Leave out the eyes (we've already got a pair ready, remember?) and don't draw a mouth yet. That will come later. Also, don't give him any arms *just* yet. That's our next step.

Another Quick Note:

If you haven't added color to your Google-eyes symbol, now would be a good time to do so. If you don't, his eyes will naturally appear transparent. I would suggest white, a very light blue, or even yellow if you want to make him look shady, sick, or irrational. (Reminder: To edit the appearance of a symbol or its artwork, make sure you double-click it so you can edit it within its Symbol Timeline... the only place you can edit it!)

If all is well so far, you can continue:

3. Create a new layer and call it **Arm**.

4. With the new layer selected, draw an arm. (Ha! I'll bet you didn't see that one coming, huh?)

5. Select the arm, right-click (PC) or Ctrl-click (Mac), and choose **Convert to Symbol**.

6. If you haven't already, move the arm into place over the Dude.

7. Check to make sure your layers are set up similar to the ones shown in the following illustration.

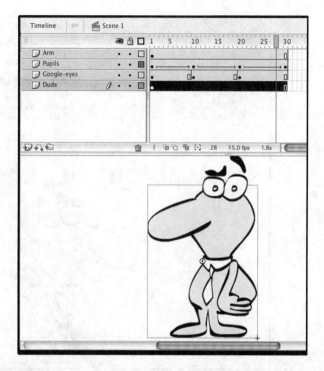

As you've no doubt guessed already, the next part of our little experiment is to rotate the arm back and forth. We'll start by selecting the Arm symbol on its layer.

8. Select the Arm symbol.

9. Right-click (PC) or Ctrl-click (Mac), and choose **Free Transform**.

10. Position your Selection tool over the upper-right corner of the selected Arm symbol until you see the circular arrow (Rotate tool). (See the following figure.)

Now, let's pause here briefly. Normally, you'd go ahead and start to rotate. But look carefully at where the large, glowing arrow is pointing in the figure. Remember talking about the registration point? If we were to rotate the arm now, around what registration point, or axis, would it rotate?

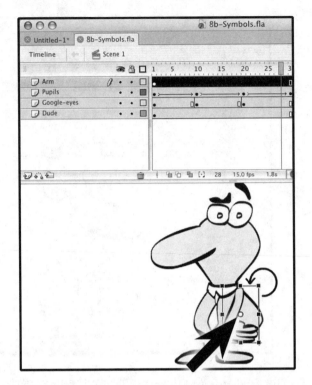

Before you rotate an anatomical feature, such as an
arm, make sure your registration point is in the
proper location. We need to drag the registration
point from the elbow to the shoulder in this example.

If we were to follow the example, it would rotate around the
elbow, wouldn't it? Weird, true, funny... well, maybe; but remember, we're trying to do believable characters (no matter how
silly-looking) and we want our humor to be *intentionally* funny. Not
the result of amateur anatomical errors. So instead of allowing his
arm to rotate around the elbow, let's rotate it from where it
should... the *shoulder*.

With that settled, we can continue without further erroneous
anatomical distractions.

11. Drag the registration point to the shoulder.

12. With the Arm symbol still selected, choose **Insert | Timeline | Create Motion Tween**.

    From that point, you should once again see the dotted arrow, which tells us there's essentially a "hold cel" there.

    Your Arm symbol should still be selected. If not, the simplest thing to do is use the assistance of my wacky pal, the Option-drag (Mac)/Alt-drag (PC).

13. Select the first keyframe in Frame 1, and Option-drag (Mac)/Alt-drag (PC) that over to Frame 10.

14. In Frame 10, right-click (PC) or Ctrl-click (Mac) and choose **Free Transform** from the pop-up menu.

    Now you've got two positions. That's basically all you need at first, because you want the arms to move back and forth. However, those are only the first *two* positions. We need more. This is what I call "hopscotching" keyframes. Basically we're just Option-dragging (Mac)/Alt-dragging (PC) alternate keyframes past one another.

15. Select Frame 1 and Option-drag (Mac)/Alt-drag (PC) that keyframe over to Frame 20.

16. Select Frame 10 and Option-drag/Alt-drag that keyframe over to Frame 30.

17. Now hit **Return** (Mac) or **Enter** (PC). Watch your cartoon and see what you think. In the case of my example, his arm swings back and forth, and his eyes look from side to side. Not bad, but what say we try to really get tricky here? Let's make that bad boy *walk*.

First, we'll try the simple approach using tweening:

18. Double-click on your character's body layer. (In my case it was the Dude layer.) You should be in the Timeline of the body symbol.

19. If your only layer is Layer 1, rename it **Body**.

20. Create a new layer and name it **Leg1**.

   Now comes the difficult bit. We're about to perform a bit of surgery on your character, so the faint of heart may wish to skip to the next chapter. Everyone else ready to continue? Okay, good. Here we go:

21. Zoom in on the general area of your character's legs; remember, your shortcut is **Cmd++** (Mac) or **Ctrl++** (PC).

22. Select the **Lasso** tool and select your character's right leg.

23. Cut the leg.

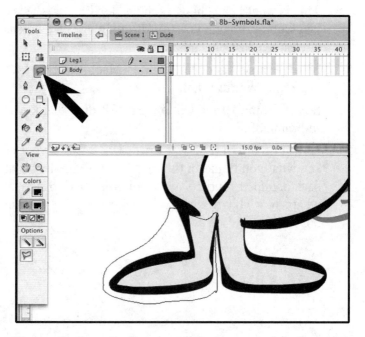

Choose the Lasso tool and encircle the area of the leg you wish to cut.

Yes, yes, I know it sounds cruel… but don't worry. We're going to put it right back where we got it, we're just moving it to another layer. And why? So the leg can move independently of the body, of course. But why so much trouble?

Well, here's the plan. We want this character walking, but essentially walking in place. (We'll move him soon enough, but first things first.) While we want his legs to be rotating independently of the body, we want them to stay in the same position in *relation* to the body. In other words, though we want the legs swinging back and forth, we don't want them to accidentally leave their sockets as he moves across the Stage.

24. Click in your Leg1 layer.

25. Go to **Edit | Paste in Place**.

Whew! The leg is back where it should be. Isn't that a relief! The main part of our operation was a success, but we still have some stitching left, not to mention a bit of plastic surgery. But before we get to that, let's make that leg a symbol while it's still selected, using the shortcut for Convert to Symbol.

26. If the leg isn't already selected, then select it by clicking on its layer.

27. Press the **F8** key, the shortcut for Convert to Symbol.

28. Click on the **Free Transform** tool in the Toolbox (another method to access Free Transform), and move your registration point by dragging it to the top center of the leg.

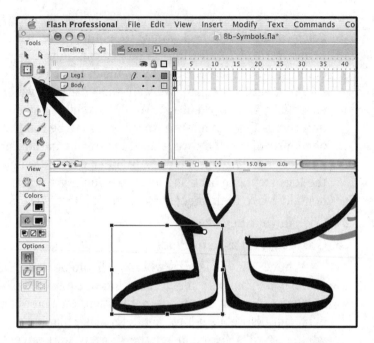

Click on the Free Transform tool as shown, and then drag
your registration point (the circle) from the default center up
to the top of the leg, the point from which a leg would
realistically rotate, on the lower hip.

All right, now back to our aforementioned plastic surgery.
You remember how much easier it is to animate one symbol and
then duplicate it, rather than animating *two* different objects,
like, oh I dunno… two legs?

Yep, I was just thinking the same thing.

But first, let's tend to our plastic surgery, which will set the
stage for our leg symbols.

29. Hide your Leg1 layer by clicking in its Eyeball column.

30. Select your Body layer, then select the remaining leg with the
Lasso tool.

31. Cut it by pressing **Cmd+X** (Mac) or **Ctrl+X** (PC).

32. If necessary, tidy up any rough edges by painting over them with the Paintbrush tool. (Most likely you'll want to use the flesh color of your character for this last bit of cosmetic surgery.)

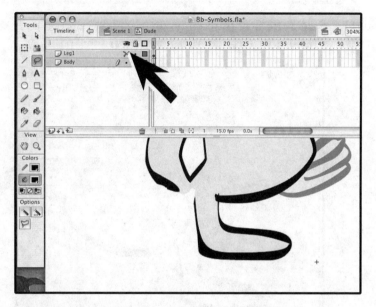

Remember, you can hide any layer temporarily by clicking underneath the Eyeball column for that layer.

Now you can unhide your Leg1 layer again.

33. Click underneath the Eyeball icon in the Leg1 layer to show the layer.

34. Click in Frame 8 of the Leg1 layer and add a frame by pressing **F5**.

35. Click in Frame 8 of the Dude's Body layer and add a frame by pressing **F5**.

Now that we've got some frames to work with in each layer, we can animate a simple, cartoony walk cycle just by using tweening.

Creating a Simple Cartoon by Using Tweening

1. Select the first frame in your Leg1 layer and go to **Insert | Timeline | Create Motion Tween**.

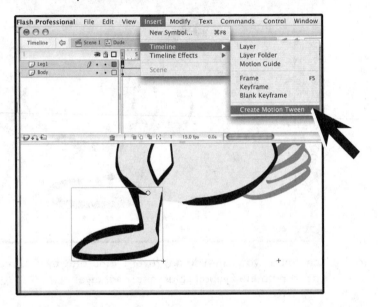

2. Option-drag (Mac)/Alt-drag (PC) Frame 1 to Frame 8.

   You should see the arrow line continuing from Frames 1 to 8. This ensures that our feet end up at the same position in which they started and keeps the cycle continuous. Of course, there's no animation yet, since both our keyframes are the same position right now. Let's change that by adding a keyframe in the middle, and then changing the rotation there.

3. Option-drag (Mac)/Alt-drag (PC) Frame 1 to Frame 4. (The leg should still be selected at this point.)

4. Click on your **Free Transform** tool in the Toolbox and then rotate the leg, preferably by dragging the upper left-hand corner of the symbol. It's probably best to rotate the leg into an *upward* position, essentially lifting it off the ground.

Rotate the Leg symbol by dragging the upper-left corner. As you can see in the example, I had to tidy up the rough edges of the top of the leg where it connects to the body. Though you can see those rounded edges now, we will easily hide them by dragging the Leg1 layer underneath the Body layer.

Now play back your animation. It looks as though our character is tapping one foot. Although not entirely convincing, it has potential.

5. Insert a new layer and name it **Leg2**.

6. Option-drag (Mac) or Alt-drag (PC) the first keyframe from the Leg1 layer to the Leg2 layer.

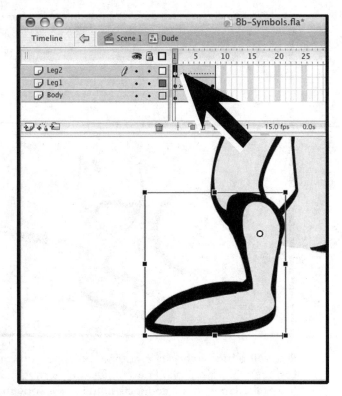

Option-drag your first keyframe from the Leg1 layer to the Leg2 layer.

You might first suppose it would be easier if we could duplicate the entire Leg1 layer on Leg2, but remember from our discussion on walk cycles that the legs move opposite each other. So in essence, it's almost easier, or less confusing, to work this way.

The only downside to duplicating the entire layer would be the fact that both legs would be sharing the same pivot point in the hip; at best, an awkward alliance. That just wouldn't work.

(At least with this method, we are duplicating a keyframe that already has a Motion Tween applied to it, so that in itself saves us a step!)

7. Zoom out a bit by pressing Cmd+– (Mac) or Ctrl+– (PC). You might need to do this once or twice, just so you can see the whole figure.

8. Drag your Leg symbol in the Leg2 layer down a bit and to the right to pretty much where you would expect the leg closest to us (the left leg) to attach.

9. As a safety precaution, temporarily lock the Leg1 layer by clicking in its Padlock column. (I usually lock the layers I'm not using to avoid accidentally changing them.)

10. Option-drag (Mac) or Alt-drag (PC) the first keyframe from the Leg2 layer to Frame 5 in that same layer.

11. Click in Frame 1 on the Leg2 layer.

12. Select the **Free Transform** tool from the Toolbox and rotate the Leg2 symbol upward by dragging the upper-left corner so that the toe is pointing up, as shown in the following figure.

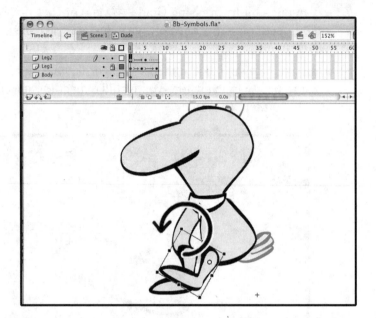

13. Option-drag (Mac) or Alt-drag (PC) the first keyframe from the Leg2 layer to Frame 8 in that same layer.

14. Now to hide the tops of those legs, just drag the Body layer up over Leg2, and that should cover it up rather nicely.

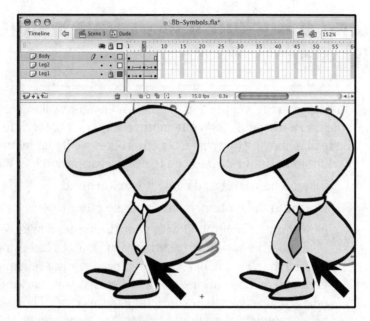

I noticed after dragging the Body layer above the two Leg
layers that I had left a "hole" in the body by not painting the
tie (see the figure on the left). See the top of the leg
peeking through? Fortunately, I managed to fix it quickly
with a dab of the Paintbucket tool in just the right spot.

Guess what! That's all you should have to do. If all went according to plan, you should have your first walk cycle animated in Flash.
Play it through a few times to see.

True, those folks from the Oscars may not be beating your door
down just yet, but let's move along just a bit.

Go back to your main Timeline by clicking on the Scene 1 icon
at the top of your Symbol Timeline. Now try playing your movie
back. If it works as it does in my example, your character should
walk along, swinging his arm, while his eyes dart back and forth.

True, for a much better walk cycle, the character would be
bending his legs, especially during the passing position. Nothing
beats animating a 2D walk cycle by hand, but sometimes budget,
file size, and time constraints may not allow such luxuries, and we
must resort, just like the folks of Hanna-Barbera during their hey-
days of the '60s and '70s, to silly tricks like this.

Adding a Background to Your Simple Animation

To help give the impression that he's no longer walking in place or stuck on a treadmill, let's put another silly trick to work for us. Instead of moving our character anywhere, we'll just move the background. But first, we need to draw a background.

1. Insert a new layer and name it **Background**.
2. Drag it to the bottom, beneath all the other layers.
3. Now draw a background with your Background layer selected.

    It doesn't have to be anything fancy; just a large green field and maybe a couple of trees. I just drew a large rectangle with a green fill and no outline. Don't forget that your background needs to be *wider* than your Stage in this case. This is going to be a panning background, a landscape that moves to the right, as the character appears to walk to the left.

    I also kept the tree pretty simple, as you can see.

Remember, if your background is going to pan (or move horizontally), then you need to make your background image wider than the Stage. How much wider depends on how long you want your character to walk in front of this background.

Of course, you've probably already realized that you only need to draw one tree, make it into a symbol, and then duplicate that symbol as necessary. You can resize that second tree to make it not such an obvious clone; maybe squash it or stretch it just a bit, and then place it on top of the green field.

4. Click in the first frame of your Background layer and go to **Insert | Timeline | Create Motion Tween**.

5. Click in Frame 1 of your Background layer to select *only* that first frame.

6. Drag everything in that layer as far as you can to the left.

7. Click in the last frame of your Background layer to select only that final frame.

8. Drag everything in that layer as far as you can to the right.

9. Now play back your movie by hitting **Return** (Mac) or **Enter** (PC).

Your character should appear to walk (however briefly) through the panning background. You can experiment with making the movie longer by extending keyframes in his arm swing, Option-dragging (Mac) or Alt-dragging (PC) those keyframes to keep the arms moving back and forth properly, and so on. You can even make your background wider by adding onto the artwork, or better yet, making it into a symbol, and then adding onto that.

I'll show you one more animation trick before we leave our little walking dude, and that's the trick of perspective for adding believability to the scene. Have you ever stared out the car window and noticed how objects closer to the highway, like trees, seem to move faster than objects farther away, like distant mountains or buildings? Watch it sometime (preferably with someone else driving) and take note.

Now let's use one of those tree symbols to simulate this effect.

10. Insert a new layer and name it **Tree-Foreground**.

11. Drag that layer in front of all your Dude elements.

12. Drag a Tree symbol into that Tree-Foreground layer.

13. Resize the Tree symbol so that it's larger than the trees in the Background layer, and place the base of its trunk so that it's below the Stage level. (This is important to the illusion we're trying to create.)

14. Place the Tree symbol on the far left of the Stage.

Adding a perspective trick by having items in the foreground move more quickly than items in the background adds believability to your movie. I added to the illusion by selecting my tree and setting the brightness in the Properties window to –30%.

You'll also notice in the above example that I added to the depth illusion by darkening my tree just a bit. Objects in the foreground are subtly darker than objects in the background because particles in the air that are nearly invisible to us nearby make distant objects like mountains and buildings look lighter.

15. Click in the first frame of your Tree-Foreground layer.

16. Go to **Insert | Timeline | Create Motion Tween**.

17. Click in the last frame of your Tree-Foreground layer.

18. Drag your tree as far as you can to the right side of your Stage.

Now play back your cartoon. Even if you've got a relatively low number of frames, like I have in the example (30 frames), you should still see the illusion we're talking about. Pretty neat, huh?

As always, you may find that most of your experiments (especially for beginners) will most likely require some tweaking. In any case, when I was at this point in my personal learning experience with Flash, I was just starting to appreciate the possibilities of increasing productivity with my projects.

I hope you are, too!

What's an Instance?

Here's as good a place as any to define the term *instance*. If you had a whole forest made out of one tree symbol, you'd want to transform each tree so that they weren't all obvious clones of one another by resizing or skewing some, even editing the color slightly on others. If you performed these transformations onstage, you would only be editing the appearance of each individual instance of that symbol... not the original symbol. An instance is best described by the synonym *occurrence*. Each time that tree symbol occurs (or appears) on the Stage in one spot on the Timeline, that's an instance. One instance may be the original size, another instance may be shorter, another taller, another skewed, another a slightly different color or even transparency level.

Let's say you had multiple instances of a single cloud symbol onstage, and you wanted some of them appearing at different levels of transparency. (See the following illustration.) You'd start by selecting one particular *instance* of that cloud symbol onstage, and in the Properties box, you could adjust the transparency by going to Color, then clicking on the word None, and dragging down to Alpha. Finally, move the resulting slider bar (which appears as soon as you change None to Alpha) up or down to your preference.

You can cut down on your workload (not to mention download time, for you webtoonists) and file size by duplicating symbols like trees and clouds onstage, and then modifying each one individually by their instance. Go to the Properties window of each selected instance to modify the transparency of that particular instance, in this case a dust cloud. Click on the word None by Color, and then choose Alpha from the pop-up menu. Once you change None to Alpha, another box will appear beside Alpha with a percentage appearing inside. Now, slide that percentage to the desired transparency.

Note how the same symbol has been resized in each instance, and each has a different level of transparency.

Now there are times when you might want to edit your *original* symbol rather than an *instance* of your symbol. You may have noticed a stray mark or pixel made its way onto your original tree or cloud, and now that annoying dot or "digital smudge" appears on every single instance of your symbol.

Note how the stray mark on one symbol appears on every instance of the symbol onstage. When you delete it from the original symbol, it will be deleted from every copy of that symbol. If you add something to the original symbol, it is added to all copies of that symbol.

To get to your original symbol and edit it, merely double-click on the desired symbol, and that will take you into the specific Timeline of that particular symbol.

When you double-click on a symbol, note how you're brought into a *separate* Timeline, outside (or inside, depending on how you look at it, I guess) the Timeline of your particular scene.

We experiment with animating a symbol in the next section. But before you do that, let me offer you a word of warning. If you want to create a symbol of something you wish to be animated, such as a sequence of moving mouths or blinking eyes (like we're about to do), make sure you select and make the first still image into a symbol *first*. Then, double-click on the symbol to go to that symbol's Timeline where you can add frames if you like.

I learned that the hard way, and whenever possible, I like to spare people the pain and frustration associated with the hard way... especially when it involves having drawn several really cool animation drawings of, oh, let's say a hand clenching or unclenching. Let's say you've done these six or seven drawings of this hand clenching, and you realize, "Hey! That turned out pretty good! I'd better make this into a symbol so I can flip it and use it for the opposite hand clenching!"

Good idea!

One unfortunate thing might happen, though, to dampen your enthusiasm.

If you were to select all those frames of your animated hand and go to **Modify | Convert to Symbol** as you did before, you would be in for a rude, nasty, and otherwise unwelcome awakening.

You'd suddenly find that every drawing after your first one disappeared. Even if you double-clicked to edit that symbol, hoping to see your now-lost drawings in the separate Symbol Timeline, well... they'd still be lost. Again, just make sure that if you know you want an animated symbol, you convert your *first* drawing into a symbol. Then double-click the symbol to edit it within its Symbol Timeline, and finally, add frames and/or new drawings as necessary.

There. You've been warned. (I feel as though I've done my good deed for the day!)

Shape Tweening

Up until now, most of our time and energy has been spent on resizing and rotating symbols. But believe it or not, there's at least one other way we can make this whole tweening symbols thing really work for us. And that's by Shape Tweening.

Simply put, when you start Shape Tweening, you're modifying the shape, or outer vector points of a shape, over time. It's pretty much akin to morphing, which was used in the Michael Jackson video *Black or White*, where he changed from one person into another, and the creature transformation scenes in movies like *Willow* (although that latter scene was partially the result of clever animatronic puppetry mixed with computer morphing).

Obviously, we're not talking about something as high-tech as that. This is pretty simple stuff, but can save us some serious time. Flash can Shape Tween simple shapes, but you've got to remember a few things.

Flash can't Shape Tween symbols, movie clips, or groups. It can only Shape Tween raw vector art. And the simpler the shape, the better. Notably it can change a square to a circle, a circle to a triangle, and an "Ooh"-shaped mouth to a smile. It will even change the colors between the shapes, like make an orange circle into a purple square, smoothly over time.

But let's start simple.

Let's say, for instance, we have a character looking wide-eyed at someone, and we want one eye to slowly narrow into an angry slit, as if he's got some serious issue with that someone.

1. In a new document, name your first layer **Face**.

2. Draw a face in that layer, but don't draw eyes just yet... not in that layer.

3. Insert a new layer and name it **Pupils**.

4. Draw a pair of pupils on that layer.

5. Lock both the Face layer and the Pupils layer.

6. Insert a new layer and name it **Eyeball Tween**.

7. Drag that layer between your Face and Pupils layers.

8. Insert another new layer and name it **Eyeball Static**. (This one won't move.)

9. Drag it below your Eyeball Tween layer.

    Refer to the following illustration to make sure your layers are set up properly.

Flash can handle simple Shape Tweening to make your life easier and your production schedule faster.

10. Select your Pupils layer, click in Frame 10, and hit **F5**. That will add a static cel, or "hold cel," to Frame 10.

11. Select your Eyeball Static layer, and do the same as before... click in Frame 10 and hit **F5**.

12. Select your Face layer, click in Frame 10, and hit **F5**.

Your screen should look something similar to the following illustration.

The reason we're only Shape Tweening one eye rather than both will soon become crystal clear in a forthcoming example. Again, it's best to keep things simple.

13. Click in Frame 2 of the Eyeball Tween layer, and go to **Insert | Timeline | Blank Keyframe**.

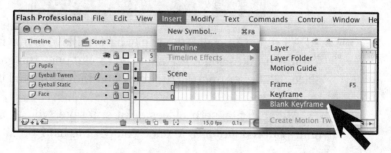

14. Click in Frame 10 of the Eyeball Tween layer, and go to **Insert | Timeline | Blank Keyframe**.

15. Click in Frame 1 of your Eyeball Tween layer.

16. In your Properties window, go to Tween and choose **Shape**.

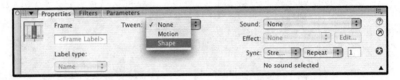

17. Click in Frame 10 of your Eyeball Tween layer.

18. Draw a second shape that will serve as your next keyframe. (I drew a sideways crescent, and filled it with the same color from my first eyeball. See the following illustration for my example.)

All right. As usual, the tricky part in Flash is moving key-frames. It takes some getting used to, but once things are in place, whatever minor irritations/frustrations should be temporary.

All incidental setbacks aside, it still saves you enormous hours of production time once you get the hang of it.

I ran through this myself several times to spare you the grief (and yes, you're welcome, incidentally) to find the quickest way to do this. And here's what I found to work best:

19. Click on Frame 1 in your Eyeball Tween layer.
20. Drag it one frame forward.
21. Next, drag it one frame backward.

I know this may sound odd, but it's what worked best... and quickest, mind you... for me.

Look at the following illustration to see what your screen should look like, and some sample frames of how your animation might look.

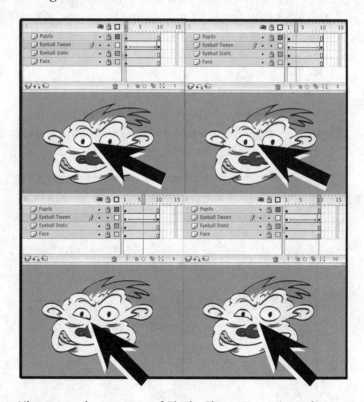

Like most other aspects of Flash, Shape Tweening takes some practice. But once you get the hang of it, you'll soon realize how simple animations like a narrowing eye or making a mouth go from a small line to a wide grin can be achieved quickly.

Also, never forget the online help available to you through Flash's Help menu. I'll gladly admit I went through it with these examples. Just go to **Help | Flash Help** at the upper-right corner of your screen, and type in some keywords.

A couple of other quick things before we wrap up this chapter. Remember that *automatic* tweening makes for stiff, uninteresting movement. The computer, unless we tell it otherwise, just moves things from point A to point B in equal increments. And that's not quite how we move in real life, is it?

No, we "slow in" and "slow out" or "ease/cushion in" and "ease/cushion out" (depending on what you like to call it). We might start out an action slowly and finish it quickly, or vice versa. Rarely do we move with predictable robotic precision. It's what makes people and characters interesting to watch.

Thankfully, Flash has the ability for us to adjust Shape Tweening.

Here's how to access it:

1. Click in Frame 1 of your Eyeball Tween layer.

2. In your Properties window, click on the down arrow and change the value for Ease in and Ease out.

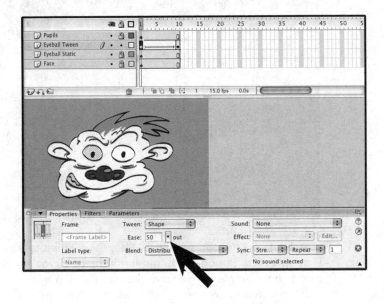

Roughly speaking, here's how the whole Ease in/Ease out thing works in Flash with Shape Tweening. If you want to start a Shape Tween quickly and then decelerate that tween toward the animation's end, just drag the slider upward... or you can simply enter a positive value somewhere from 1 to 100.

You've probably already guessed that if you want to go the opposite direction, or start slowly and accelerate, then enter a value from –1 to –100.

Just don't forget that unless you tell Flash differently, the default rate of change on tweened frames is constant. Easing in and out has a more natural appearance. I was told by one of the local animation studios that outsources for Cartoon Network's shows something to this effect on the subject of tweening: "Every time we try to use tweening, particularly the default settings, the producers on the show catch us and make us redo the scene. But if we use Ease in and Ease out, it has a more natural appearance, and we can usually get away with it."

For obvious reasons, I won't say which studio said that; I don't want to get anyone in trouble, and I certainly don't want to interfere with their production schedule. If a trick works, use it. If it doesn't, find something else that works.

One last word of warning on Shape Tweening: As usual, it's best to keep things simple.

As you can see in the following example, I tried to get fancy too fast, and wanted to have TWO eyes narrow into slits on my character. You can see what happened in the following illustration.

By keeping your shapes to tween simple, you avoid problems as indicated by the arrows. I thought I was dealing with relatively simple shapes, but the computer showed me otherwise. It's best to use Shape Tweening on one shape at a time!

I remember back in the early '90s, when I was just getting into animation, my animation instructor, Mr. Holcomb, told me even then about similar computer shortcuts they were seeking with hand-drawn 2D animation. With the first PSA I worked on (a running dog in a Sherlock Holmes getup was my scene), they had attempted some "tweening"-type shortcut on a character's arms swinging during a walk cycle.

The results were less than spectacular; in fact, they were downright laughable. It had problems similar to those in my example above. The elbows, I was told, bent in ways that were both physically uncomfortable and downright impossible.

You've got to remember that when working with a computer, it thinks the shortest distance between two points is a straight line. And because of that, it doesn't take into account that our arms swing like pendulums from our shoulders. Instead, it's like getting bad directions from a map website that doesn't take into account things like rivers, buildings, and one-way streets. It just plows forward between those two points, start and end, that we give it, and considers its job done.

So for simple matters, it works fine. Just don't expect to get too complicated. As frustrating as that may seem, just consider it like I always have: job security.

The nice thing about Shape Tweening is that it's so simple, and it cuts down considerably on your production time.

Chapter 9

Libraries, Scenes, and Special Effects

Sezquatch, Thurman, and Deadbeat
© Mark S. Smith/MarkToonery.com

Flash has a lot of strengths, and it's time to delve into yet another.

Have you ever drawn something simple, like a tree, cloud, or animated puff of smoke? Sure! And then maybe you thought to yourself, "Gee, it's almost a shame I can't put this tree, cloud, or animated puff of smoke on a shelf somewhere. I'm bound to need this sort of thing again, and when I do, I'd like to pull it down from that shelf for my convenient use. It'd be a shame to animate the exact same thing all over again. What a shame I don't have something along the lines of... a library!"

Lucky you!

That's exactly what we're going to talk about now.

You can really save yourself a lot of time and trouble if you take a few moments to organize your libraries, so you won't have to go recreating artwork you've already done!

Nested Symbols or "Meta-Libraries"

I hate that we have to come up with fancy and/or potentially intimidating names like "nested symbols" or "meta-libraries" for some of the most particularly useful aspects of animating our cartoons with Flash, but this leads to one of the best tips I got during my "one-on-one" tutorial session at Cartoon Network. It was a groundbreaking revelation to me that made that little light bulb pop on over my head and say, "Hey, this Flash might be pretty cool after all!"

That tip is the ability to use an animated symbol as a sort of library. Recently, one of my students told me how incredibly helpful this tip is. He says quite often he has an animated symbol... within a symbol... within another symbol, and so on.

For instance, maybe I'll draw a character walking and decide the head (since this character will be talking during the walk cycle) might need to be a separate symbol by itself. I'll select the face and make that into a symbol. Then I'll get inside that symbol and start to edit it, and decide that the eyes really need to be a symbol too.

I'll select the eyes, and make them into a separate symbol. Perhaps it's an extreme example, but once you learn this trick, you might be surprised how helpful this concept is to your work.

A variation on this is using a symbol as a "library." You might have within a symbol a series of blinking eyes, mouths in different positions, or even hands holding a variety of props like a pencil, a laser gun, or a rubber chicken. You just have to place that instance of the symbol on Single Frame (rather than Loop), and it will "hold" those eyes on that given frame, that mouth in the "ooh" position, or that hand holding that rubber chicken.

Read on, and I'll try to explain...

Breaking Down a Character into Component Symbols

As usual, let's start out with the basics. As I mentioned before, the best thing to do is start out any task *simply*. When I started on a series proposal for a client recently, I did a rough pencil sketch for a character I'll call "Jenny." I've grown accustomed to a new process I've recently developed, which starts by scanning in my rough sketch (at 150 *ppi*, or pixels per inch, if it's a small drawing; I'll scan at 72 if it's larger), and saving it as a JPG. I take it into Photoshop (especially if it's a grayscale image) and adjust the brightness and contrast so that the lines are nice and dark. Naturally, this is not the finished artwork; it's merely a tracing guide.

I'll go into Flash, and start the setup of my document as follows:

1. Go to **File | Import to Stage**.
2. Resize the artwork so that it comfortably fills the Stage by **right-clicking** (PC) or **Ctrl-clicking** (Mac) the art and selecting **Transform**. (Don't forget to hold down Shift while you transform art to keep the scaling proportional; that is, to keep a square intact without squashing or stretching it into a rectangle.)

3. Name the layer **Guide Layer**, Sketch Layer, or something descriptive.

4. Lock the Guide Layer.

5. Insert a new layer, and rename it. (In this case, I'll call it "Face.")

Don't forget that by locking a layer, you can prevent accidentally making unwanted changes to that layer.

Okay, now you've got a blank layer you can trace your character's face on. This is as good a place to begin as usual; it's where we usually start our design process anyway. What we're going to do is break down the character's face into areas that can be easily managed. We'll start with Granny Addams' advice when wondering how to dig into one of her meals: "Start with the eyes!"

You can see here that I may have gotten ahead of myself in the example by placing everything on one layer. Let me advise you to be a *bit* more cautious. Although you can certainly do this, and then break it apart, it may prove more time effective (at least if you know ahead of time) to draw parts that may move individually from others on separate layers in the first place.

For instance, if you drew everything on one layer to begin with, as I have in the example here, you'd have to go back, cut the eyes off one layer, paste them (Paste in Place) on a separate eye layer, and then go back to that face layer you started with, and fill in the holes left behind by the absentee orbs. This might be even further complicated if you gave the flesh tone a gradient fill... as I did here.

So let's try to think ahead, before it gets too late... which facial features might be grouped neatly onto what separate layers?

As always, it might be different depending on your character, but let's try these groups for a starting place:

- Neck (and necklace, or necktie, which would conveniently hide any separation of "cel layers," like our old friend Yogi)

- Face (which could be subdivided into upper skull and lower jaw, for reasons that might soon become obvious); nose and ears would probably go on the same layer

- Hair (at least one layer of hair for one side of the face, and another layer for the side away from the viewer)

- Eyes and/or eyebrows (depending on how wide a range of expression your character has)

- Mouth/lips

Again, all characters are different, which helps keep our job that much more interesting, but any guide I give you will be general at best. Each will vary according to preference and necessity.

In the example I've got, I'll let you in on a little secret that you've probably guessed: This face was prebuilt, and I just brought it out as an example. The reason I mention this is to give you a preview of what's to come. (Sometimes I like to give students a "sneak peek" of coming events, to give them an idea of what can *really* be done with this program.)

Do you remember how we "broke apart" a JPG image so that we could erase parts of it, and later have images show up behind it? You can do the same thing with a piece of an image that's been built out of symbols (or symbols *within* symbols). That is, you can break apart a "greater symbol" into its components of "lesser symbols."

This character has already had a bit of work done on her, but it will still show you what this is all about. Since she's already been built out of some symbols, I can do this:

1. Select the Face layer.

2. Go to **Modify | Break Apart**, or better yet, use the shortcut **Cmd+B** (Mac)/**Ctrl+B** (PC).

   As you can see in the following illustration, the character now has been "broken down" into her component elements: Face and Hair.

By selecting a symbol that is composed of other symbols and then going to Break Apart (or Cmd+B on the Mac, Ctrl+B on the PC), you can break apart the symbol into parts that can be individually manipulated. Note the multiple selection squares as indicated by the arrow.

But I'm not done... I can make my work more convenient still!

Because you see, at this point, if I tried to do *any* kind of tweening in the Timeline, it would affect *everything* in that layer. I mean, if I tried to rotate her hair a bit, that would rotate her whole head at that point on that layer.

So you may be asking yourself at this point, "Isn't it a shame there's not *some* way to distribute these different elements that should move exclusively from one another to different layers? I mean, I'm sure there *must* be, but wouldn't it be great if I didn't have to do a whole bunch of manual cutting and pasting to get everything distributed to those different layers?"

Guess what! There *is* such a way, and it's fairly simple at that. Before I deselect this item with multiple symbol elements, I need to:

3. Right-click (PC) or Ctrl-click (Mac) and drag down to **Distribute to Layers**.

Using Distribute to Layers

Wow! Doesn't that look handy?

That's only because it is, kiddies... All right, though; as you can probably see in *my* case, I ran into an unexpected problem.

4. I already had a layer named Face within my symbol, so as to avoid confusion, I'd better rename it. I'll call it **Mouth**, for now.

Another thing you might notice in the following illustration (and that's something that will further make this business more convenient) is something called layer folders. If you have several objects on stage that belong to different characters, you might want to consider adding layer folders, which are just like real-world folders. They keep things neatly tucked away inside, and make objects or symbols easier to find when you go looking for them.

As you can see, I already had another layer named "Face" within my character's head symbol (see top arrow), which I discovered after breaking it apart. It's best to rename it to avoid confusion. (I'll probably call it "Mouth" or something.)

To make a layer folder, just click on the Insert Layer Folder icon (see bottom arrow). Then I can place related items within that folder simply by dragging them inside.

Now back to those eyes.

5. Click the **Insert Layer** icon.

6. Name your new layer **Eyes**.

   If you haven't yet, go ahead and trace the eyes onto this layer. (In my case, since I was "working backward," I had to go *inside* my Face layer (by double-clicking, since it had already been made into a symbol) and remove the eyes by selecting them with the Lasso tool, cutting them, and then going back and filling in the holes left behind in the next timeline. Then I went *back* to the Eyes layer, and pasted them. Whew!)

7. Okay, I'm keeping in mind that these separate layers are going to be animated. I select her Eyes layer, which should contain only her eyes and/or eyebrows (in my case they contain both), and convert them into a symbol (**F8**).

    With that done, I:

8. Double-click on that **Eye** symbol (I named mine "JennyEyes") to go into that symbol's Timeline.

    Once inside the symbol's Timeline, I like to go ahead and give myself a blank frame to start with. You might decide to go to **Insert | Timeline | Blank Keyframe**, but as usual, I prefer my Option-drag method. I select the first frame, and **Option-drag** (yes, on my Mac; of course that's **Alt-drag** for you PC folks) that keyframe to Frame 2.

    It's more than laziness in this case; it's closer to efficiency this time around.

    I want her eyebrows to remain still and unaffected for this first frame. All I want to happen is for her eyes to look from her left to forward. In Frame 1, they're looking to her left, and in Frame 2, they look directly at the viewer.

    So if you haven't already:

9. Option-drag (Mac)/Alt-drag (PC) Frame 1 to Frame 2.

10. Use the Lasso tool to select only the eyes — not the eyebrows.

11. Delete the eyes (and you guessed it, leave the eyebrows untouched, in place).

12. Turn on **Onion Skinning**, so you can see the previous eye to trace for reference (see the following illustration).

13. Trace the second set of eyes in Frame 2, only looking forward (instead of to one side, as in the previous frame).

After deleting the copy of the character's eyes on
Frame 2 (but leaving the eyebrows untouched),
turn on Onion Skinning (upper arrow) so that you
can see the previous eye to trace from.

Once I'm done with my Guide Layer, as I now am at this
point, I'll go ahead and drag it to the trash. It's served me well,
but now that I'm done with it, it's best to keep our workspace
uncluttered. (Of course, if I went *strictly* by that rule, I wouldn't
have these Muppet and Roger Rabbit beanies hanging off my
computer desk!)

Next, it's time to add some frames, so we can appreciate
this work we've been up to.

14. Go to Frame 5 (or rather, where Frame 5 will *soon* be), and drag
all the way down so Frame 5 in all the layers is selected.

15. Hit **F5** to Insert Frames.

If you were to play the movie by hitting Return (Mac) or Enter
(PC), you'd quickly see that we've got a problem. In my case, Jenny
may be pretty, but she's a little shifty-eyed. Did you notice? That's
because the default setting on any *animated layer* (and by that I
mean a layer that contains a symbol with *multiple* frames in its own
Timeline) is set to Loop. See the following illustration for a further
explanation.

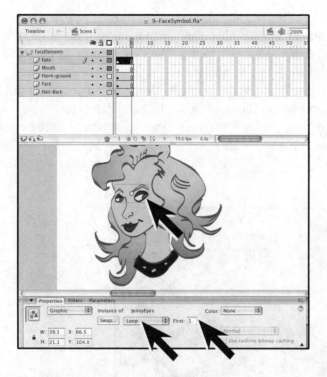

As long as you have multiple frames on your stage, animated symbols will (or can, depending on how *you* apply their settings) loop through their Timeline frames. Note how the Eyes symbol is selected (top arrow). Because it's selected, we can read details regarding its settings in the Properties window. The default settings for this particular *instance* of JennyEyes, as previously mentioned, is set to **Loop** (bottom left arrow). We can further modify this by choosing the first frame in which to begin the loop (bottom right arrow). Since the JennyEyes symbol now only has two frames, our only logical choices to type in are 1 or 2; naturally this depends on how many frames your symbol has available. For instance, if we wanted Jenny to start out the animation looking to her left/our right, we would leave the First frame setting of the loop at **1**, as it now is. If we wanted Jenny to start out looking forward, we would set the First frame setting to **2**.

Again, I'm hoping all this is starting to help you realize how helpful this can be. But there are even more options at our disposal. You've probably already thought, "Well, as usual, this is all fine and dandy if I want Jenny to be a shifty-eyed little sneak, looping through those frames continuously. But what if I actually want her to look someone in the eye? What if I want her to just look in one spot by holding that one particular frame, or what if I only want the animation to play through once?"

Check out the following illustration for a reply to any of these questions.

You can choose whether you want your symbol animation to **Loop** continuously, with control over which frame plays first (as previously discussed), or you can decide to **Play Once**, which will play the animation frames within that symbol once and then stop. Or, you can choose to only display a **Single Frame**, and naturally tell Flash which frame you want that to be by entering the number in the box beside the word First. Choose either of these three options by dragging down on the Loop box and releasing on your choice.

Meta-Library Defined... Finally!

Hopefully you've already begun to realize the widespread applications this can grant you. You can use each of these symbols as what some call a meta-library. Simply put, each symbol can be like a library of eyes in different positions, or mouths forming different vowels and consonants, or even hands holding different objects. The hands can grasp a book in Frame 1, a stick of dynamite in Frame 2, and even be clenched into a fist in Frame 3. You just choose which frame is displayed by going to Single Frame, and then tell Flash which frame number you like. Keeping track of what is in each one of these meta-libraries is a job called *asset management*. Assets, in this case, are any objects that you've created and made into symbols. It would be well worth your time to keep track of which assets have already been created so you're not spending valuable time drawing something that has already been drawn.

Why reinvent the wheel, as they say?

It's difficult to say whether more time is being wasted if you're redrawing a character's hand holding a cartoon bomb if someone else down the hall already drew it last week, or if you're redrawing previously completed drawings by yourself. Why waste time? Great cartoons take so much *time* to make, so let's utilize that time best by minimizing the recreation of work already done!

After all, recycling cartoon elements is one of the things Flash does best!

Lip-Synching with a Meta-Library

All right, back to Jenny. In my case, I need to get back into her Face symbol, because her lips are still part of that symbol and not on a separate layer by themselves, as they should be. I want to do something high-tech, like adjusting her mouth positions frame-by-frame in order to lip-synch with a prerecorded soundtrack.

As you may recall from our experiment with Jenny's eyes, we're going to cut the mouth from the main part of the Face symbol.

The first thing I need to do is to put her mouth on a different layer:

1. Double-click on the **Face** layer, which will take you inside the Timeline of the Face symbol.

2. Insert a new layer and name it **Lips** (or Mouth, if you like).

3. Select the area around the mouth using the Lasso tool.

4. Cut the lips from the Face layer.

5. Select the **Lips** layer and go to **Edit | Paste in Place**.

    Once again, you might have to do a bit of tidying up on each layer by selecting any leftover bits of flesh color on the Lips layer and deleting them. Likewise, you'll probably have to go back to that Face layer and fill in that hole with flesh color that resulted from removing her mouth. (Eventually, you'll get used to little bits of housekeeping like that.)

6. Extend your Face layer to 5 frames by selecting that layer, clicking in Frame 5 and pressing **F5**.

7. Start **Option-dragging** (Mac)/**Alt-dragging** (PC) Frame 1 in the Lips layer, and do that for each frame until you've got all five frames filled with an individual Lips drawing. (See the following illustration.)

8. Activate Onion Skinning so you can see between layers.

9. Select **Frame 2**, delete the artwork there (so you can start anew), and draw the mouth in another position, slightly open.

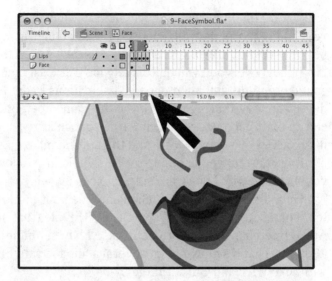

Once again, by turning on Onion Skinning (as indicated by the arrow), your work will be much easier when performing tasks like lip-synching dialogue.

Now repeat this technique for all five frames, and draw all the mouth positions you'll need for the word "Hello." Refer to the illustrations back in Chapter 5 if you need help, or just mouth the word to yourself in front of a mirror, and observe. Remember that we don't always *enunciate* words with annoying precision; more often, we have a tendency to kind of slur syllables together. The rule of thumb, though, is that observation is the best method.

You'll probably need a mouth position for "eh," "ehl," and "oh." What about the letter "h"? If you notice in your mirror, we don't make any particular mouth position for the letter "h," especially in "hello." (Regardless of whether you pronounce it like the little British worm from *Labyrinth*, "No, I said 'ello.'") In this case, it's just the same mouth position — that vowel best spelled as "eh" (not "ey," as some Canadians might say) — that follows that "h" in "hello."

Once you get the drawings you need, you'll use a sound recording of the word "hello" to synch them up with. (This may be a little backward from my usual practice, but try whichever works best for you. You're perfectly welcome to get your soundtrack digitized before you start drawing; that's how I usually prefer to work.)

I know everyone will quite likely have at least a dozen different sound programs and microphone combinations to do their dialogue digitization with (using Final Cut with a camcorder, or SoundEdit and an external mike, etc.), but for no particular reason (other than it's quick), I just used iMovie and the built-in mike on my computer.

(For those of you listening to the sample in the download file, you'll realize why I don't do female voices myself.)

Once I've recorded the audio using the built-in mike, I export it (or "share" it, as iMovie calls it) as an AIFF file (that stands for Audio Interchange File Format, in case I haven't mentioned it already). That's simply one of several audio formats Flash can deal with, like WAV and QuickTime movies.

Now back to Flash. To import my girlish "Hello" bit of dialogue:

1. Go to **File | Import to Library**.

2. Locate the audio you wish to use. (If you want to use the sample included in the download file, then I would suggest copying it to your hard drive first.)

3. For the next bit, we don't want to be inside our Symbol Timeline of the face, but in our regular ol' Scene 1 Timeline, so click back on **Scene 1** at the top left of your screen's Timeline.

   One little thing I'll let you in on that I didn't realize at first: We might not need that Lips layer we made on the Scene 1 Timeline (I'll explain why shortly) as originally planned. I've thought of a *better* use of it.

4. Select your Lips layer in the Scene 1 Timeline and rename it **Audio.**

5. Drag it to the top of your Timeline.

6. Extend the Audio layer to about Frame 22 by clicking in Frame 22 and then hitting **F5**.

This will obviously be different if you've done your own audio for this exercise. If you're not sure how many frames your audio lasts (or if you're lousy at math), you can always just sort of guess. You may go to frame 60 or more (perhaps just beyond where you might need), select that frame in your Audio layer, and then hit F5. Quite likely, you'll have some frames left over. You can trim them back by holding down the Cmd/Apple key (Mac) or the Ctrl key (PC) over the last frame, hover there briefly till you see the double-arrow, and then drag back to where you can see the little Audio waveform stop in that layer.

You can look at your Audio layer's waveform readout, and easily see how long the sound lasts by the presence (or absence) of the small line in the center of that layer.

First of all, before we go any further, we need to make sure the instance of our dialogue in the Audio layer is set to Stream, as shown in the following illustration. This will enable you to "scrub" back and forth within your Audio channel. In other words, when you drag back and forth, you can listen to the exact moment of the dialogue played with the frame of animation that belongs to it. It's imperative to use this in order to synchronize (or "sync") audio to artwork.

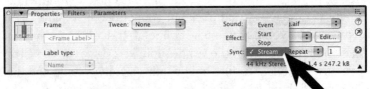

Make sure you have your Audio selected in
Channel 1 of your Audio layer, and that the Sync option is set to
Stream (as indicated by the arrow).

If you've already looked at the Audio track in the example, you'll notice there are a few frames of silence before the dialogue actually begins. We certainly don't want the lips moving during this time, so let's put a stop to that right away.

1. Select the instance of Jenny's face on the Stage by clicking on it.

2. In the Properties window, drag down from Loop to **Single Frame** (see the following illustration).

If you click on an instance of a
symbol onstage, you can control whether that symbol will loop, play once, or play a single frame of its animation. You can choose which frame of the animation shows up onstage by entering the frame number in the First box. This is especially handy with dialogue, eye blinks, or even selecting a range of objects a character may commonly carry.

I took a look (or should I say a *listen*), and discovered by scrubbing back and forth that the dialogue in the first syllable of "Hello" doesn't start until Frame 7. In that case, I want the animation to hold for the first six frames of that Face layer. So I'm going to Option-drag (Mac)/Alt-drag (PC) that first keyframe to Frame 7.

3. Select the first keyframe in the Face layer.

4. **Option-drag** (Mac)/**Alt-drag** (PC) that first keyframe to **Frame 7**.

I inserted another keyframe by using my non-patented Option-drag (Mac)/Alt-drag (PC) method, but you could just as easily do the same thing by selecting the frame within the layer in which you want the new keyframe to appear, and right-click (PC) or Ctrl-click (Mac).

Now since Frame 7 is where we begin to hear the first syllable, we'll probably want to start with that "eh" mouth position. You can simply start typing numbers in the First box (remember to make sure that layer of that instance is still selected), then Return (Mac)/Enter (PC) and see which mouth position best fits that sound, but it would probably be wise to come up with some sort of chart that keeps track of which mouth positions are in which frame number.

Anything to make life easier (like eliminating guesswork) is probably worth doing.

As a matter of fact, some animation studios have two sets of mouth positions for each character within a given mouth symbol. Frames 1 through 7 might be the "happy" mouth positions, next there's a blank frame within the symbol (for separation reference), and then Frames 8 through 15 might be the "unhappy" versions of those mouth positions.

Some of these things may very well be determined by your personal preference (if you're working by yourself), or the studio you're working for.

By going through your animation and setting keyframes, then choosing which frame of your symbol to display within that keyframe (see arrow), you can make your work easier and your finished web movies download faster.

All right. Very briefly, here's what I did next. For the first couple of mouth positions, I found they worked out all right being onstage for two frames. That's basically "shooting on twos," remember? (You can refer to the folder for Chapter 9 in the download files to see what I ended up with.) Frames 11 through 13 worked all right with the "oh" position being held three frames, and then I went back to two frames for the next mouth position, just before Jennyy closed her mouth again completely.

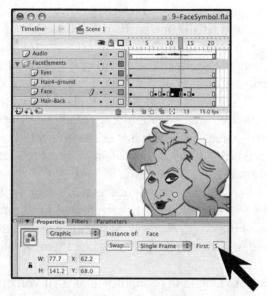

Insert keyframes as needed, click on
that instance of your symbol in each keyframe, and
then tell it what frame it needs to play. Here in Frames
11 through 13, Jenny's mouth is in the "oh" position of
Hello. In my case, that mouth position is saved in
Frame 5 of Jenny's mouth symbol (see arrow).

Once you've set up your mouth positions properly, there are
just two more things I would mention that might make dialogue
more believable. For a demure girl, there might not be a whole lot
of jaw movement as she speaks, but that depends on the particular
scene you're dealing with and her emotional state within that
scene. If she were angry (or even screaming her dialogue, for that
matter), she might actually move her lower jaw as she speaks...
violently, in some extreme cases.

In such a case, you might decide to place Jenny's lower jaw
(say, from below her cheekbone to her chin) on a separate layer,
and actually have her face change shape subtly (or not so subtly) as
she speaks.

Another way we emphasize our particular words during a sentence as we speak (usually one particular syllable of one particular word, let's say) is with our eyes and eyebrows. If you look at this chapter's dialogue example in the download files, you'll see I had Jenny's eyebrows go up on the first bit of her "oh" mouth position.

To do this, I just went into her Eye symbol, duplicated a frame by (yep, you guessed it) my Option-drag (Mac)/Alt-drag (PC) method. In that frame, I selected her eyebrows with the Lasso tool, and right-clicked (PC)/Ctrl-clicked (Mac) to do a Free Transform on only her eyebrows... *not* her eyes.

Then I just enlarged her eyebrows ever so slightly. True, my first thought was to merely *raise* her eyebrows, but I thought... no. When we raise our own eyebrows, they change shape, ever so slightly. I thought both raising and enlarging them would be more convincing.

Next I went to look in my soundtrack for that verbal *accent*. In this case, the second syllable of "hello" looked louder, judging by the waveform readout. That's where I decided to place my accent, which just happened to be in Frame 11. I selected my Eye symbol in Frame 11, and in my Properties window, I clicked on the First box and entered the frame number of my new "raised eyebrows," Frame 3.

Note how I've set the eyebrows to go up slightly on the second syllable in the word "Hello." Doing subtle things like having the eyebrows go up, or maybe having the eyes squint on a particular syllable or go wide on an important word — all these are subtle ways to make dialogue more convincing by adding a visual accent to a verbal accent. Naturally, all this can go in more dramatic directions by having a character point on a certain word or perform any number of physical accents during a particular line of dialogue.

Using the knowledge you've gained with this exercise, try that with one of your own characters, and hopefully you'll agree that little details such as accenting dialogue with eye movement (and occasional jaw motion) make our character's performance more convincing... and more entertaining.

Working with Scenes

You might have already decided that as your movie starts to grow in complexity with all these layers upon layers, even layer folders aren't helping you keep them under as much control as you'd like.

Now might be the time to start working with scenes.

Scenes are fairly straightforward to deal with, and I would suggest breaking each sequence into a different scene every time you change your background; possibly even every time you change your camera shot (naturally some shots may share the same background, just resized and/or repositioned for each variation of camera angle).

Every time you want to insert a scene, go to **Insert | Scene**. A new scene will be added *after* the current scene, and the numbering system isn't terribly creative. You'll have Scene 1, Scene 2, and so on.

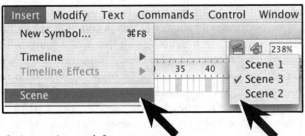

Going to Insert | Scene
(see left arrow) will add a new scene to your movie; you'll probably find it convenient to change scenes whenever you change a background or camera shot. But don't forget that even if scenes are numbered properly, they'll only play back in the order they're listed at the top right of your screen beside the Clapboard icon (see right arrow).

The thing to remember, though, is that the scenes will play back in the order they're listed, which you can view by clicking on the little old-fashioned Clapboard icon at the top right of the Timeline. So be careful to add scenes in order; by that, I mean, if you want to add a scene *after* Scene 8, make sure you've got Scene 8 open when you add it. That will add Scene 9 after Scene 8.

However, if you do add scenes in the wrong order, all is not lost. If you need to change the order of a scene, all you have to do is drag the scenes into your desired order by dragging the scene name to a different location in the Scene Panel. In order to get to this, go to **Window | Other Panels | Scenes.**

Special Effects: Creating Glows with Flash

As usual, there is more than one way to apply special effects to your characters and Flash artwork. I'll start by showing you how to apply a glow to a Flash symbol. I have a toad wizard, as you can see in the following figure, and though I could quite happily get away with mere flashy colors flying from his fingertips, I think it would be more effective if they had an otherworldly glow. We'll start with that.

1. Create a new layer and name it something like **Sparks**.

2. Draw a series of lightning-like strokes on that separate layer.

Part of the "special effects" in this picture are really just creative applications of color. I noticed something recently when watching *The Rescuers* with my Intro to Animation class. What I had once thought was some sort of special effect really wasn't. Those alligators' (or crocodiles') eyes weren't *glowing*, as I'd thought long ago, but actually were just painted bright yellow, and everything around them was painted in *darker* colors. By contrast, they appear to be glowing, like the "magical reflections" you see on the edge of the toad wizard's cloak (see arrow).

3. Now, with your sparks drawn, change them into a symbol by selecting them and then pressing **F8**.

    Here I will mention, though, that these effects have their limitations. They're only applicable to text, movie clips, and buttons. In that case, we have to change this spark into a movie clip. (It's obviously not text and wouldn't do us much good as a button.)

4. In that case, I need to go to my Properties window and change it from my favorite symbol format, Graphic, to **Movie Clip**.

In order to apply a filter like a glow, blur, drop shadow, etc., you first need to change your symbol from a graphic to a movie clip (or button).

5. Next, click on your **Filters** tab (beside the Properties tab), and click on the + sign you see there, in order to add one of the special filters.

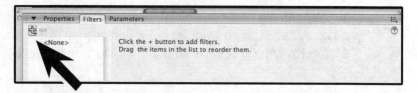

Add filter

6. As you can see, you've got quite a few choices, like Drop Shadow, Blur, Glow, and so on, but for now, let's drag down to **Glow**.

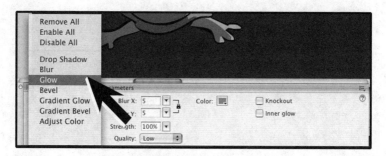

Adding a glow effect

The glow actually looks pretty good (on a single frame), but here's the problem I ran into. Because it was a movie clip, it wouldn't play my animation through (oddly enough), even though I made several frames of various "zaps" for it to cycle through when it played. I could probably get around this by doing each spark as a separate symbol (and you're certainly welcome to try experiments of your own), but I decided to take a different approach to my glow, as I hinted at earlier. (I always like to have a backup plan, and this approach might actually play back faster, I suspect, if download time is a concern.)

Once again, I made a lightning-bolt artwork symbol, this time called Spark 2. I went into that symbol's Timeline by double-clicking, and made about three frames of various lightning bolts, with the Onion Skin option activated as my guide. First off, though, I did one thing different: I used a much wider brush to create my bolts, and here's why.

You can also use your radial gradient fill in the Color Mixer to make a gradient with an outer color that is transparent, via the Alpha channel. Look what I did in the following example.

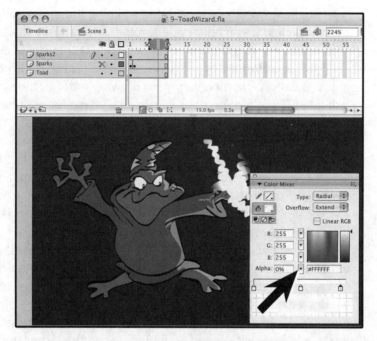

By creating a radial gradient fill with your Color Mixer, you can lower the Alpha channel of your outermost color and have it fade away to nothing for a glow-like effect. My first color is yellow, my second color is white, and my third color is "white" with an Alpha channel lowered to 0%, as indicated by the arrow.

You might have to adjust your gradient on each frame by using the Gradient Transform tool (located just beneath the Subselection tool, or "white arrow" tool, as some may call it). You'll see that doing so will give you more control over the effect.

One final word on special effects like lightning, fire, and even watery cycles: If you only cycle through two or three drawings, the mechanical effect will become immediately recognizable and dull, even to the *untrained* eye. Instead of cycling through three drawings repeatedly in order, vary your drawing order in the symbol's individual Timeline. In other words, don't have three drawings that continuously loop 1, 2, 3, 1, 2, 3, 1, 2, 3, etc. Rather, vary that cycle somewhat by going 1, 2, 3, 2, 1, 3, 2, 3, 1, 2, 1... and so on, in a more seemingly random order. That's what separates lackluster "computery" animation from more naturalistic, random, and I dare-say *organic* animation.

It's those subtle variations of shape and cycle that make real life, or even great animation, worth watching anyway.

Go through the other filters like Drop Shadow, Bevel, and so on to see what kind of effects you can come up with on your movies.

As always, I encourage you to experiment, and even *more* so, as we draw closer to the end of the book. As I noticed myself, the more I worked with Flash, the more comfortable I got, and the more bold I got with my experiments... and the better my Flash cartoons looked!

Chapter 10

Preparing Your Work for Video or Web Downloads

Sezquatch, Thurman, and Deadbeat
© Mark S. Smith/MarkToonery.com

A Brief History of Dubbing Homemade Cartoons to Video

A former coworker at Alabama Public Television years ago (around 1998, I think) told me that a new era in video production was on its way. He told me that the day would come when there would be a new breed of video producers; they would be called "prosumers," or professional consumers. He explained that within the next decade there was going to be a drastic drop in the price of professional-grade video production equipment that average consumers could soon afford. I can't remember the exact words of my reply, but I had to admit that I harbored my doubts at the time.

THERE'S ALWAYS A CHANCE
IT'LL MAKE A COMEBACK...
OF COURSE, I SAID THE SAME
THING ABOUT MY
BETA COLLECTION...

Deadbeat © Mark S. Smith/MarkToonery.com

I had paid roughly $1,600 for a Panasonic S-VHS editor (that stands for Super-VHS) that would enable me to make "semi-professional" dubs of my computer cartoons. S-VHS has roughly twice the screen resolution (which we'll discuss shortly) as plain ol' VHS. Back then, if you wanted to make dubs of your work, getting things transferred from computer signals (digital) to a consumer-brand VCR (analog signals) was a somewhat laborious (not to mention expensive) process.

If I wanted a full-fledged professional-quality video editor to dub my computer cartoons onto, I needed a $3,000 to $5,000 Beta machine. And that's not all; as I mentioned, going from digital to analog wasn't as simple as getting a cable. You had to have a video card installed in your computer and/or something called a genlock. A *genlock* was a device that translated the computer's output into a format that a consumer-quality VHS machine (or in my case, S-VHS) could understand, and therefore record.

Fortunately, however, my former coworker at APT turned out to be right.

I was absolutely thrilled when I heard about the iMac G4, a half-globe-shaped CPU with a screen extending above its main body. (I describe it to others as R2D2's head with a TV dinner tray sticking out from the top.) Although the unusual shape was mildly amusing, and the surprisingly small size for such a powerful computer inviting, the thing that got me was this: You could burn your own DVDs right on the machine's built-in drive!

Up until that point, I prided myself on staying a step *behind* the "state of the art." You heard me right — a step behind! When a new computer would come out, I'd buy last year's model when prices dropped dramatically on the release of this year's latest model. Or better yet, I'd occasionally buy a refurbished model (from someplace like Sunremarketing.com or Shreve Systems) from places that would buy used computers and then restore them to "like new" for considerable discounts.

But that time I knew this was the verge of that "prosumer era" of video production my coworker was talking about. I bought the new iMac, and roughly three years later, I'm still working with it. (I'm typing this very book on it, no less!)

Naturally, my point to all this is that "you kids" just don't appreciate how easy you've got it nowadays! Once you finish that fabulous Flash cartoon you've been working on all this time, all you have to do is pop a blank DVD into your computer's DVD burner and start burning, right?

Well, yes… and no.

There are a few things you need to take into account before you start exporting your Flash movie, no matter how great it is.

And that's what this chapter is about.

Title Safe and Action Safe Areas

One of the most important aspects of screen layout is a concept called Title Safe and Action Safe areas. While not so much of an issue in film animation, it's a vital topic in video animation. Title Safe is a little less forgiving because of something called overscan, so we'll talk about that first. When I started producing computer graphics for video production, one of the first things I learned was the danger zone on your computer screen called the "overscan area."

If you look closely around the edge of your computer monitor, you'll notice that you can see every last pixel your computer illuminates. The active area of your screen stops about 1/8" away from the edge of your monitor. (I'm sure even this area varies from screen to screen and platform to platform.) However, if you were to look carefully at a television when it's on, you'd probably notice that a small portion of the picture is actually *covered up* by the border of its monitor. That's what's called the overscan area. (See the following illustration.) The television scan lines (horizontal lines that the TV "draws" at 30 frames per second) actually show up "underneath" the frame around your monitor, so that you can't see a certain outer portion of the video.

If you have a character's name, a crucial bit of text information, or even credits to be shown, make sure you allow yourself at least three-quarters of an inch around the edge of the screen. That's what I was always told.

However, don't leave a black border visible in that "unsafe area." By all means, let the edges of your background sit tight, whether it's a jungle, forest, cityscape, or even a plain empty room. What I am saying is that you need to make sure no crucial pieces of information are sitting along that line.

As a frightening example, I was horrified to be watching a newscast one night, and a little beeping sound started on the television. I could tell there was some sort of severe weather alert (tornadoes are pretty common during certain times of the year in the southeast). At that point, they usually inform the viewers by running a computer graphic banner at the bottom of the screen, and

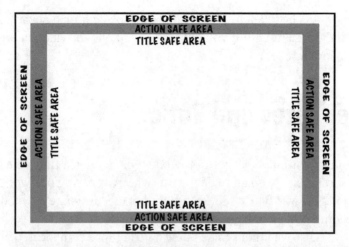

It's important to design your artwork with Title Safe and Action Safe areas in mind, especially when it comes to text. Don't cut off the background at the edge of the Action Safe area. Once I was horrified to see that a student had actually shrunk down his entire video image to fit inside the Action Safe area, surrounded by a black border. Instead, go ahead and let it bleed beyond the edge of that screen. The TV will cut it off for you.

warn the viewers whether a tornado has been sighted and what counties need to take emergency precautions.

I couldn't read the banner.

I could only see the top of the banner, which read "Severe Weather Alert/Tornado Watch," but the banner at the bottom of the screen was *outside* the Title Safe area. I could not read which counties were included in the tornado watch.

That was poor planning on the part of their computer graphics artist… and downright dangerous.

By contrast, the Action Safe area is a little wider, and therefore somewhat more forgiving. It's not as great a tragedy if the very bottom of a character's foot ends up in the overscan area. But if a character is pointing at something of interest, it's highly likely that its hand needs to be well within the Action Safe area.

The earlier incarnation of Flash (Flash MX) had a handy TV broadcast template. Regrettably, it was absent in Flash MX 2004, and to the best of my knowledge, hasn't been seen since. It might not be a bad idea to create your own, place it on a separate layer, and delete it before you export your movie for video or web download purposes.

Screen Sizes and Ratios

As I mentioned earlier in the book, once upon a time, the only screen size we had to deal with (when preparing our work for video output) was 640 x 480. Done. End of discussion, everybody go home, it's been a great day.

That was then; this is now a little more complicated.

640 x 480 means that the screen is 640 pixels wide and 480 pixels tall. That is roughly a 3:4 ratio, or more precisely a 1.33:1 ratio, so when I was preparing my storyboards, I'd make sure they were roughly that same ratio. If it was three inches tall, it would be four inches wide, or any fraction based on that ratio (1.5 inches to 2 inches, etc.); again, those were simpler times.

The most common broadcast size now (if we can make such a hasty, generalized statement) would be 720 x 540 pixels. That's what I generally set my screen size to when I'm starting a new Flash project.

But what about this new complication called HDTV?

As most of you well know by now, HDTV stands for High Definition Television, and it has made life slightly more complicated for those of us preparing work for broadcast. It has a wider aspect ratio, of 1.78:1, if you compare it with 1.33:1 (and that's *exactly* what we're comparing it with).

So if that wasn't enough of a trick to deal with, HDTV comes in three formats!

The smallest format is 1280 x 720 progressive scan. The next is 1080 I, which means 1920 x 1080 interlaced, and finally 1920 x 1080 progressive scan.

Interlaced means that the video image you're seeing is being drawn alternately in odd and even scans. What does that mean to you as a designer? It means you should avoid drawing perfectly horizontal lines that are exactly one pixel tall.

What do I mean by that?

I'm glad you asked. (Well, not altogether *glad*, but I've gotta explain this anyway, so here goes...)

On the normal video images we're generally watching, the television actually draws two pictures for every one of those frames you heard me mention earlier. Remember that we have 30 frames per second of NTSC video. Well, each one of those frames is actually broken down into two *fields*. So for that matter, you've actually got 60 fields per second of video.

What happens is this: The television draws all the odd horizontal fields in one pass, and then all the even horizontal fields in the next pass. So for every one of those frames, you're watching two fields; you're seeing an odd field and then an even field.

The reason I said we therefore need to avoid one-pixel tall, horizontal lines is because that one-pixel line will be visible on one field and gone the next. The result? An annoying flicker. The remedy? Avoid one-pixel-tall lines; draw them thicker.

These are naturally just guidelines. If you have any doubt about the size your screen needs to be, the best possible thing to do is ask a video professional. Even if I gave you every specific detail for every specific situation (a virtual impossibility for a book of this scope), there's the odd chance things might change, as they have a nasty habit of doing, by the time you're reading this.

Before you even start setting up your files for broadcast, it's a good idea to ask the creative services director or video producer at the agency or video production house you're working for. They will much prefer to answer these questions beforehand than for you to have to resize your stage for your Flash movie... moving characters back into the Action Safe area, resizing text so that it fits in the Title Safe area.

Fixing a movie you thought was finished can be a weary, time-consuming process, especially if you're on a tight deadline!

Screen Resolution

Now that we've covered screen sizes and ratios, let's touch briefly on the subject of screen resolution.

Screen resolution is simply the number of pixels you'll find within a square inch on your computer monitor. That's where we get the acronym *ppi*, or pixels per inch.

Hey! Remember me? Yeah, Tangent Man! You haven't heard from me in a while, so I've decided to put in my two cents worth right here, before you guys forget about me altogether! Ahem! Anyway, ppi, as you may or may not know, is generally used in terms of video production and web graphics, while dpi, or dots per inch, is generally used for print production.

As a general guideline, most video production graphics, like animation, are at 72 ppi. If you were preparing something to print out, however, like you wanted to export a Flash image to Photoshop or Illustrator for a flyer or something, then you'd want to export that image at 300 dpi or better. As always, ask your client, art director, or creative services professional as a safety precaution *before* the day of the deadline!

There! Well, with that out of the way, I guess I'll go get some coffee... maybe an espresso. Can I get you guys anything? A croissanwich, or maybe a cinnamon bun...? Which reminds me of a funny story, actually...

Since we're talking about video and not print, for all practical purposes you'll be dealing with 72 ppi, because that's what video monitors are capable of. Therefore, there would be very few occasions when you'll need to scan your artwork at anything more than 72 ppi.

If you scan it in at 300 ppi, you're taking up almost three times as much disk space as necessary with that one drawing, and then multiply that times 30 frames per second (or 15 frames per second if you're shooting on *twos*, or 10 frames per second for *threes*), and see how that adds up.

Naturally, there may be exceptions when you may need to scan in a bit of artwork at a higher resolution for your cartoon. For instance, you might scan in a background you're going to import as a JPG file, and you happen to know you're going to need a close-up of a particular section for a cut-in of a character. If that were the case, you may decide it would be helpful to scan it in at 150 or even 300 ppi, depending on how close Flash's "imaginary camera" is going to get to that extreme close-up of artwork.

It's okay; in that case, you have my permission.

Movie Format: FLA, SWF, or MOV?

All right, not only do you have your movie complete, but you've talked to the video producer (or webmaster, as the case may be) and have decided on the perfect output size and resolution for your movie.

Now, what format does our movie need to be in?

The initial thought to the "first-time Flash filmmaker" might be, "Oh, it's just a Flash movie. I'll send them the Flash file I've been working on!"

Naturally, this first idea might *not* be the best for a number of reasons.

First of all, there's no guarantee your viewer will have Flash on his or her computer. Let's face it: Flash is an expensive program for some of us, and not every home office or production suite has a copy.

Another reason this might not be advisable is that other people can therefore "dig into" your original files, and because of Flash's ease of use (not to mention character "recyclability") might decide to use *your* symbols to make their *own* cartoons... without your permission!

There's a scary thought. And perhaps worse still, who knows what gosh-awful website your characters might show up on? Yecchh!

So your next most obvious choice might be a SWF file. That's just a Flash Player file. That's a far more reasonable conclusion.

Many people already have it on their computers and don't even know it. Because so many websites have Flash content, it's already been installed, so to speak!

Just as a precaution (and you all know by now what a cautious fellow I am), before you export your movie as a SWF file, you can do a "Publish Preview."

1. Go to **File | Publish Preview | Default**.

    That's simple enough, isn't it? And it's a nice — not to mention quick — way to double-check your movie before you go making anything final. It's a good way to make sure that your scenes are playing in the right order, your sounds are okay, and so on.

    Your movie will open up in your default web browser, and you'll get a looping preview to see how well your cartoon plays back. Just don't forget, if you've got a particularly fast machine, it might play slower on someone else's laptop, or vice versa.

    I did a short Flash presentation at home one night on my computer, which you know by now is an iMac G4 (at least at the time of this writing). The next day, I played my presentation at school for an animation workshop, and the machines they have at school are G5 Macs. They played the movie back so fast, there wasn't ample time to read the onscreen text in certain parts of my presentation.

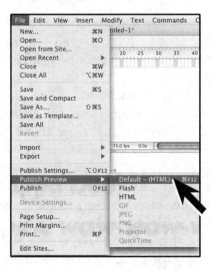

Before you go exporting files, it's not a bad idea to do a Publish Preview.

Now if all went well with your test, and you're ready to export your movie as a SWF file, then here's what you should do:

2. Go to **File | Export | Export Movie**.

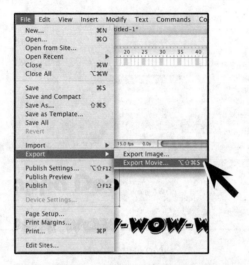

When you wish to export your movie as a SWF file, begin by going to File | Export | Export Movie.

3. In the window that pops up, select **Format** and drag down to (for now) **Flash Movie**.

By now, you've already begun to ask yourself a quite logical question: "What format do I wish to export this movie in?" I would say the possibilities are endless, but in reality, you've got a mere *11* choices, as you can see in the following illustration. We're only going to hit a couple of highlights, for purposes of brevity.

The first one we're interested in is the Flash movie, otherwise known as SWF format, which we've mentioned.

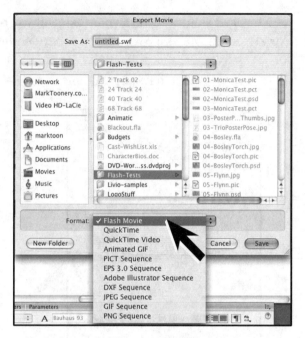

Movie formats

Once you export something as a SWF file, after Flash is done exporting, you can double-click on the item, and it will begin playing automatically. The SWF format is the file I send to my webmaster (Craig of c-eye.net, who does all my website design with cunning expertise, while I just do the actual drawings and animation) when I've got a new Flash cartoon I wish to post on my website.

Refer to the following illustration for your various options on exporting a SWF movie. Myself, I generally leave them at the default settings. The one item I *would* recommend adjusting, particularly on a case-by-case basis, would be the JPEG Quality setting, which determines the picture quality, and therefore the file size as well.

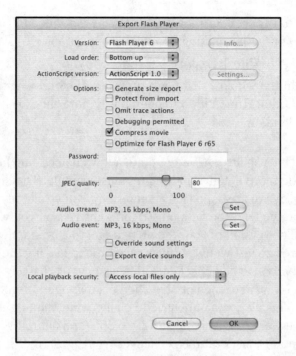

Flash Player export options

Exporting as QuickTime for Video

On the other hand, when I've got a file I want to burn directly to DVD (with a program like iDVD, for us Mac folks, or any number of applications for you PC users), or even one I wish to touch up by adding filters with Adobe After Effects, or edit together with a bunch of other shots with a nonlinear video editing program like Final Cut, then I'll select the QuickTime Video option. As with the others, you'll find you've got a variety of choices and levels of quality. The suggestions I'm going to offer are merely a starting point for your own experiments; they've proven to work for me.

To export your movie as a QuickTime Video file for burning to DVD or further editing in outside applications:

1. Go to **File | Export | Export Movie**.
2. In the window that pops up, select **Format** and drag down to **QuickTime Video** to open the Export QuickTime Video window.

Once again, you've got quite a few choices, and here I'll go into a little more detail than the previous example. The dimensions of your movie are supposedly something you've already determined before you got too far along. If for some reason you wish to make a smaller version of your movie to email to a friend, here's where you can resize it. I would *strongly* recommend leaving the **Maintain aspect ratio** box checked. Otherwise, your characters might end up looking squashed or stretched in an altogether undesirable fashion. This way, you only have to change one number; for instance, if you were to change from 720 to 360 (and naturally left that Maintain aspect ratio box checked as suggested), Flash would automatically cut the second number (480) in half to 240, which would be directly proportional to its original size.

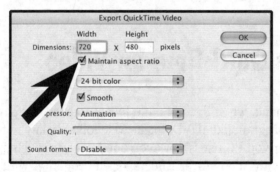

Export QuickTime Video window

Your next choice worthy of mention is **Format**, and in this case, that refers to color depth. Generally, you'll be safe with 24-bit color, which is millions of colors. 16-bit color may work in some cases, but the only time I would suggest trying it out is when you have characters that are colored in flat colors. There is a slight risk of your gradients (if you have any) *banding*, or turning into nasty pixelated stripes rather than smooth transitions of color.

32-bit color is recommended if an Alpha channel is an area of concern.

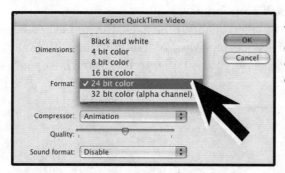

The Format options let you choose a color depth.

As you can see from the following illustration, you've got a wide variety of choices for compression method. Again, we've got way more choices than I had when I was just working with plain ol' Macromedia Director. And also, once again, I'll tell you what works for me. For the obvious reason (the fact that we're making cartoons), I leave my **Compressor** setting at the default of Animation.

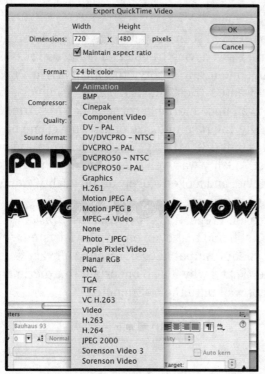

Choose a compression method

If you're uncertain of which method is the most desirable, consult with that handy ol' creative services director or webmaster for his or her particular preference.

In the case of video quality, I'll choose the highest possible quality of export rendering. Most of the time, the stuff I'm doing is for either broadcast quality or DVD, so I want the best possible setting.

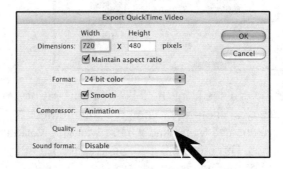

I generally choose the highest Quality setting.

In a somewhat related scenario (although with a different software program), I was having trouble, for some odd reason, rendering a QuickTime file in any quality other than "High." I was determined that I wanted "Best" quality, but as deadlines sometimes force us into an uncomfortable corner, I had to settle for "High." Surprisingly, the resulting size of my QuickTime file on "High" quality was only 138 MB. By contrast, an almost identical file saved in "Best" quality was well over 1 GB. I opened up the "High" quality movie, and looked closely at the quality. Admittedly, I didn't notice a great amount of difference.

This is one reason I repeat this advice almost *constantly*: Try it out for yourself. You'll find that even on your own system setup (and within your clients' output needs), results will vary drastically from time to time. That's why it's so important to experiment beforehand and not wait until the last minute.

As you can see in the following illustration, we've got quite a few choices as far as our **Sound format** options. While as always, I encourage you to experiment, I will say a few words about sound quality. In the following illustration, you see that 44kHz 8 Bit Stereo is the default setting. While I'll generally leave it at this setting, you might want to consider whether your client will approve of this. If it's for the Internet, and people will be watching on unpredictable processors of various speeds, the default might be all right. It's just a bit less acceptable than 44kHz 16 bit Stereo, which is CD quality, or therefore broadcast-quality sound.

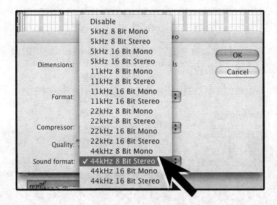

The Sound output options

But if this is something that has essential sound embedded in it, and you're going to be using this rendered video file for broadcast or DVD, I'd recommend going for the best.

The higher up the list, the worse the quality of sound but the smaller the file size. The farther down the list you go, the better your sound quality gets.

Which is more important? File size or sound quality? That's up to you — and/or your client — to decide.

Creating a Projector

All right, there is one other option we'll explore for sharing your movie (before closing out this chapter) and that's by creating a projector. As mentioned earlier, you can generally be fairly certain that most computers will have some form of Flash Player installed.

But if you're going to meet with an important client, and you're uncertain whether they've got Flash Player, and you just can't take chances... there is such a thing as a Flash Projector.

For this technique to work, you must have already created a SWF file. Once you've done that, we can begin.

1. Open up the SWF file that you've created, and you'll be taken into Flash Player.

2. Once inside Flash Player, go to **File | Create Projector**.

Flash Projector

This technique is particularly useful for distributing your movies via CD-ROM and various other media. What makes it great is that the person doesn't even need to have Flash Player for it to work. It creates an executable application, and Flash Player realizes that the file must begin to play by itself. True, there's a slight increase in size when you create a Projector file, but it's a relatively small price to pay, all things considered.

There is one downside to be taken into account, however. If you create a Projector with this method, regrettably a Projector made on the PC can't run on a Mac, and a Mac-made Projector can't run on the PC.

(Yeah, it just sounded *too* darn good to be true, didn't it?)

The good news is, though, that via the Publish Settings command of Flash, you can create a Mac-PC "hybrid Projector." But you have to tell Flash that's what you want it to do.

To try this method:

1. Go to **File | Publish Settings**.
2. Click on both the **Windows Projector (.exe)** and **Macintosh Projector** boxes.

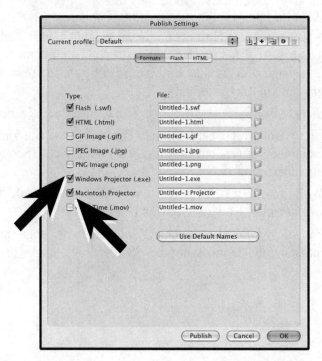

Choose both options to create a hybrid Projector.

Possible Cross-Platform Conflicts: Fonts, in Particular

Do be warned, however, that although the SWF file format is intended to be cross-platform compatible (equally viewable on the Mac and the PC), there are always possible setbacks to be encountered. You may want to consider that sounds, bitmaps, and particularly fonts shouldn't give you problems (and, of course you knew this was coming…), *but* I'm always paranoid that some favorite novelty font I've included on my file might not display correctly on someone's computer. Even if the font appeared okay, there are still issues like leading, kerning, and all sorts of other irritating text details just waiting to rear their ugly heads.

What do I do to avoid this would-be catastrophe? (Or would that be ca-text-trophe?… Hmm… no. No, it wouldn't…) Just like Adobe Illustrator (or Photoshop, for that matter), I convert my font text to either a shape or a graphic. In the case of Flash, to preserve the integrity of your favorite fonts:

1. Select your font text by clicking on it with the Selection tool.

2. Go to **Modify | Break Apart**. This will break the font into individual letters, but they'll still be "font text." (See the following illustration.)

3. With the object still selected, go to **Modify | Break Apart** a *second* time. (Now they're text objects.)

4. For safety (and with the object still selected), make the object into a symbol by pressing the **F8** key.

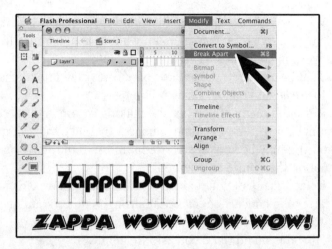

To preserve the fonts you designed for your movie, you may wish to "break apart" your text, and therefore convert it to a graphic. Do keep in mind, however, that a slight risk (changing your file size) might be involved. If you're ever in doubt, always do a "Save As" to see what the difference in your file sizes would be with text broken apart into graphics, or as plain text.

If you're using a standard standby font like Helvetica (yawn) or Times (double-yawn... pardon me!), it's probably not going to be an issue. But if you have a tendency like yours truly to use more "cartoony" fonts (like Bauhaus 93 or Bertram, as pictured), you may want to take these precautions.

Well, as you can see, we're getting closer and closer to the end of this book! Hopefully that means by the end of this chapter, you've got a cartoon ready to show the world, whether you've burned it to DVD with any of the easy-to-use software readily available with most new Macs and PCs, or a SWF or Projector file.

Whatever your method of distribution for your Flash cartoon, perhaps the most fun part of making animation (admittedly after all that work is done) is sharing it with others.

That brings us to the subject of our next (and final) chapter...

Just *who* do you show this cartoon to?

Although many of you may be making cartoons purely for your personal enjoyment, I strongly suspect that, like most of my students, you may be seeking a little bit more from the world of animation than mere amusement.

In fact, many of you may be seeking that career satisfaction that (as far as I'm concerned) can come from no other source...

You want a *job* in animation.

How do you do that? you ask. Read on...

Chapter 11

Jobs, Colleges, and Film Festivals

Sezquatch, Thurman, and Deadbeat
© Mark S. Smith/MarkToonery.com

One of the most common questions I get as an instructor from students and parents alike is, "How do I get a job in animation?"

Deadbeat & Sezquatch © Mark S. Smith/MarkToonery.com

Many of us have always suspected the truth behind this illustration. Sadly, there may be more to this scenario than you might think. There is a way around it, but what is it? Read on, and I'll be happy to share the "secret information."

Finding a Job

The answer is both simpler and more complex than they hope for. (How's that for an evasive reply?) The answer is, "It's different for everybody."

The reason I say that is because it's always such an ongoing struggle to make a living at animation, even if you're good at it. As I've realized during the course of writing this book, you cannot get complacent, whatever stage you're at. Your career is an ongoing process, and like gardening, you've always got to continue to water it (keep sending out updated demo DVDs to previous clients), fertilize it (send out demo DVDs to *potential* clients), and prune it (turn down "offers" to work for free or turn away projects that otherwise sound suspicious).

If there's one thing I can tell you (there's more, which will follow, but this is a *golden* key), it's network, network, network.

Networking, for those of you unfamiliar with the term, basically just means to find out who the industry experts are and talk to them. Find out what organizations they're members of and attend the meetings. You may have to drive an hour or two (it was *three* from Montgomery to Atlanta), but you may find an improved career is worth the price of a tank of gas.

In my case, I found that most of the people at Cartoon Network (and the local studios they outsourced to) were members of ASIFA-Atlanta, the International Animated Film Association (yeah, that's from a French acronym, if I haven't mentioned it before). So I found out when the next meeting was and attended. Show up early and stay late afterward. And don't hang about shyly in the corners, *hoping* someone is going to come talk to you. Find out who the club officers are, and talk to *them*. Tell them you're a lifetime animation fan (if that is indeed true), whether you're an art or animation student, and that you're trying to make it into a career. They'll probably be happy to tell you who to talk to. *Occasionally*, they can even tell you which studios are seeking freelancers.

Interview with Joe Peery, ASIFA-Atlanta President, and Animation Director, Turner Studios

On ASIFA membership, the importance of networking, and how Flash has returned American animation to American shores!

MSS: How important is networking to the career-minded animation professional?

JP: Extremely important, just because animation is a collaborative effort to begin with. You have to know how to work with people, and you have to be able to communicate with people. One of the things I tell people who are freelancing is… have a phone. Have it with you all the time, and *answer* it. If you're not able to answer it, return your calls immediately. It's as simple as that. If you meet somebody, they say, "Hey, I do animation, call me," and when you do give them that call, they don't answer; you leave them a message. If you don't hear back from them right away, you call somebody else. And they've missed the job.

MSS: Right. Good answer. How can a beginning freelancer keep his or her career moving forward?

JP: I think by continuing to work on your own projects. Like if you have something you're passionate about that you're working on. So the next time you call the person you want to do some work for, you have something new to show. That always helps. I have a figure drawing class, and I always encourage people to do as much figure drawing as possible to keep their drawing skills up. That's pretty much it. Just continue to work on your skills. Keep drawing every day, and keep studying animators and animation that you love. Freeze-frame it, study it frame by frame, and draw from it.

MSS: That makes for a good follow-up question. Who are some of the animators that you admire? Some of the popular ones, and maybe some of the less well-known ones… independents, maybe?

JP: Well, let's see… John Kricfalusi, of course, is just great because his stuff is so *extreme*. Really groundbreaking. I mean, the stuff that he did was on the heels of one of the worst times of animation in recent history. Everything had just sort of taken a dive. There was just nothing but [junk] out there. He nearly single-handedly brought it back with just hilarious animation. He was a big student of animation as well, as you see now with his blogs and books that he's written, and with his liner notes on *The Flintstones* animation. The more I think about it the more I really appreciate him, not only because of the example he set with his animation, but also the knowledge he was able to impart and share with other animators. He seems really anxious and willing to do that, to be a teacher as well as to direct.

MSS : What is ASIFA, and how did you get involved?

JP: (Ahem!) It's a French acronym [Association International du Film d'Animation, translated as International Animated Film Association]. The official website is ASIFA.net. It's a worldwide animation organization that was started in France in the '60s, and now there are groups all over the world, including here in Atlanta. So this one was started in '97, and I just took over this last year after the passing of our last president, Lou Hertz. So we've kinda built it back up, with the help of a lot of people. This year I went to my first international film festival, which absolutely floored me. It was incredible. It was in Zagreb, Croatia. And I met all the other board members that were representatives of all the other groups around the world. It was just incredible. I learned a ton about just how ASIFA works, what it is, and what it's *trying* to be. One of the main things that they do is try to share, inform people what animation is, so they try to educate and then bring animators together. And one of the ways that they do that is by hosting these international film festivals. And these top international film festivals are the ones that have been [officially sanctioned] by ASIFA. So they actually have a group that, when there are new festivals for people trying to get on the festival circuit, they check it out and rate it, and say whether or not it's approved by ASIFA, and that carries a lot of clout. Several of the board members are judges, and that's a really big deal.

I didn't realize what a big deal it was until I went, because we don't really have them here in the States, where it's very limited. Especially here in the Southeast, we [didn't] have international film festivals. Now I realize what that was, because once a year we [do *now*] have a film festival, which is an international week-long film festival, of which one evening is animation. [That's] two showings of about a three-hour show, so that's what we see. Every year we see about three hours of animation, and at the international animation festival I went to, it was about six or seven full *days* of animation. It started at nine in the morning and ended at midnight, every night. Nothing but animation for a week long. And these were fantastic films like I had never seen before. When you go to a film festival, a lot of the audience are just fans who come to see the films. Then at the animation festivals, the majority of the audience are actually filmmakers.

So the first question I was asked by everybody I met there was, "Do you have a film in the festival?"

I admitted, "No, I don't."

[Then they'd say], "So what do you do?"

I'd say, "Well, I'm an animator."

"Then why don't you have a film in the festival?"

Then I'd tell them, "Actually, this is the first international film festival I've been to." And they would pretty much look at me like I was some sort of hillbilly that just [wandered in]. And y'know, I've been animating, fifteen, maybe twenty years now, however you define it.

MSS: You never really wanted to do any of your "own stuff"? Or maybe you just never set aside the time?

JP: No, I have some things that I've done, but I just wasn't aware of the sort of gravity of these international festivals outside the U.S. It's sort of like Sundance, or something like that, but it's international. I've kind of had my eyes opened in a lot of ways about ASIFA and film festivals. I did find out that next year there's going to be a festival in the States, in Portland. It's called the Platform Festival, and I'm going to go to that for sure, and maybe I'll have something together for that. I do have some side projects on the back burner… just waiting for some time. (Laughs)

MSS: So how can someone without a nearby chapter get involved with ASIFA? Or how many chapters, I guess I should say, are there in the States?

JP: Well, in the States there are six: Atlanta (GA), Central (MI), Colorado, East (NY), Hollywood, and San Francisco; then there are two ASIFA groups with less than 10 members: Northwest and Washington D.C.

You can go to ASIFA.net to find out more. You can have an International Membership with a single member, but chances are there's a group nearby if you live in one of these major cities. They're always looking for members, especially *active* members. That's something you can never have enough of. Active members get a lot out of it. Like I did. I basically just took over the presidency this last year. I didn't realize that meant I got to go for free (basically) to this film festival, so it ended up paying off in the end.

The big deal is that it's a network. If you come to these things and you're involved with the board, or directly involved with the group, you network with a lot of people in the business. That's a really good thing, and that's one thing we're trying to push locally, with the next event we have coming up called "Blowin' Smoke." We've had "Roll Your Own," which used to be [an all-in-one event]. It was anything anybody had been working on in the last year.

MSS: [That was] more like personal, students, and independent films?

JP: [Before] it was pretty much everything. It could be that, or it could be commercial work, could be anything, but it got so big we had to break it into [two events]. "Roll Your Own" for the personal work and student work, and then "Blowin' Smoke" for the professional work. So that's coming up really soon... October 16. It's great, because it's an opportunity for these professional outfits to show their work (or show off), and it's also great for students and people interested in the business, because professionals are going to be there. It'll be a great mixer, and it's real low key.

MSS: That's one of the things I was really happy about when I first got involved with ASIFA. There's just a sort of camaraderie among most artists, but particularly among animators I've seen.

JP: It is, and that's something Clay [Croker] used to have. [He'd have] parties at his house during Dragon-Con among animators, and people from the [L.A.] industry would be in town and come to his party, and they would see what the scene is here. They would say, "It's really 180 degrees from the way it is in L.A., which is really cutthroat, and people are after each other's jobs." Here, it's very loose among friends, and everybody helps everybody out. I'm kinda grateful that it's still that way, even though it has gotten a little tougher in the past couple of years. There are more animators, there's more competition, but still, I like to think that the younger ones who have come up through the system here in town see how that worked for them. It doesn't hurt *me* to help somebody out. If I'm too busy watching my back because I'm scared somebody's gonna take my job, I'm not looking in the right direction.

MSS: Oddly enough, at one of the other studios, I think Primal Screen, they suggested, "Y'know, over at Radical Axis, they're looking for animators, why don't you try over there?"

I said, "You're sending me to another studio?"

And he said, "Well, we'd help anybody trying to get started in the business." So it was just really a pleasant surprise.

JP: It serves all of our interests to keep freelance animators busy. So we try to even coordinate amongst ourselves, especially us and Primal Screen. Jim [Threlkeld] is a good friend of mine. He's always in contact to see who's busy. "Who are you using right now? Who's available? When are they gonna wrap up on that job?" We'll go ahead and book them, and try to do the same thing here if we've got somebody. We'll try to let them know when we'll be done with them so they can plan to be back over at Primal Screen next week. It just serves everybody, because if freelancers don't stay busy, say you just keep them to yourself, when you don't have work for them they're out wandering the streets. They have to take another job, and that takes them out of the pool. And that's happened *too* often, in too many ways. Especially when we opened up the Flash department here, a lot of my favorite freelancers that I was using, my right-hand men, were swallowed up by that group. And all of a sudden I had to find new animators.

That helps if you have a good relationship with the other studios. We call in and say, "Hey, who's good? Who are you using right now?" That way, especially if you're in a pinch, you [don't accidentally] hire somebody that's not at the level they need to be to pull you out of a hole. If I can call somebody at Primal that I trust, and say, "Look, this is really a tough job. Who can you recommend?" It works out really well for everybody.

MSS: Here's a popular question from my students: How does one get a job with Turner Studios' Cartoon Network?

JP: Heh-heh! Good question! I got in with Turner Studios just because they needed somebody with the skills I had, and I just happened to walk in the door. Actually, I had a tip from a friend of mine. And this is another thing about networking; also, about helping other people out. The way I heard about the available job here (as animation director) was through an animator friend of mine, Sam Leyja, who was working here. I just happened to ask him how things were going, just testing the waters, having freelanced at Primal over three years under a verbal contract. He said it was actually going very well; as a matter of fact, they were looking to hire somebody. And one of the reasons Sam told me that is because a few years before, when I was working at Primal Screen, I had been introduced to him and saw that he was a really good artist. I said, "Hey, this guy's great," and they of course saw he was great, and hired him on the spot. So it was just perfect because several years down the road, he repaid the favor. And that's how you'll find it works in this business; you'll meet people over and over again. And sometimes what you think is a simple favor can turn into a really big deal, and they can pay it back. Usually for me, it's just the talent. I wanna work with talented people and help them any way I can. (Sighs) I strayed from the question.

MSS: No, I think that's fine. I think everybody wants one easy answer, and my experience has certainly proven that there is no easy answer, that it's a different answer for everyone.

JP: Here's *another* answer. So outside of that, I've known some people who have gotten in at Cartoon Network in some ways at Turner Studios. They did that by working for Turner Temps, a temp agency. They got their foot in the door, anywhere they could. I know a lot of people at Cartoon Network who got in that way, and did a really [outstanding] job. Once you get in the door, you impress a few people with your work habits or skills, then people tend to move laterally. They'll jump over from whatever particular department that they're in. It's like a college campus; you're constantly running into people all the time, having lunch. So once you get in the door, you see all these people. If whoever you're working for sees you're doing this great job, they're going to tell others. Your manager may know the manager of a department you want to get in. They might say, "We've got this temp who's about to leave; she's really good, you may want to give her a shot..." You're going to have a lot better chance to get in the door if somebody knows you, as opposed to you being just one [name] in stacks of resumes.

MSS: Do you see the in-house production of Cartoon Network increasing in the near future?

JP: I hope so. We're set up and have developed a whole Flash department, a digital department, in order to do more shows in-house. With the success of *Harvey Birdman*, I think we've kinda floored everybody involved in how quickly our animators learned Flash, and learned how to use it in a way that it wasn't being used. They got to where they could draw in the program, and animating it to make it look like it wasn't done in Flash, but like it was done traditionally. The benefit is that it's a fast way to create a library full of assets. The more shows you do, [the more] you can use old assets from previous shows. But you're still able to draw new things when you need to. But really, the biggest thing was that they were able to work directly with the writers and the producers; we're on the same "campus." They could just come downstairs and talk to the animators as they were working, instead of having the animators create scenes, send them out, take a look at them [and say], "I dunno about that..." then send them back to the animators and have them rework the scenes. They can walk right down [and approve] scenes and make suggestions. So that show was able to be done a lot more on the fly.

There were also a lot of timing issues on that show. It's really quick, quick timing. There's really some offbeat sensibilities that don't necessarily translate to, say... Korean.

MSS: That's a pretty good point you've hit on there. I've heard a lot of people say one of the main advantages of Flash is to bring American animation back to America, so they can keep American animators working on these shows.

JP: Right, that's exactly right. In a couple of different ways. One way is that you storyboard something, and you send it to one of these awesome studios that were cheap but really good, but there's that cultural difference. So if you have something with those American sensibilities, and we send storyboards over, depending on who handles it, they may not *get* it. But we don't get their humor either.

MSS: So much of humor is culturally based.

JP: Especially if it's topical or if it's very recent, there are going to be certain things that just don't translate well. [Another thing] is even if your producers have instant messaging and your animation directors are in different states, say up in New York. They can IM and send them a clip back and forth, but there's just something about being in the same room with people. You can convey things with body language. IM just doesn't convey the same thing. Especially as an animation director, you want to be able to talk, and you want to be able to use your hands, by *showing* an animator when they're working on something. You might need to act something out. It's really hard to replace that with email.

That's one thing. And the other thing is that the individual animators are able to do so much more. Traditionally, in the animation production line, you'd have an animation director who's gonna storyboard everything out, and hand it out to maybe a lead animator to do part of it, who passes it down to an assistant animator, who passes stuff down to the inker. But the way they're doing the stuff now [in Flash], one animator gets one scene, doing everything. So you don't have anything lost in translation. That scene is owned by that one animator, from beginning to end.

MSS: One of the things I like about it is that I'm able to do my storyboards essentially directly in Flash. I can do an animatic almost instantly.

JP: That's really one of its highest qualities. And even if you have traditionally drawn storyboards, you can put it right there [in Flash] instead of making Xeroxes, and blowing them up, and waste a ton of time.

MSS: At first, I thought I would just do my animation key drawings traditionally and do my inbetween drawings in Flash, but I've gotten so comfortable with my drawing tablet that now I'll do a rough story sketch, scan it in, and work the whole scene from that. Sometimes I just draw it "from scratch" in Flash.

JP: Yeah, and you get better and better at drawing in the program. It's weird how it makes the hardest parts of animation the easiest. Like one of the hardest parts when you're animating is to do really subtle movement, keeping all the "wobble" out of the lines. It's a *breeze* in Flash! You can take that same line, and just move it... just a little bit.

MSS: Thanks so much, Joe, for taking the time to talk to me. I think my readers will get a lot of useful direction from this interview! I know I have.

Or if you can't find "experts" (whatever the word means; it's sorely misused), simply find people who are doing what you want to do and talk to them... locally or otherwise. Ask them how they got started. Better yet, ask them how they'd get started if they had to do it over again today! Oddly enough, we have an inborn tendency to think of these people we admire as demigods or superheroes (like movie stars), but they're people just like everybody else. And it took them work to get where they are, and mostly they'll appreciate the efforts and hardships of others. Again, careers don't "just happen" to people; it's up to you to make your career happen. In other words, take *action*!

Some of these people may occasionally be difficult to reach, some may not wish to be reached (and please respect that when it is the case), but those who *are* willing to be reached you might find surprisingly helpful.

Just as an extreme example, when I was watching *The Ren & Stimpy Show* during its premiere season, I had already started my habit of reading the credits to find people to contact. I saw the name of a lady animator (who I also happened to recognize from a photo in a *Ren & Stimpy* fan magazine), and decided to contact her. For some reason, I felt less intimidated talking to a lady animator; I suppose since I was then somewhat shy by nature. I knew the name of the company that produced the show was Spumco ("the Danes call it quality"), so I went to the phone, dialed directory assistance for Los Angeles (where I figured, in this case *correctly*, the studio was then located), and when the receptionist answered, I asked to speak to the animator. I'm sure when the receptionist asked who was calling, I probably responded something like, "This is Mark Smith, with MarkToons Video Animation." (That was the name of my freelance company back then.) If she had asked me anything about what MarkToons was (I don't think she did), I would have just responded truthfully, "It's my freelance animation service."

I found the animator in question to be very polite, cheerful, and helpful. I even wrote her a letter, and she wrote me back (I still have it somewhere). She did tell me that though it was really "hard to make the grade" there (meaning it was tough to get on board with them), she'd be happy to look at my work and offer constructive criticism.

One quick word of advice there on criticism before I move on...
if an industry expert offers you "constructive criticism," accept it
cheerfully. And that's even if you don't necessarily agree with it.
(Find polite ways to keep the conversation moving, if needed.
Wordless nodding helps, and noncommittal responses like, "That's
a unique insight," with the occasional, "Hmm...") Advice is free,
and they may point out some weaknesses in your work that you
genuinely need to improve. Remember, someone told me my inking
skills sorely needed improvement (a comic book editor), and so
when I started my job at the T-shirt company, I started inking with
a brush. I learned on someone else's time clock, and now that former weakness is currently something people compliment me on.
(Go figure!)

Also, don't forget that my own brother once told me that my
drawings of women (at one point) weren't "all that attractive," and
so I worked on my female anatomy skills. After a year or two, I was
greatly complimented when an artist friend asked for one of my
first drawings of Jayle Bat, commending her... well, shapely figure.

Interview with Brian de Tagyos, Lead Animator, and Steve Vitale, Lead Animator, Turner Studios

All three of us are "career cartoonists." Brian and Steve work as
lead animators for Turner Studios (working on Cartoon Network
and Adult Swim projects), and I (as a 2D animation instructor) work
across the street at Westwood College's Atlanta Midtown Campus.
I figured the best way to make time for this interview was during a
break from a figure drawing session, sponsored every Thursday
night by ASIFA's Atlanta chapter.

MSS: How did you get interested in animation, Brian?

Brian: I was studying for illustration, mostly comic book stuff, but
that went to the back burner. When I got to college and started
looking at my other options, illustration and such, animation was a
sort of a love of movies and all that, drawing and illustration. [So] I
sort of fell into that, because it's more consistent work than
"job-to-job" illustration stuff, and it grew and became something
that I liked.

MSS: What were some of the particular animated projects that got you interested in animation?

Brian: Hmm… There was this big gap when I got disinterested in Disney, and then back in college, I started seeing it again, and was blown away. I hadn't realized how good Disney was. As a kid, you see it and you know you love it, but you don't realize that it's… incredible.

MSS: As a kid, did you ever realize the difference between Saturday morning cartoons, Disney cartoons, and feature-length animation?

Brian: As a kid? No. I didn't notice it then. But I look at some of those other [Saturday morning cartoons] now, and… oh my gosh, they're hideous… except for *ThunderCats*. *ThunderCats* is still pretty cool. But then there were classics [on Saturday morning] like the *Smurfs*, which were as soundly animated as they needed to be. They were exactly how I remembered them.

MSS: How did you get over to Cartoon Network?

Brian: I just shot my portfolio around Atlanta after getting out of school, and did some work for Cartoon Network, mainly through commercials. After years of doing freelance for Turner and Cartoon Network, then *[Harvey] Birdman* came into town.

MSS: How did you get into Flash?

Brian: Completely on the job. *Birdman* was the start of Flash [with me]. I was completely traditional, and learned Flash on the job, as most of us did. Some [of the others] had *some* experience, but the way we use it is almost like doing traditional animation.

MSS: What's the most important thing somebody new to Flash should know about it?

Brian: I think the first thing you should think of is, if you want animation to look good, don't think of it as using "Flash tricks." Don't [think], "How can Flash make this easier for me?" Basically, use it how you would traditionally, and maybe one or two places you'll see where you can save yourself time cutting and pasting, and maybe not having to redraw a head. Ideally, sketch out the motion first without trying to use "finished pieces of art," and you'll get a lot more life.

MSS: Steve, how did you get interested in animation?

Steve: [I did] probably the same thing everybody does when they're kids; watch Saturday morning cartoons, go to the Disney movies, and that sort of thing. It never really dawns on you that there's somebody out there drawing it. It's created by people.

MSS: Most kids just think it's magic?

Steve: Exactly. It's not till you get a little bit older that you start to really appreciate it. You buy books, and find out about the people who create the characters. You then become a fan of "that animator" like some kids become fans of baseball stars and football players.

MSS: What are some names of animators you've become a fan of?

Steve: Absolutely guys like Frank Thomas and Ollie Johnston... [and other Disney animators like] Milt Kahl and Marc Davis, Ward Kimball.

MSS: And all the rest of Disney's "Nine Old Men"?

Steve: Ward Kimball is especially one of my favorites, who animated Jiminy Cricket.

MSS: Some of the more realistic stuff Disney did blows me away, like Milt Kahl's scene of Shere Khan, the tiger, getting up and walking away. I later found out it wasn't rotoscoped (traced over live-action footage of a tiger), but he did it without any photographic reference. He just knew where the weight was on every frame because he'd already studied so much animal anatomy.

Steve: Yeah, and guys like Marc Davis on *Bambi*; he was basically the animal anatomy [expert]. You look at [his work] and you say to yourself, "How can that be a *drawing*?"

MSS: If you were talking to someone considering animation as a career, how would you recommend they get started?

Steve: Absolutely, drawing is the most important thing. Life drawing is probably *the* most crucial thing you can do.

Brian: Life drawing is the biggest key. And you don't stop. I mean, we're on a break from a life drawing session right now! We're in the career, professionally doing it every day. We know the goal of life drawing is the stronger it gets, the more solidity to your drawing, the more natural the posing of your drawing, the more balance… you learn everything. In animation, [the importance of] life drawing is *huge*. I walked into my first animation job interview with life drawings in my portfolio. I didn't have an animation portfolio. I have a [lousy] little reel of the first thing I ever did in animation, and just a massive book of life drawings. And it was the life drawings that got me the job.

MSS: I went to the Disney Animation Studio in Florida, when it was still open, and I was kind of naïve. I just took a bunch of Disney cartoon drawings in my portfolio, and I found out they didn't care about seeing that; they wanted to see just life drawings.

Steve: Again, that's the number one thing to do. Just draw. Get your drawing skills, and keep drawing as much as you can. You should especially [learn to] do some quick gesture drawings… one minutes, and two minutes… as fast as you can, get the essence of the figure. That's what we translate to in animation, that's what you're looking at; it's the form. [Your goal] is not to come up with a finished illustration of a single picture, you're ultimately seeing what the character is *doing*.

MSS: I think you've pretty much said it. If you want to caricature real life, you need to be able to draw from real life. Well, thanks very much guys, I appreciate your time, and I think they've started again without us!

Don't Wait for Your Fairy Godmother to Appear

I've done my best to talk to those that I consider industry experts (Richard Williams, Don Bluth, Gary Goldman, and an ever-growing list of others) for training and guidance, and I was always thinking one of them would give me some magical piece of advice that would make me instantly successful, or even arbitrarily offer me a job… just because they liked my "moxie."

I'm sorry to admit, neither of those things ever happened. However, talking to these people has resulted in some golden nuggets of information, that when melded together with personal experience, do provide some useful guideposts, and may even land that "dream project" we're all hoping for.

Top Five "Reality Tips" for Animation Careers

1. **Realize you are an individual, with individual talents, strengths, and shortcomings.** Getting the job you want may be *seemingly* easier (or tougher) for somebody else. Guess what? Fair or not... that's life. (As a matter of fact, one of my favorite quotes I saw written on a restaurant menu, of all places, read something like this: "Life *is* fair... because it's equally *unfair* to everyone.") When you do get an interview, try not to dwell too heavily on your successes (that's called "bragging") and even less so on your shortcomings (that's called "putting yourself down").

2. **Don't expect success to happen overnight.** Any worthwhile success, much less a *lasting* success, is going to require time and endurance. I've heard a saying attributed to Eddie Cantor (and repeated by *The Muppet Show* performers), "It takes twenty years to become an *overnight* success." (That doesn't mean you have to *starve* for 20 years, mind you!)

3. **Don't expect the jobs to come to you; you are going to have to go *look* for the jobs. This may possibly require moving out of your "comfort zone."** When I met fantasy illustrator Boris Vallejo at an Atlanta art show years ago, I was "moaning and groaning" about how hard it was to find an art job. He said I'd have to go where the work was. Boris had come to this country from Argentina, and learned English by reading comic books. I certainly couldn't beat that, but I finally had to move away from Montgomery, Alabama. There I was teaching animation once a year (every spring), and struggling at other jobs like the T-shirt company (good experience, but not spectacular pay), and KinderCare (before they moved out of state), part-time at TV stations, and then freelancing to fill in the gaps.

I could have continued like this for years, emptily hoping for a "dream job" to show up, or I could grit my teeth and move to Atlanta, the home of Cartoon Network, three hours away. I gritted my teeth and made the move. I think I made the right choice.

Although I had to accept an office job to pay for the initial move to Atlanta, within eight months I was able to leave it and teach graphics, multimedia, and animation classes. I had to leave my "comfort zone" of the animation programs I knew and learn new software. (Don't get me wrong; Atlanta is not the answer for everyone. If in doubt, refer back to Number 1.)

4. **Always seek new sources of inspiration to keep you going.** As most of you know, Richard Williams is my "animation hero." It was *Roger Rabbit* that opened my eyes to the fact that animation doesn't have to be "just for kids." Although it was *Roger Rabbit* that got my attention, it was Williams' more "artsy" films (for lack of better terminology) that kept my attention. Watch *The Thief and the Cobbler* if you ever find yourself faltering in your dedication to this art form. Or if that doesn't keep you going, find something else that does, whether it's the Disney classics like *Fantasia*, the 1940s *Looney Tunes*, or the Italian classic *Allegro Non Troppo*. That last film began as a parody of *Fantasia*, but ended up being a rather impressive mix of animation styles in its various sequences. (It even has some amusing black-and-white live-action segues between the musical numbers, with an overweight truck driver conducting a captive orchestra of old ladies.)

There are plenty of other films I list in Appendix A for recommended viewing, some of which you can find in the dollar stores or in the bargain bins at the big-box stores. (Don't forget that most of them you can buy *used* on Amazon.com!)

5. **Even when you** *do* **get that "dream job" in the field of animation,** *don't* **get complacent.** Although I've greatly enjoyed my teaching job, I still have to freelance to keep myself up to date, both for my own and my students' sake. As a matter of fact, this past weekend, it just occurred to me that I'm finally getting close to finishing this book! This very book you're reading has been my chief freelance project over the past several months. That made me realize, "I've been so involved in this temporary writing job, I need to look ahead to my *next* freelance check!"

With that in mind, I did a web search with some words I thought might be helpful, and came up with several advertising agencies that might utilize freelance animators. I sent out roughly eight emails after writing one letter, mentioning my animation teaching experience and that I was writing a book on Flash animation. Naturally, I copied and pasted text from the letter, switching out the greeting (of course) and an introductory sentence that let each reader know I'd actually *looked* at their website by mentioning something I liked about it.

And I know this is an unusual case (let's face it, each of us has a truly *unique* experience in our differing lives; if in doubt, refer back to Number 1), but within half an hour, I had a reply from a lady in Pennsylvania who owned an advertising agency, and at least one other local video producer who liked my work. The lady from Pennsylvania called me within 20 minutes of her email. She informed me that her former freelance animator had moved to Ireland (of all places), and she was looking for someone to handle her occasional animated commercial requests. As a matter of fact, she sent me a link to a graphic for a client who wanted a 5- or 10-second tag for their otherwise live-action TV spot.

Furthermore, she requested that I send her not only a DVD demo of my work (she was looking at my website while we spoke on the phone), but she asked me to also send two more demos to her two producers!

On the Art of Working for Free...

(A story about the author's brother, freelance artist/full-time graphic designer Michael W. Smith)

My brother Michael once told me of an incident when he was working for a T-shirt printer, and one of the wacky clients (yes, one of *many*) was telling him that more time needed to be spent on this particular illustration to be printed. Michael pleasantly reminded him that for the "art charge" (or lack thereof) that this aforementioned client had utilized, he had spent all the time his boss could afford to pay him for said "fee." (They did have other clients.)

The client then suggested to my brother that if he couldn't spend time drawing it on the "company's clock," then perhaps he could use his outside hours to further "perfect" this illustration. Perhaps Michael could devote further attention to the drawing... on his "free time."

Client: "It would be a great portfolio piece for you; it would really help you out."

Michael: "I don't need a portfolio piece. I have plenty of portfolio pieces; in fact I have to turn work down because I have a great portfolio. I need *money*; I don't have enough of that."

Another story, in Michael's own words...

I had a friend who had an idea for a comic. I asked him about his idea. I told him I was very interested in hearing about his idea. (Okay, not really; but he *was* a friend.)

Me: "I am very busy and I don't have time to do illustrations, but I would love to read what you have written."

Friend: "Oh, I haven't written anything."

Me: "What about dialogue or characters?"

Friend: "Oh, I don't know about that either; I'm not too good when it comes to stuff like that. But I got the idea from a line from a song."

He did not *just* want me to illustrate it, he wanted me to write it and come up with all the characters.

UGGH!!!

In conclusion, in the beginning you will get screwed over (occasionally), but you will get a paycheck and *not* have to cook fries. Unless that is your second job because your first job does not pay enough.

Freelancer's Secret Best Friend: *Artist's & Graphic Designer's Market*

Sensing I was on a roll (and knowing I'd be spending some time at Office Max anyway, making color copies of my DVD cover insert), I figured I'd best go ahead and make a few more calls. I picked up my old 2003 copy of *Artist's & Graphic Designer's Market*, an annual publication that lists not only advertising agencies by state, magazines that buy illustrations and cartoons, newspaper cartoon syndicates, and so on, but also the contact information for each of these companies. (If somebody else has already done the legwork for you, why reinvent the wheel?)

I looked up the entries for Georgia Advertising Agencies, and sure enough, there were three agencies that listed freelance animators under their video production needs. I called them up, and two of them were still active (the number of the third was disconnected). I even remembered previously talking to one of the creative directors (though I couldn't recall whether I'd ever sent him a demo), so I made sure to send him an updated demo DVD the next day.

And then here's another golden key... once you send off these demo DVDs, do a follow-up call a week after you send them. Ask them whether they've received your demo, whether they've had a chance to look at it, and whether they think your work will be useful to them. If they haven't received it yet or had a chance to look at it yet, call back... next week. Not that afternoon or the next day. Remember, these are busy people with schedules and deadlines of their own (just like you), and like it or not, we have to respect other people's schedules.

I know the age of email is great (just like instant oatmeal), and when you can't (for whatever reason) speak to someone in person, email works great as a filler or "instant reply." But in these days of the instant (and to a degree, impersonal) information age, the personal touch of a brief phone call (try to keep it no longer than three to five minutes) will help fellow animators, producers, and creative directors remember you just a little better than that "next guy."

When I was creative services director at ABC-32, and we had just held auditions for on-air talent, out of all the 87 or so applicants we had, one person, Sherry, sent me a "thank-you" card for taking the time to interview her. She had also sent a card to our promotions director, Laura. Although there were other people involved in the decision-making process (like the owner of the station), I was actually "on the committee." I'm not sure whether she was aware of this or not, but Laura and I were the ones conducting the interviews (I just happened to be running the camera). The owner and station manager asked Laura and me who we thought were the best personalities. Sherry was one of the three final people we ended up hiring. Though her personality was what sparkled on camera (and ultimately got her the job), the card was a nice touch. Even if she hadn't made that first cut, we used all the applicants' contact info for our TV commercials when we needed extras for restaurants and such. And when Sherry later moved out of town, we ended up moving to the next "attractive, funny blonde" on our list of extras for a replacement.

How long do you think it took Sherry to hand-write, address, and stamp that thank-you card? And how long did we remember her after that? (Well... I took the time to mention her in this book, didn't I?)

All that aside, I can give you some decent starting places for personal guidance and job postings. The first thing you're going to need, though, is a great sample of work. Before anyone will give you a job, they want to see what you're capable of.

All that aside, I can give you some decent starting places for personal guidance and job postings. The first thing you're going to need, though, is a great sample of work. Before anyone will give you a job, they want to see what you're capable of.

You need to have a great cartoon completed if you want to get a job. I didn't say a *long* cartoon; certainly not an animated feature. I mean a great cartoon, and that can be short. Brevity is the soul of wit, they say. And the shorter a cartoon you set out to complete, the greater your chances of completing it, and the greater your chances of doing it well.

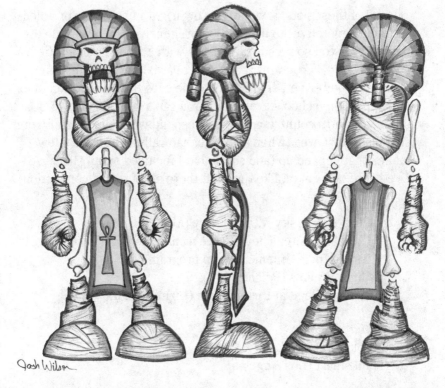

Mummy Model Sheet © Josh Wilson

Here's a great model sheet of a mummy from one of my character design and 2D animation students, Josh Wilson. Josh won a character design contest at Westwood with this drawing. Something I like about his work is that he manages to mix the weird and the wacky in a perfect combination. I especially like the exaggerated proportions of the fists and the feet. It kind of has the visual flavor of those old-fashioned Halloween specials I enjoyed in my younger days.

Hopefully at this point in the book, I've at least given you the basic information that will nurture your skills to make a great short cartoon.

Once you've got that great short cartoon, how do you decide who to show it to? If you've already read the previous advice in this chapter, let me follow it up with the following organizations, film festivals, and so on... the aforementioned outlets for your work.

Colleges and Schools

Like all of these lists, it would be downright impossible (or at least time-uncooperative) to make a comprehensive list, but I'll do my best to give you some starting places with schools, universities, and educational programs that (last I heard) offered animation classes or, better yet, degrees. Also, be sure to check awn.com for updates (http://schools.awn.com/). You can select a nearby city, a state, or even a country, and it will respond with a list of animation schools in that area (when available, naturally). Here are a few names that popped up (and some that I included simply because I've heard of them or, like the first, there's a personal connection).

Alabama
Auburn University Montgomery (Montgomery)
(Author's note: They offered a character animation class as part of their Graphic Design program)
Twilight Studios (Pelham)
Virginia College in Birmingham (Birmingham)

California
Brooks College (Long Beach)
Thinksmart (Los Angeles)

Colorado
Digital-Evolutions — Smoky Hill High School (Aurora)

Florida
Ringling School of Design (Sarasota)

Georgia
  Art Institute of Atlanta
  Savannah College of Art & Design (Atlanta and Savannah campuses)
  Westwood College, Atlanta Midtown Campus
    (Author's note: They offer an associate degree in Animation and Game Art & Design)

Kentucky
  Louisville Technical Institute (Louisville)
  Spencerian College (Lexington)
  University of Kentucky (Lexington)
  University of Louisville (Louisville)

Florida
  Ringling School of Design (Sarasota)

New York
  Alfred State College (Alfred)
  Cyber Arts (Rochester)
  Digital Film Academy (New York City)
  School of Visual Arts (New York City)
  The Center for Character Animation (Levittown)
  The Mac Learning Center (New York City)

Pennsylvania
  Art Institute of Philadelphia (Philadelphia)
  Art Institute of Pittsburgh (Pittsburgh)
  Future Media Concepts (Philadelphia)

Texas
  Art Institute of Dallas (Dallas)
  Austin Community College (Austin)
  San Antonio College (San Antonio)

Axeman © James Bridgens

James Bridgens did this illustration for a character design contest at Westwood while he was in my Adobe Illustrator class a couple of terms ago. I think I just liked the style of this particular illustration, both in the cartoony treatment of the muscles and overall anatomy, and of course, the distorted proportions.

Film and Video Festivals

Again, like the others, this is *far* from a complete list. It barely scratches the surface. Even if I were silly enough to try to list them all, it would constantly change, because new festivals arise just as quickly as older festivals die out. I'm just beginning with a sampler, so feel free to investigate these as a starting place. You might even want to pick up an issue (better yet, subscribe) to *Animation Magazine*. If you can't afford the magazine, ask your school or local library to start carrying it, and then you can just read the issues for the price of a library card (free). On the last page or so of the magazine, they have a list of upcoming film and video festivals that accept animated entries.

Also, on awn.com, you can check the Communities heading of the menu to find a listing of festivals.

> The Academy Awards (Los Angeles, CA)
> > (Well! Ahem! They *do* have an animated short category, y'know? Yeah…yeah, well, I can dream, can't I?)
> Atlanta Film Festival (Atlanta, GA)
> Dragon-Con Film and Video Contest (Atlanta, GA)
> Flipbook Festival (Honolulu, HI)
> Kalamazoo Animation Festival International (Kalamazoo, MI)
> Nashville Independent Film Festival (Nashville, TN)
> Sidewalk Moving Picture Festival (Birmingham, AL)
> SIGGRAPH (location varies annually)
> Toon Makers, Inc. (Granada Hills, CA)

The importance of getting your work seen is it gives you an excuse to network with other animators, filmmakers, and the occasional network executive who cruises these festivals looking for talent. (Hey, it *does* happen.) Whenever possible, invest that odd tank of gasoline to attend the festival your film appears in.

Networking is key. (Read the interview with animation director Joe Peery earlier in this chapter for more information on that subject.)

Animation and Cartooning Jobs

Yeah, here's the one you were waiting for. Do keep this in mind, though: Animation is a seasonal business at best, sometimes quite literally, because a show goes into production for a certain number of months. Sometimes producers have to wait weeks or even months to find out if a show is going to be picked up for the next season. At those periods of the year, it's difficult to say how many animators they'll need when their hectic production schedule suddenly kicks back in (or worse yet, lay off afterward).

The first place I would recommend would be awn.com. That's the Animation World Network. Once there, click on the Careers tab and choose the area you're interested in.

- *Career Connections*: This has monthly advice columns for animation professionals from artists to voice actors. They've also got a nice archive of previous articles with career advice from professionals.

- *Search For a Job*: Yeah, you know this is the one most everyone is looking for.

Another great website, if you're more interested in comic book illustration (and there are surprising numbers of crossovers between animation and comic careers), would be Digital-webbing.com (http://www.digitalwebbing.com/talent/). If you go there, you'll find links to the major comic publishers, and specifically, their Submissions Guideline pages. You'll also find a Talent Search Classifieds page, in the categories of Pencilers, Inkers, Writers, Colorists, etc., and even a Submissions page for smaller and beginning studios.

Don't forget: It's not a good idea to turn up your nose at smaller and beginning studios; they're usually the ones that are more receptive to new talent. My only advice would be for you to exercise extreme caution toward anyone that asks (much less *expects*) you to work for free, for the all-too-popular excuse, "Just because it would look fabulous in your portfolio!"

(Yeah, just like those overdue bills would look fabulous in your portfolio, too!)

Let Your Fingers Do the Walking

While you shouldn't forget the Internet (obviously), that old saying of "Let your fingers do the walking" still holds true. Because the only problem with the Internet is that sometimes you can come up with irrelevant keyword results that you have to wade through... page after page, in some cases. Better yet, go to those good ol' yellow pages. If you're near a large enough city (New York, San Francisco, Los Angeles, or even Atlanta), there's probably a listing for Animation. But if you're in a considerably or even comparatively smaller city (Montgomery or Birmingham come to mind), you might want to check the listings under Video Production and Advertising Agencies.

If you're looking for a job doing freelance animation only, then be sure to find out where your local TV stations are. In Montgomery, we had local affiliates for ABC, CBS, NBC, Fox, and PBS. Those are the basic national affiliates that have been around for a while, but nowadays some cities also have offices for the CW and possibly other networks.

Also, don't forget your local cable company. If your city has one, they've probably got a rival nearby. Montgomery's big company was (at the time) AT&T; they seemed to change owners every other month for a while, but I can't remember offhand who they are now. (Oops! Now I *do* remember, but won't mention their name for fear of getting sued regarding that last snide comment.) Anyway, I got the offbeat idea of having an introductory "animation sale." I came up with a price I thought local folks with a halfway decent budget might afford (I'll just say it was in the lower four-figure range). I put a time limit on it that didn't tie me down to that price on the off-chance that I got a lot of interest (and got overwhelmed with under-priced animation to do). Also putting a time limit on the sale (say, a winter animation sale for a month or two) gives people the feeling they should act *now*! Limited time offer! Operators are standing by!

When people are putting you off, they usually won't come right out and tell you no; they usually say, "Let me think about it" or

"Let me get back to you." That's not *always* an eternal no, but it's about as close to a real answer as you'll get with some people.

Occasionally, you may strike it lucky by approaching a local business owner like a restaurant or hardware store with an offer to do an animated TV spot. One paint store owner who had a cartoon mascot on his outdoor billboard liked my demo and told me, "Oh just do me a TV spot and I'll see if I like it." (You can bet I got to work on *that* one right away... Hah!)

But you'll get a lot more rejections and put-offs than solid answers. Instead, I would suggest going to the places where business owners go when they're *ready* to spend money on advertising... an advertising agency or video production company. Seriously; just think about it. Each one of these places (including local TV stations that show locally produced TV commercials) already has a staff of salespeople whose very job is to go around visiting local business owners and find out who's ready to spend money on making a TV commercial. Wouldn't it be simpler to let somebody *else* do the legwork for you? And if you've got some good work on your demo, these salespeople will quite likely be happy for you to make their job easier by offering their client a nice-looking TV commercial... a *different*-looking TV commercial that no *other* advertisers can offer them!

My point is this: Don't spend your time chasing the outer spokes of a spinning wheel... go to the center. Save energy when possible.

Don't be mistaken; the local folks don't have the advertising dollars of their national headquarter offices, but they're a good starting place.

Few local businesses would be able to make a 30-second animated TV spot worth your trouble (it might take me a month or two, depending on my schedule), but what about 5- and 10-second animated tags? Even a beginner should be able to knock one of those out in a couple of weeks. If they could just pay you a couple hundred bucks for that, it might be worth your while, right? Just make sure to keep up with your time and expenses spent on the production. Figure out how much you're making per hour. If you spent so much time on a project that you're only making minimum wage, you might want to raise your rates a bit, or offer your work elsewhere. It's all right to make just a couple hundred here or there at the beginning, to pay for some new software or that royalty-free sound effects CD you've had your eye on... maybe even that digitizing tablet! But ask yourself, "Am I just in this to make some extra money, or to try to make a career out of it?"

Top Five Freelance Business Tips

1. **If you're going to freelance, go ahead and get a business license.** It obviously varies from city to city, but I bought my first business license at the Montgomery City Hall. It could differ in your city, but most cases it's the city that will handle business licenses. If for some odd reason they don't, they can probably tell you who can help you. A Commercial Artist license only costs me about $30 annually, and that makes my business nice and legal. (If I was an advertising agency, it would have cost me about $250!)

2. **Make sure you save and organize your receipts... and don't wait until April to start.** Start a folder or box, and ask your accountant what categories he'll need to know about next April. Save receipts for everything from drawing paper to pens to office supplies, industry-related magazines, computer hardware and software; *anything* that's relevant to your business! Even your animated DVDs, wildlife nature videos, and comic books might be considered visual reference material! (Naturally, consult with an accountant if you have any doubt whether or not an item may be tax deductible.)

3. **Consider becoming incorporated or an LLC.** Depending on how much business you expect to do (notice I didn't say *wish* to do), you might decide whether it would be worth your while to incorporate your freelance business. Some people do it for tax purposes, some do it for protection. In this day and age of lawsuit-happy citizens, all it would take is one disgruntled client to claim that you didn't live up to your part of the bargain, want to sue you for damages, and want your car to ease their mental anguish... or your house.

Consult a lawyer to find out how much it would take to incorporate, or possibly become an LLC (that's limited liability corporation). The LLC has become very popular over the past few years, and seems to be helpful in protecting the small businessperson.

4. **Always get it in writing...** *before* **you start work.** That's right, I said *before* you start work. I'll agree to doing storyboards "for free," but I'll get my client to sign a written agreement before I start animation so we know what we expect of each other and on what terms. Although you may not know the exact time frame it will take you to complete each particular project, you can usually have a fairly educated guess within a couple of weeks or so, and you can put the words "estimated production schedule" in your contract.

   Never trust anyone who says "a handshake is good enough." That in itself is a signal for trouble. Proceed with caution, if at all. Not every opportunity is a good one, much less a wise one. Just because someone offers you an animation job doesn't mean you're obligated to take it.

5. **Consider getting an agent.** Already? It's easy to get bogged down in the fun and/or work process of completing your current animation job, and carelessly forget about how you're going to pay your rent next month. In other words, where's the next job coming from?

   An agent can do your legwork for you. You can focus on doing the work, and he or she can focus on finding you the work. Most agents charge 10% of whatever the job is. Some charge more, some charge less. Some might whine or grumble about what an agent charges, saying, "I'd rather find my own work and keep all the proceeds myself." Don't forget that finding work is a job in itself, but I'll leave it to you to do the math. What's better: 100% of nothing or 90% of something?

How do you find an agent? Admittedly mine was, once again, an unusual case. I was attending a faculty orientation here at Westwood one weekend, and the young lady who sat down next to me mentioned that she was an "entertainment attorney." I mentioned I was an animator, and though she didn't usually represent animators, we exchanged business cards. Within a week, she mentioned a friend of hers in L.A. was a music producer who was looking for some assistance putting together a pitch for an animated show. She worked up a contract for us.

In that particular case, this was someone the school had hired to teach their business management classes, so I knew her credentials were good.

If you want to find an agent, you might start with the Internet. There are larger agencies that represent talent, such as International Creative Management, but they're difficult to get on with, and I do mean *difficult* (they represent big-name movie stars and voice artists)! You might need to start at a more modest level; just do a web search for talent agencies: animation, entertainment, artist, or agency and see what comes up. (If they do birthday parties, you might wanna move on.)

Here's one I came up with that might just prove a good starting place. They might even be able to recommend other artists' agencies closer to you: http://www.njcreatives.org/graphic-animation.htm.

As always, check things out for yourself first, and do a little detective work. I wouldn't dare guarantee results from any one method (for legal reasons alone). Do some thinkin' and plannin'.

My favorite quote from good ol' Uncle Scrooge McDuck: "Work smarter, not harder!"

Prices Divisible by Three

My prices are almost always divisible by three. Why? Here's a neat math trick: Add up all the individual digits in a number, like 750. If the sum of those numbers is evenly divisible by three (no fractions), then that number you started with is also evenly divisible by three. 7 + 5 + 0 = 12. Since 12 is evenly divisible by three (12 divided by three is four), then so is the number we started with. 750 divided by three would be three "installments" of 250.

Because I get paid in three installments. Once the customer approves storyboards, I get a deposit before I start drawing actual animation. If they ask why, it's because I have to buy supplies... maybe a particular royalty-free music or sound effects CD will be needed. The customer usually doesn't know how much animation paper, royalty-free music, sound effects, or background paint supplies cost, and doesn't need to. You're not operating a charity... you're operating a business, and a business takes funding to run. But do be *polite* and cheerful during all these responses, naturally! You want repeat customers, right?

The first thing I start on with the delivery of the deposit check is the animatic, or pose test, which we discussed in the first half of the book. That will give the client a good idea what the camera shots are going to look like before you start doing all those drawings. I recommend doing it in color, because as Dick Williams said, "Black-and-white animatics came back with numerous requests for revisions... color animatics came back with approval." (It's probably because the people you're showing these to are not of the artistic persuasion, and need our help to visualize the forthcoming product for them.) I'll usually even have an explanation on a video slate, or still graphic, at the beginning of the animatic, that reads something like, "What you are about to see is an animatic, or pose test. While the drawings don't actually *move* yet, this is merely a test, like an onscreen comic book with a soundtrack, to ensure the camera shots and voiceovers are working properly together before starting work on the numerous drawings." It would probably be a good idea to break this into two screens of about five to six seconds each. Make sure you have time to read it, maybe even twice, before changing to the next screen of text.

That way, even if you've explained it to your client, they may be showing it to other decision-makers who may not yet fully understand the process.

Upon approval of the animatic, I get my second check, and start the process of doing "all those little drawings." Make sure it is clearly understood to the client (in writing) that any changes must be made at the animatic phase, because of the time-intensive nature of animation. Have it in *writing* that any changes beyond the animatic phase (perhaps except for mutual agreement between you and the client) will be charged at an hourly rate. Some clients may think it's kinda fun to "play director," but once you start charging them by the hour, that should make them calm down and decide which changes are absolutely essential.

Of course the next stage is final animation. If you've heeded my precautions, you shouldn't have to make many changes (if any) once the customer views the final piece. If all goes well, they'll be absolutely delighted to have an animated character singing their praises via television or web animation. If there are some areas that need to be revised, try to pleasantly arrive at a mutual agreement. While you don't want to give away work for free, you do want repeat business. And business owners know other business owners. If you do a great piece of work for one, they'll tell their friends about it, which will hopefully lead to other work.

The pricing! Ughhh... I was afraid you would ask that, and for fear clients may pick up this book, I'll try to give you as much information as I can afford to. For a 30-second TV spot, I wouldn't dare charge less than four figures. If you're desperate for rent money, that figure may occasionally change. If it's a national ad, you should be getting closer to five figures... at least. (You should get another figure still for a Super Bowl ad!) As always, the more they can afford to spend on the spot, the more time (and/or assistants) you can afford, and the better the ad will look. If you're uncertain of how much they can afford, my best advice is to let them speak first. They're usually willing to offer more than you're willing to ask. (At least that's my experience.)

If they offer one price, say, well, I can do a 1960 Yogi-level quality for that price, certainly. But if you were able to pay this price, it might be a little closer to Scooby quality, and for this price, it could be a little closer to classic Looney Tunes.

That's just an example. But the owner of a TV station I did some work for had a very wise saying regarding price negotiations, as he told their sales department, "Whoever speaks first loses. Don't be afraid of an awkward silence. Someone will have to speak eventually." I later found out the guy's a millionaire and owns several TV stations across the country, so I figure he must know what he's talking about.

In summary, three things should affect your price negotiations: quality, length, and delivery date.

Character art © Scott Pruett

One of my first nearly published comic artwork pieces was of what's called anthropomorphic (or sometimes referred to as "furry") characters. Anthropomorphic characters are animals that are given human attributes (walking upright, talking, wearing clothes, etc.), and have become rather popular in their own right over the last decade or so. My own Jayle Bat is probably a pretty good example of this. Maybe that's why I like this character illustration by Scott Pruett so much.

Character art © James Roberge

Here's one of the things I love about teaching animation. What other class would not only encourage you to draw caricatures of your instructor, but actually reward you for it? James Roberge drew this illustration of me in (I believe) Character Design class, and I liked it so much I told him I'd include it in this book, in exchange for a copy. Thanks to a book titled *How to be a Villain* (a Halloween/birthday gift from my webmaster), I picked out the nickname for myself, Professor Death-Hammer. Hence, the sketch you see here.

In Closing

Now that I've shared with you the magic of this art form of techniques (drawing), tools (Flash software), and even the freelance business of animation, let me implore you all to heed what a very wise man once said, "With great power comes great responsibility." That was Uncle Ben, if I'm not mistaken. (No, no, not the rice guy, the one from *Spider*… oh, never mind.)

In any case, I just want to tell you that you have the power to create some wonderful movies and elicit genuine emotional reactions in people.

Though I obviously can't control what you do with it, I just want to formally request, like a karate arts instructor might tell his students, "Just because you know *how* to break somebody's leg doesn't mean you *should* go out and break somebody's leg. I teach you only to do this in self-defense. Hopefully the discipline I've tried to instill has developed with that knowledge."

In animation, I'm asking you to use this knowledge and these skills that you will develop for good… use them to inform, to educate, but also to make people happy.

The world doesn't need more filth, anger, and resentment. Lord knows, we're already overflowing with that. (Ughh!) We've got plenty.

The world needs laughter. It's hurting, and we have the healing power of laughter and hope to make it a better place; a power that can make it a better place and a cleaner place than we found it. A very wise saying goes, "Laughter is God's hand on the shoulder of a troubled world."

I don't know about you guys, but now that this book is finally finished, I'm gonna go have some fun. I'm gonna go make myself some Flash cartoons!

Thanks for reading!

Recommended Reading and Viewing

Recommended Reading

There are way too many good books to mention, so I'll just list the top 10 here. If I had to start an "animation bookshelf" from scratch, I'd start with these three:

- *The Animator's Survival Kit* by Richard Williams
- *Cartoon Animation* by Preston Blair
- *Action! Cartooning* by Ben Caldwell

And then, if I had a few more bucks, I'd add these:

- *The Illusion of Life: Disney Animation* by Frank Thomas and Ollie Johnston
- *The Art of Animal Drawing* by Ken Hultgren
- *Animating the Looney Tunes Way* with Tony Cervone

And I don't recommend always just drawing cartoon style. Improve your figure drawing skills with the following photographic reference books:

- *Comic Artist's Photo Reference: People and Poses* by Buddy Scalera
- *Concise Illustrator's Reference Manual: Figures* by Peg Osterman

Buddy Scalera's book is a great sequence of action photos of muscular male and slender female models from different ethnic backgrounds posing with swords, guns, and capes, and fighting.

Why try to draw from your head when it's so much more convincing to work from reference material? I'm guilty of causing several innocent, starving college students to put books like this on Christmas wish lists when they should be asking for far more practical gifts, like sampler gourmet cheese variety packs and jeans without holes.

Peg Osterman's reference book is similar in nature, with models going through everyday actions like opening an umbrella, having a cup of tea, putting on socks, and even smooching.

The last two books on this list are more along the lines of business reference. As I often tell my students who are complaining about having to take classes in business administration: "If I was going back to college again, I'd double-minor in theatre and business."

- *Artist's & Graphic Designer's Market* by Mary Cox and Michael Schweer
- *Unofficial Guide to Starting a Business Online* by Jason R. Rich

Don't forget, these books aren't going to do you any good if they're collecting dust on your bookshelf, or worse yet, lying on your coffee table in an attempt to impress friends. Open them up, read them, and practice what they preach.

Again, it's unlikely that any *one* book (or any list of books) is an end-all answer to everything you need. Any of them are a good starting place, and these are books that I've found particularly helpful in one sense or another. I hope they prove useful to you!

Recommended Viewing (Currently Available on DVD)

- *Who Framed Roger Rabbit* (two-disc set)

  Thank goodness I never bought the one-disc version that came out; it was completely without special features. Completely. (Unless you count "restored color" as a special feature. I don't.)

  Disney *more* than made up for the first lackluster DVD release with this one. Numerous interviews with Richard Williams, Bob Zemeckis, and animators and special effects crew from the film are informative for the older viewers; a "Behind the Ears" featurette is slightly faster-paced for the kids. You can search through Eddie's office for character designs, conceptual art, model sheets, and other goodies. Even the Acme Factory has some hidden surprises. A 3D version of Benny the Cab acts as your tour guide. (Admittedly, this was kinda inappropriate, since the film was an homage to classic 2D animation.) My favorite is the deleted "Pig-Head Sequence," when Eddie Valiant is captured by Doom's Weasels and painted with a toon pig head. He has to go back to his office and wash it off with turpentine. This sequence had even been in the original movie trailers, despite being trimmed from the final release.

  Another great feature is the bonus material of the test film they shot to prove they could pull off the illusions in *Roger Rabbit*. The set even has all three Roger Rabbit theatrical shorts — *Tummy Trouble*, *Rollercoaster Rabbit*, and *Trail Mix-up*.

- *Chuck Jones: Extremes and Inbetweens, A Life in Animation* from Warner Home Video

  Besides great interviews with Jones himself, fans, and collaborators — including Coyote layout artist Maurice Noble — this indispensable disc also contains fan favorite Jones cartoons *Duck Dodgers in the 24½th Century*, *Feed the Kitty*, and a Grinch pencil test.

■ *Wizards*

A sizable set of extra features is here with theatrical trailers, model sheets, and early character designs. The highlight is easily an interview with Ralph Bakshi ("The Wizard of Animation"). I don't know what I expected Ralph Bakshi to sound like, but he doesn't match his voice. But seriously, you won't hear me bad-mouthing Ralph Bakshi. Just because I asked his website shop about the possibility of a two-disc set of *Cool World*, it made Ralph laugh so hard he gave me a T-shirt.

Seriously! His webmaster said he has a soft spot in his heart for teachers.

Matter of fact, here's the original correspondence:

MSS: Longtime fan of Bakshi films (especially *Wizards*, *Fire and Ice*, and the animated version of *LOTR*) and I'm currently an animation instructor. Thanks for all the inspiration for independent animators! (I'd love to see a *Cool World* expanded DVD with the missing "Sweet Place" musical number we saw in the DC comic book! Any chance?)

Sincerely,

Mark S./www.marktoonery.com

RalphBakshi.com: Hi Mark — Thanks for your order and for your comments — Bakshi laughed when I told him. He says keep teaching those kids. You better be teachin' them the real side of animation — stories from their hearts — that's where it's all at. We'll put your tee in the mail to you as soon as we receive your payment. And we will throw in a black Peace one on Bakshi's request for you (he admires teachers).

Best Regards,

The Shop

(Parental warning: This film is PG. It's got some scary — and briefly bloody — battle scenes that may frighten younger viewers, and Princess Elinore's costume throughout may frighten protective parents. Like any film, watch it first to decide if it's appropriate for your family, and learn to time the mute button just right when Mr. Bakshi lets one particularly naughty word slip during his interview!)

■ *Fire and Ice* (two-disc set)

For a long time, my only copy of this movie was an old VHS I bought at a discount store that was released by GoodTimes Home Entertainment. I was really glad it made it to DVD. The characters were rotoscoped (fancy word for traced over) from live-action footage shot of real actors, but still had to be exaggerated to make them match the superhuman visions of character designer/producer Frank Frazetta's spellbinding fantasy illustrations. An evil ice sorcerer is crushing the peaceful villages of a kingdom with a wandering glacier, and the lone surviving villager, a princess, and a solemn, mysterious warrior must overthrow him and his sinister mother.

There's an interview with Ralph Bakshi and Frank Frazetta, a documentary on the making of the film (dubbed from director Bakshi's only surviving VHS copy), and numerous production photos. Disc two, *Painting with Fire* is an extended interview and documentary showcase of the legendary Frazetta, best known for his cover paintings from *Conan the Barbarian* and numerous adventure novels.

■ *Allegro Non Troppo*

I wouldn't have known about this film if my very first video animation instructor, Marc Holcomb, hadn't told me about it, so thank you, Mr. Holcomb, wherever you are!

It's an Italian parody of *Fantasia* by animation director Bruno Bozzetto. I know I astonish some people by saying this, but I think it actually turns out as a more successful film (although not financially upon its theatrical release, but neither was its source of inspiration, for that matter) than *Fantasia*. Perhaps not better animated, true, but as an independent animator, I enjoy the widely varied styles of the different sequences. My favorite piece is either the "Valse Triste" (abandoned cat) sequence, or Vivaldi's music set to a prissy honeybee's picnic; she is trying to enjoy a quiet meal while an amorous picnic couple is... well, interrupting her attempts.

The film in itself is worth the price alone, but the DVD also has a terrific hour-long documentary of Mr. Bozzetto himself (subtitled, naturally) with clips from his animated and live-action films accompanied by 10 of his best short films (in their entirety).

(Parental warning: This film is also PG, mainly for an interpretation of DeBussy's *Prelude to an Afternoon of a Faun*, where an aging satyr is chasing naked wood nymphs; some other casual nudity is peppered throughout.)

■ Disney's *Atlantis: The Lost Empire* (two-disc set)

I really wish Disney had made more movies like this before they shut down their 2D animation department.

It's got terrific animation, one of the few Disney heroines in a bikini, and perhaps best of all... no musical numbers! Not one single character breaks out into song!

Just buckle yourselves in for a terrific, old-fashioned adventure story, in the vein of an animated *Raiders of the Lost Ark*.

■ Disney's *The Emperor's New Groove* (two-disc set)

Admittedly, I went to this film because our niece was visiting for the weekend (and *despite* the participation of the perpetually smug David Spade). However, I found myself liking the film far better than I *suspect* our niece enjoyed it (who *did* like it, incidentally).

Yzma, voiced by the purr-fectly voiced Eartha Kitt (one of the campy TV *Batman*'s Catwomen), is probably my favorite Disney villainess since *The Rescuers'* Madame Medusa (and I even liked Ursula, too). Her sharp-tongued exchanges with the dull-witted Crunk are the highlights of the film, along with some spectacularly stylized character designs.

John Goodman is on board as a heartfelt, good-natured peasant trying to convince the selfish emperor (Spade) not to destroy his village in order to make way for a royal vacation home.

■ *Ziggy's Gift*

Directed by Richard Williams, this charming Christmas special has Tom Wilson's favorite comic strip everyman donning a Santa suit to earn some Christmas cash. Inexplicably, he ends up with a "magic kettle" that gives out cash, but only when the user is giving out of unselfish motives. (A nameless Pickpocket character seems to be the disowned descendant of the thief from Williams' *The Thief and the Cobbler.*)

■ *Rock & Rule* (two-disc set)

Thank you, Unearthed Films, for digging up this terrific movie, the first animated feature from Canada! (Also possibly the first animated feature featuring a full cast of anthropomorphics, or human-like animal characters.) The demon at the end might be a little scary for younger viewers, but a stirring music track by Blondie's Debbie Harry and others make up a soundtrack that you won't be able to get out of your head for weeks.

The bonus features include a "making of" documentary; *The Devil and Daniel Mouse*, a Halloween special; and yes, even a "making of" documentary of that film, as well!

■ *Disney Treasures: Behind the Scenes at the Walt Disney Studio*

Walt Disney was clever enough during his lifetime to command some charming self-promotional materials, and this bundle of documentaries is probably the best example of that era. I find myself showing this to my students repeatedly, to showcase the early years of the animation industry… all the way back to the first "animated character," Winsor McCay's Gertie the Dinosaur, whose film is included almost in its entirety.

It also has some fascinating recreations of the very first animated film devices, one of which even predates the motion picture camera!

I would also strongly suggest watching the original Max Fleischer *Popeye*, *Superman*, and *Betty Boop* cartoons, which have oddly enough fallen into the so-called "public domain" and are available in various sets throughout discount stores nationwide, as well as on Amazon.com.

Ten Most-Needed Animated DVDs (Currently Unavailable)

Yeah, I didn't know where else to put this wish list in hopes that some of the current copyright holders on these films hear me so that they'll hopefully release these sorely missed (and in some cases endangered) classics of animation.

■ *The Thief and the Cobbler, Recobbled*

A "complete director's cut" for Richard Williams' unsurpassed masterpiece of animation, nearly 30 years in the making, does not exist. (It has been suggested that he accepted the task of *Roger Rabbit*'s animation director just so he could get the funds to complete *Thief*.) Six months from completion, it was yanked from Williams' control by nervous financial backers (fearing obvious comparisons with the forthcoming *Aladdin*, even though *Thief* was in prior production — easily by a couple of decades). It was handed over to a Saturday morning cartoon producer, and jam-packed with sappy song numbers and needless celebrity narration. Huge chunks of animated sequences were cut and patched back together with visually inferior animation.

Animation was produced by Richard Williams himself, Art Babbit (Disney's Goofy), Ken Harris (the Coyote's animator), and Grim Natwick (Betty Boop and Snow White), all of whom were coaxed out of various stages of retirement to work on this film.

The only consolation prize is that an independent animator has taken the trouble to attempt patching the work together (or "recobbling") from the best available resources, including foreign versions of the film that had some of the missing footage, as well as from a VHS "work-in-progress" version of the film that circulated through the animation community for decades. You can look up *The Thief and the Cobbler "Recobbled"* on youtube.com, and watch it in low-resolution bits and pieces.

■ *Song of the South*

Say what you like about the controversial racial stereotypes allegedly presented in the film, but they're no worse than *Gone with the Wind*. (In fact, the black characters in this film seem to be treated with somewhat more dignity than in the MGM classic.)

Even though the NAACP originally denounced the film as racist, they currently have no stand on the film.

Controversies aside (or even the vague threat of such, which has undoubtedly kept the movie from DVD release), this film was thankfully what helped the Disney studios recover from lost overseas revenue following World War II. The charming animation is some of the best I've seen from Disney's Golden Age, and my favorite character is undoubtedly the conniving Brer Fox. Not many people know it, but James Baskett, the first black man to receive an Academy Award (for his portrayal of Uncle Remus), also provided the fast-talking voice of Brer Fox.

If Disney won't release the film because of the live-action sequences, why not release *Disney's Tales of Uncle Remus*, which could just have the animated sequences from the film? (Just a suggestion, if anyone at Disney is listening.)

(Incidentally, if you get the two-disc set of Disney's *Alice in Wonderland*, there's a feature on the bonus disc called *An Hour in Wonderland*, Walt's first TV special. During the special, the Magic Mirror (played by veteran radio and voice actor Hans Conried, performer of Disney's Captain Hook, *The Hobbit*'s Thorin Oakenshield, and *Dudley Do-Right*'s Snidely Whiplash) is taking requests. Bobby Driscoll, the voice of Peter Pan and a young actor from *Song of the South*, asks the Magic Mirror to show him one of the Uncle Remus stories. The Mirror obliges, and Disney thoughtfully includes "Zip-A-Dee-Doo-Dah" in its entirety and the first Brer Rabbit sequence from the film... in full, glorious, restored color.)

■ *Faeries*

Not to be confused with an inferior version using the same title (and spelling) that came out in 1999, this 1981 animated TV special was based on the character designs from the book illustrated by Brian Froud (now famous for his conceptual work for *The Dark Crystal* and *Labyrinth*). Some truly imaginative faerie characters seek the help of a young human hunter, as their Faerie King has lost his shadow, which gained a sinister intellect and developed itself into a malignant, red-eyed dragon shape. This CBS special directed by Lee Mishkin won an Emmy.

■ *A Christmas Carol,* directed by Richard Williams

Similar to the style of the titles he animated for *Charge of the Light Brigade* (the only watchable sequences from that film, by the way), these characters look like "living illustrations." Highly detailed character animation is the showcase in this Academy Award-winning production, in the style of nineteenth-century British magazine *Punch*.

■ *Gary Larson's Tales from the Far Side* (Volumes 1 and 2)

Based on the humor and panel cartoons by Larson, this mostly pantomime Halloween special has four major sequences (with a few extra scenes): a title sequence about a farmer performing some mad experiments in his barn, an airplane full of insect passengers, a wild west ranch exclusively for zombie tourists, and a man trapped out in the woods on a dark and stormy night.

■ *Witch's Night Out*

Another of my favorite obscure Halloween specials, this story has a witch (expertly voiced by the late, great Gilda Radner) masquerading as a fairy godmother to duotone townsfolk. The simplified character designs (and colors) make for a few terrific shots of exaggerated perspective and character animation, notably when the witch transforms trick-or-treaters into their favorite Halloween monsters. Another noteworthy character voice was Catherine O'Hara (the red-haired housewife from *Beetlejuice* and *Home Alone*), who performed Malicious.

■ *Twice Upon a Time*

Possibly one of the most unique animated features, at least in its technique of stop-motion animation. Characters are cut out in bits and pieces from colored paper and plastic, but you soon forget about the method and get immersed in the story, produced by *Star Wars'* George Lucas. I happened to catch it once on Cartoon Network, and think it's available (sorta), or at least used to be, on VHS. The peaceful dream-makers for the Rushers of Din (humans, who live fast-paced lives running from one place to another, in stock black-and-white footage) are captured by an evil overlord. Synonamess Botch (the aforementioned villain) wants to keep humans asleep forever and deliver unending nightmares to them via his giant buzzards. Ralph, the all-purpose animal, a changeling beast, is voiced by the late Lorenzo Music, who also voiced the 2D-animated *Garfield*.

I found it ironic that on *The Real Ghostbusters* cartoon, Bill Murray's character was voiced by Lorenzo Music, and later, when they made the *Garfield* movie, Garfield's voice, formerly supplied by Lorenzo Music, was now supplied by Bill Murray.

■ *Captain Caveman and the Teen Angels*

Why they called these characters angels is anyone's guess, but the most likely answer is they were trying to cash in on the success of *Charlie's Angels* (much like *Casper and the Angels*). The fact that Taffy, the blonde leader of the group, had suspiciously Farrah-like hair is almost a dead giveaway. And the nerdy Brenda bore more than a passing resemblance (at least in my opinion) to Kate Jackson's character on *Charlie's Angels*.

Of course, why I remember this show with such nostalgia is anyone's guess, as well. (Heck, I even had the lunchbox for this show!)

Captain Caveman was a hairy superhero (supposedly the "world's first") who looked like a cross between a circus peanut and Cousin Itt. However, his design was recycled heavily from the Slag Brothers of the previous Hanna-Barbera hit, *Wacky Races*.

"Cavey," as Taffy affectionately referred to the hero, had one of the most enviable super-powers. Besides being able to fly (with various levels of success from his gadget-heavy "power club"), he could pull out almost any possible cartoon prop from his fur, which usually involved a living dinosaur with *Flintstone* household-gadget-like appliances. Now *that's* a super-power!

Of all the Saturday morning cartoons to be made into a live-action feature film, I never would have suspected this one (well, maybe right after *Wacky Races*). But according to Wikipedia.com, that exact treatment is planned for Cavey in 2007.

■ *Richard Williams' Personal Work*

Yeah, you knew at least one more Richard Williams "wish title" would weasel its way onto my list, so here it is.

I've seen many of Dick's films that I think should be more widely available to the public. We were treated to a couple of these in the Animation MasterClass, like *Love Me, Love Me, Love Me* and *I Drew Roger Rabbit* (by London's Mentorn). *Animating Art* is a film about his friendship with late Disney animator Art Babbitt, and there are more of his short films like *The Little Island*. Then there are all his TV commercials, which look more like "moving fine art" than commercial art (ever see his Harlem Globetrotters ad or the Pink Panther insulation commercials?). He's also done movie titles for *Return of the Pink Panther, The Pink Panther Strikes Again, Charge of the Light Brigade*, and *A Funny Thing Happened on the Way to the Forum*...

Sure, I'm probably talking a licensing nightmare, because all this work was done for all these different studios. And sure, I'm probably talking nonsense, because some of the titles are already commercially available... and you *could* buy at least *some* of them separately... but it sure would be *nice*...

■ *Roger Rabbit 2: The Toon Platoon*

Don't get your hopes up. This film was never even made. I'm not a fan of sequels (Williams said he wouldn't want to be involved, in the unlikely event the film were ever made), but I'm just such a *Roger Rabbit* nut, I'd be up for directing it just to see the film made (and I *know* I ain't no Richard Williams, by a long shot)! I picked up a screenplay from an Atlanta Dragon-Con vendor one year. According to the script, Roger Rabbit came to Hollywood after finding out he was an orphan (raised by humans) to find his toon mother, and ended up working in pictures, meeting future wife Jessica, who was a prim and proper secretary... with glasses and her hair in a bun, naturally! The United States enters World War II about this time, and Roger is drafted along with a bunch of other toons, since they can't be killed (Doom's Dip hasn't been discovered yet). The only problem is though they're quite adept at dodging bombs and bullets, they don't want to *hurt* anyone! (Nope, not even those nasty Nazis!) Eddie Valiant has a cameo role (he and Roger hadn't met yet, remember?) in a barber shop; his face is covered by a hot towel until Roger leaves, so they don't "see" each other.

So what do you do if you want to see any of these terrific films on DVD? Pick an executive from the video distribution division of the copyright holder (Buena Vista, Warner, etc.), look up the address of the company, and tell them you'll buy them if they'd be so kind as to release these movies on DVD. If enough people offer an executive money, chances are, at some point, he or she will be inclined to take it.

List of Suppliers

The following sections describe several of my favorite online vendors for various supplies needed to create animation.

Art Supplies

www.cartoonsupplies.com

I get my animation paper and purchased my light table from these guys.

www.cartooncolour.com

They have my favorite animation pencils, the light blue Col-Erase pencils, available in boxes of one dozen.

Music and Sound Effects

www.musicbakery.com

Best known for their royalty-free music (pay one price, use it for a lifetime), they have music available both in their legacy/variety CDs (usually around $70 at the time of this writing) and in their categorized music CDs (Drama, Symphony, Action, etc.).

www.sound-ideas.com

Probably my two most highly recommended sound effects libraries are listed under their multimedia FX CDs. *Captain Audio* (450 sound effects in WAV format, have cartoon, realistic, and sci-fi sound effects) and *Mzzz Music* (200 tracks of various music styles from jazz and rock to classical cuts, most between 15 to 30 seconds). The CDs go for $29 each.

I also highly recommend their Hanna-Barbera *Lost Treasures Sound Effects Library*, if you have a little more to spend ($129, at the time of this writing). They have everything from classic Scooby and Yogi-style silly "cartoony" sound effects to realistic animal sounds (elephants, gators, and a giant bird squawk) to sci-fi sound effects from *Jonny Quest* and *Space Ghost*.

Educational Discount Software

www.academicsuperstore.com

This site offers fully functioning versions of the software (Flash and Photoshop included), but they are available only to registered students and instructors, and only for educational purposes.

Refurbished Hardware

www.shrevesystems.com
www.sunremarketing.com

As with all of these websites and suppliers, don't forget to do a little of your own research, since business are ever-changing. For instance, you might try entering words in your search engine like "used mac computers," or something along those lines.

Appendix C

Flash Professional 8 Tips, Tools, and Terms

Everything You Ever Wanted to Know About Flash But Were Afraid to Ask For

The Timeline is spread out in both a horizontal and vertical layout. Horizontally, the cells are spread into frames, or over time.

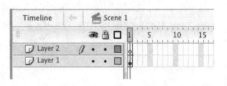

You'll find it helpful to organize your scenes into layers. You can insert a new layer by clicking on the leftmost button below your existing layer in the Timeline.

The layers are vertically stacked. In the example at the bottom of this page, the Storyboard layer is behind the character layer. You would do the same with a background stacked "below" a character.

Keep track of what's in each layer by naming each one accordingly. Just highlight the layer by double-clicking the name, and type in the new name.

Avoid selecting the wrong layer by clicking on the Padlock column, which will prevent changes (or drawing) on that layer.

One of the greatest features of Flash's drawing capabilities is its Onion Skinning. Here I've scanned in my first rough thumbnail, traced it in Flash (using my digitizing tablet) on a separate layer, and hidden the original storyboard layer. Now I've made it into a symbol and stretched this drawing over two frames. The quickest way to make an empty frame is to Option-drag the frame and then delete the drawing itself while it's still selected (leaving an empty frame). Then I'm free to draw in the new available frame, and with Onion Skinning on, it works just like a light table, showing several frames at once.

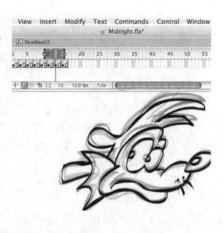

Managing Symbols

Here's what I wish someone had shown me about managing symbols when I started using Flash.

Once you've drawn your artwork on the Stage, select everything on that layer, go up to Modify and drag down to Convert to Symbol. Then name your new symbol.

Now it can appear in the library, and be modified, rotated, skewed, etc. If you want to modify that symbol, say you want to add blinking eyes to your character or mouth positions and such, double-click on your character. Though at

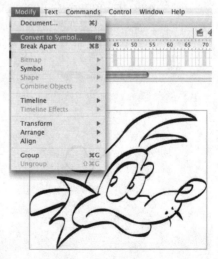

first it looks like you're still on the same Timeline, look carefully at the space next to the words "Scene 1" for the symbol icon and the name of a symbol.

See how my new symbol named Deadbeat now follows the Scene 1 icon?

That shows you can now edit your new symbol by adding frames, layers, etc.!

The Properties window for your symbol is also a pretty handy utility.

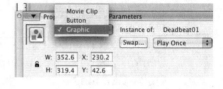

With your symbol still selected, click on the Instance behavior description of your symbol. Its behavior is either Movie Clip, Button, or Graphic. Though some people swear up and down by the Movie Clip format, it has its disadvantages. I like Graphic for starters.

An "instance" is merely a given appearance of your symbol on the Stage.

Again, you have choices. Do you want the symbol to loop your animation, play once, or merely display a single, designated frame of the animation? It's up to you what's best for the scene. (Hint: Single frame works best with lip sync.)

The Toolbox

If you float your cursor over any tool for a second, a tool tip will appear and tell you what it is. The following describes each tool from left to right and top to bottom, as shown in the figure.

The arrows, as usual, are your selection tools.

The dark arrow is your Selection tool (for moving or transforming objects), and the light arrow is your Subselection tool (to move or adjust individual points within that object).

On the left, you see the Free Transform tool for your selected shape, and on the right is the Gradient Transform tool for modifying gradients.

The Line tool draws straight lines, and the Lasso tool selects a freehand-drawn area of your art.

The Pen tool is great for drawing perfect diagonals and curves. No one really knows exactly what the Text tool is good for... (gotcha!) Yeah, it makes text.

The Oval tool will draw ellipses or circles (if you hold down Shift), and the Rectangle tool will make rectangles or perfect squares (again, holding down Shift).

Your Pencil tool will make outlines for you (and can later adjust thickness), but my personal favorite drawing tool is easily the Paintbrush, because you can choose your brush shape and size.

The Ink Bottle tool modifies stroke color, and the Paintbucket tool fills shapes with color.

The Eyedropper tool picks a color and applies it to any selected object or line. The Erase tool removes unwanted lines or shapes; if you have a digitizing tablet, some pens (when you flip them over) automatically act as an eraser.

Your two tools for adjusting the view are the hand (or "Grabber") tool, which scrolls around in your screen, and the Zoom tool, which zooms in or out on your selected area.

The area right next to your pencil designates your stroke color. In this figure, the red line drawn through it indicates that whatever shape we draw will have no outline.

The next tool is naturally your fill color. By clicking on the area next to it, you'll choose what color a selected object will be filled with. Remember, your paintbrush color is determined by fill color!

The farthest left button will set your Stroke Color to black and your Fill to white. The center button will choose No Color, and the farthest right button will switch black and white.

The Magnet here will snap to objects. Below you'll see the Smooth and Straighten features.

Personal Favorite Tool: The Paintbrush and Its Options

The main thing to remember about your brush sizes is that they are dependent on how far you're zoomed in or out on your character artwork.

Though at first it's tempting to just go with a perfectly round brush, I strongly recommend trying the odd-shaped brushes for fun and effect. The look of a real-world brush and its handsome line width variation is what can really help a character stand out from its background.

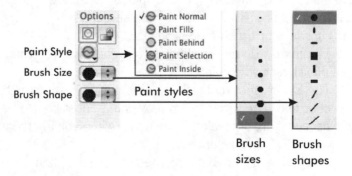

About the Author

Mark S. Smith, the founder and animation director of
MarkToonery.com Animation, has been drawing since age two (or
before, so his mother tells him), and graduated with a degree in
graphic design from Auburn University Montgomery. While working in AUM's Graphic Design Center as a lab assistant, he animated
his first scene for television in a public service announcement
warning children not to accept rides from strangers. He took Video
Animation four times: twice as a class (it could be repeated for
credit), once as an independent study, and once as his senior portfolio. Mark interned at the Alabama Department of Public Health
video production facility, doing animation and graphics on various
germs and text, as well as animated caricatures of the state health
officer in an informational video. He went on to start his freelance
animation career in 1992, and while later employed as a multimedia
specialist for KinderCare, he took the Animation MasterClass
from Richard Williams, the "Animation Maestro" and three-time
Academy Award-winning animation director of *Who Framed Roger
Rabbit* and the "semi-unreleased" animated classic, *The Thief and
the Cobbler.*

Mark was recruited by Phil Coley, head of AUM's Fine Arts
Department, to teach video animation in 1995, as well as take the
helm as animation director for a department project, *Gladys the
Octopus Nurse*, a 13-minute children's video, funded by a private
producer. Since taking Richard Williams' Animation MasterClass in
1997, Mark has taught his animation classes using the MasterClass
notes.

Mark then went to work for Alabama Public Television as a
computer graphics operator in 1998, moving to ABC-32 in 2000,
doing pretty much the same thing for their evening news broad-
casts — making subtitles and full-screen graphics of exciting
quotes from politicians. During this time, he continued to teach
video animation at Auburn University Montgomery, and one

summer he also taught full-time at Trenholm Technical College, while maintaining his full-time status at ABC-32! (Some folks will do anything for health benefits...) In December 2003, Mark was promoted to Creative Services Director.

In 2004, Mark's wife, Albalis, was offered a job in an architectural firm near Atlanta, and since he was quite fond of being married to her, left his day job to join her there in "Peachytown." Mark began teaching graphic design and digital video editing classes for Westwood College's Atlanta Midtown Campus (conveniently located "across the street" from Cartoon Network) in 2005, and started working on his second PSA for the Georgia Public Library, tentatively titled, "A Barnyard Fairy Tale." (It was later renamed "Once Upon a Time," but Mark preferred the tentative title, so being a bit stubborn, he simply felt strongly inclined to mention it here...)

Mark wrote DVD reviews for the website www.dvdtoons.com (until its digital disappearance sometime in 2006), and his reviews have included *Ziggy's Gift* (a Christmas special directed by Animation Maestro Richard Williams), *Fat Albert's Halloween Special*, *Count Duckula*, *The Scooby Doo/Dynomutt Hour*, and *Yogi Bear: The Complete First Season*.

Mark and Albalis are both members of the Atlanta chapter of ASIFA, the International Animated Film Association (a French acronym accounts for those letters not quite matching, in case you're wondering), where they get to hang out with all kinds of cool people from Cartoon Network.

Index

3/4 view, 47-49

A

A Christmas Carol, 444
acetate vs. animation cels, 255-256
Action Safe area, 378-379
agents, 428-429
Allegro Non Troppo, 439-440
animatic, 136-137
    client sign-off for, 214-216
animation,
    adding background to, 326-329
    alternatives to, 9-11
    and classical music, 82, 87
    career tips, 413-415
    disc, 40
    finding job in, 398, 424-427
    influence of vaudeville on, 150-151
    paper, 41-42
    peg bar, 41-42
    pencils, 38-40
    playing, 291-292
    programs, 420-421
    tools for, 37
    vs. illustrated radio, 145-148
animation cels vs. acetate, 255-256
Animation MasterClass, 5-8
animation methods, 162
    pose-to-pose method, 164-168
    straight-ahead method, 163-164
    the best method, 169-180
arm, rotating, 313-315
art markers, using to color backgrounds,
    110-112
art supply vendors, 448
Artist's & Graphic Designer's Market,
    417-418
artwork,
    animating, 301-311
    converting to symbol, 297
    flipping horizontally, 303-304
    recycling, 294
    resizing, 298-299
    rotating, 298-299
    skewing, 299

ASIFA (International Animated Film
    Association), 398
asset management, 357
Atlantis: The Lost Empire, 440
audio channels, 133

B

back story for character, 50-51
backgrounds,
    adding to animation, 326-329
    coloring with markers, 110-112
    creating, 109
    importance of simplicity in, 108-109
balance, 86
banding, 388
bitmap, 248-249
    converting to vector image, 249-250
black-and-white mode, scanning in, 233-235
blur pan, 106-108
books, recommended, 435-436
breakdown drawings, 166
breakdown position, 169, 177
brush, inking with, 227-232
Brush Mode options (Paintbrush tool),
    262-268
Brush Shape options (Paintbrush tool),
    260-261
brush size, in relation to screen size,
    261-262
Brush Size options (Paintbrush tool),
    261-262

C

camera, common pitfalls with, 101-102
camera moves, 103-104
    panning, 103, 104
    tilting, 103, 104
    trucking in/out, 103, 104
    zooming, 103, 104
camera shots, 91
    close-up, 92, 94-95
    cutaway, 98-99
    cut-in, 98-99
    extreme close-up, 92, 95-97
    full shot, 92, 93-94
    medium shot, 92, 94

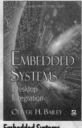